D0197568

GOOD WORK

Also by Howard Gardner

Intelligence Reframed
The Disciplined Mind
Extraordinary Minds
Leading Minds
Multiple Intelligences
Creating Minds
The Unschooled Mind
To Open Minds
The Mind's New Science
Frames of Mind

Also by Mihaly Csikszentmihalyi

Becoming Adult
Being Adolescent
The Evolving Self
Creativity
Finding Flow
Flow

Also by William Damon

The Youth Charter
Greater Expectations
Some Do Care
The Moral Child
Self-Understanding in Childhood and Adolescence
Social and Personality Development
The Social World of the Child

HOWARD GARDNER

MIHALY CSIKSZENTMIHALYI

WILLIAM DAMON

GOOD
WORK

When Excellence and
Ethics Meet

BASIC
BOOKS

A Member of the Perseus Books Group

FOR JOHN W. GARDNER

Good Worker

Design by Jane Raese
Set in 11-point Adobe Garamond Roman

Library of Congress Cataloging-in-Publication Data
Gardner, Howard.
Good work : when excellence and ethics meet / Howard Gardner,
Mihaly Csikszentmihalyi, and William Damon.
p. cm.
Includes bibliographical references and index.
ISBN 0-465-02607-9 (hc); ISBN 0-465-02608-7 (pbk)
1. Job satisfaction. 2. Quality of work life. 3. Work ethic. 4. Professional ethics.
I. Csikzentmihalyi, Mihaly. II. Damon, William, 1944-. III. Title.

HF5549.5.J63 G355 2001

174'.4—dc21   2001025950

04 05/ 10 9 8 7 6 5 4

Contents

PART FOUR—GOOD WORK IN
THE FUTURE

PREFACE

How We Came
to Write This Book

In 1994–1995, we three authors spent a year at the Center for Advanced Study in the Behavioral Sciences (CASBS) in Palo Alto, California, each working on a separate book. Although we had known each other and admired each other's work for many years, we had never collaborated on a project. Our fields of interest overlap but are different. Gardner, a cognitive psychologist, is best known for his theory of multiple intelligences, which led him to study creators and leaders in different realms. Csikszentmihalyi, a social psychologist who writes from an evolutionary and motivational perspective, is best known for discovering the psychological state called "flow," in which an individual's skills and challenges mesh in absorbing ways. His studies of flow have included groups ranging from surgeons to mountain climbers, and like Gardner, he has a special interest in creativity. Damon is a developmental psychologist who has long focused on social and moral issues. He has written definitive texts on moral development and, with Anne Colby, has carried out a pioneering study of individuals who have led exemplary moral lives. Despite our different foci in psychology, we had enough in common to enjoy exchanging ideas whenever we ran into each other on the cloistered CASBS grounds, overlooking nearby Stanford University.

One afternoon, our conversation turned to the question, If you had the choice, what sort of problem would you work on for the next ten years of your professional life? As we talked it became clear, first, that we *did* have the choice; and second, that our envisioned projects were in many respects very similar. Each of us had begun to struggle with the relationship between high-level performance and social responsibility, between excellence and ethics. We had been thinking about several key questions: Is it true that most creative scientists and artists are selfish and ambitious, unconcerned with the common good? Why is it that experts primarily teach *techniques* to young professionals, while ignoring the values that have sustained the quests of so many creative geniuses? Is the impact of science, technology, and communication predetermined—for good or ill—or do we have some control over it?

This set of questions revolving around excellence and ethics proved so seductive that we returned to it again and again, gradually refining how we could study what we first (somewhat clumsily) called "humane creativity." We envisioned interviewing and observing professionals at the cutting edge of perhaps a dozen fields that are essential to individual and social well-being—fields ranging from journalism and genetics to law and theater. The idea was to take stock of the kind of people who entered such professions and succeeded in them. We wanted to learn about their backgrounds, values, and goals. We planned to look at the ways they approached their work, as well as the opposition they encountered and the strategies they used to overcome it. We envisioned asking them to describe their dreams and nightmares about the future course of their chosen pursuit. Given our collective backgrounds in the study of creativity, leadership, and moral excellence, we were particularly interested in learning more about those persons who succeeded in melding expertise with moral distinction.

After leaving CASBS, we started assembling research teams at our respective universities and began applying for financial support to carry out our plans. At first, fundraising met with little success, perhaps because of our own inarticulateness in laying out the project, perhaps because the issues that engaged us were not yet seen as important by outsiders. Within a few years, however, our ideas seemed to gain momentum and garner gratifying interest among funders, whose support is gratefully noted in the Acknowledgments. The increasing interest in our work reflected a growing realization within our society: leading professionals currently face a particular challenge as they attempt to carry out their central missions, since conditions are changing rapidly, market forces are extremely powerful, and our sense of time and space is being radically altered by technological innovations like the Internet.

As our ideas coalesced and our planning proceeded, we moved away from the notion and terminology of "humane creativity" and toward that of *good work*—work of expert quality that benefits the broader society. What, we asked, promotes or impedes good work today? The first two fields we decided to investigate in depth were genetics and the media. At first we thought of these as two important but distinct fields—two professions in which the practitioners are grappling with how to do top-quality, socially responsible work at a time of extremely rapid change. But as our work progressed, we began to see instructive analogies and discrepancies between them. We came to conceive of the present book as a "parallel study" of two professions, one poised to control the composition of our bodies, the other with the potential to control the content of our minds. And we decided to focus on what it means to carry out "good work"—work that is both excellent in quality and socially responsible—at a time of constant change. Thus was born what we now call the Project on Good Work.

From the beginning of the project, our concerns have spanned diverse professional realms—law, medicine, theater, higher education, philanthropy, and more. In all of these we have recognized the same set of forces operating: the emergence of powerful and still dimly understood technologies; the overwhelming power of market forces and the concurrent decline of various competing ideologies and "isms"; the waning of an agreed-upon set of principles and of an ethical framework that has been designed to govern the decisions and behaviors of all members of a profession; the loss of powerful "heroic" role models that inspire the younger members of a profession and a concomitant foreboding sense that the future course of the domain is wrapped in uncertainty. Accordingly, throughout this book, we draw in examples from a variety of professional realms, because we are convinced that the challenge of "good work" confronts every professional today.

We knew, however, that an in-depth analysis of selected professional realms was necessary to tease out answers to our central questions and to gain a nuanced view of the challenges professionals are facing—hence our decision to focus on genetics and journalism. From the time of our initial interviews, we viewed what was happening in these two realms as being of signal importance for the future.

Our basic approach can be quickly sketched. We conducted semi-structured in-depth interviews with leading practitioners in several areas of specialization within journalism and genetics. Our initial sample consisted of 56 geneticists and 60 journalists, but we have now spoken to well over 100 individuals from each professional realm, including 40 mature professionals and a score of young practitioners. Most of the subjects in each group were well-known figures who had been nominated by experts in the domain; but in each realm we also spoke to a handful of "midlevel practitioners"—long-term professionals who would not be widely known. Interviews lasted about two hours; they covered a wide range of themes, from the backgrounds of the practitioners to their current aspirations and concerns, to their predictions about the field. The interviews were tape-recorded, transcribed verbatim, reviewed by the interviewees who then stipulated the use that could be made of their words. In what follows, we identify all speakers by name unless they indicated that they did not want to be so identified. Further details on the procedures are found in the opening chapters of Parts Two and Three and a detailed discussion of our methods and data-analytic procedures can be found in Appendix B.

When we began the interviews in the mid-1990s, we could not foresee the unfolding of these two professions nor the new issues confronting their practitioners. Since that time, genetics has emerged as a profession in which the scientists, the general public, and the shareholders of corporations agree substantially about their goals. In sharp contrast, journalism has emerged as a profession in which the reporters, the general public, and the shareholders of corporations differ sharply in their aspirations. And since the mid-1990s, these two realms have come increasingly to dominate public discourse. We could not then anticipate that the human genome would be mapped by the turn of the millennium; that experiments in genetic therapy would lead to an unanticipated death; that genetically modified foods would become suspect. Nor could we foresee that the Internet would become a principal source of the news; that a major newspaper like the *Los Angeles Times* would secretly split the profit of its magazine with an advertiser; that Time-Warner and AOL would lead a set of mega–media mergers; that the lines between news and entertainment, between faithful and contrived photography, would become even more blurred. We became aware that what had begun as a series of casual conversations on an academic campus had thrust us into central issues of our time.

ACKNOWLEDGMENTS

Support for the work reported in this book was generously provided by initial grants from the William and Flora Hewlett Foundation and the Ross Family Charitable Foundation, supplemented by grants from the Carnegie Corporation of New York and the Ford Foundation. We owe special debts of thanks to Ray Bacchetti, David Gardner, and Courtney S. Ross-Holst, who were the first to see promise in still incipient ideas. Support for the additional phases of this project, some of which is reported in this book, has been provided by the following:

The Bauman Foundation
Berger-Mittlemann Family Trust
Carnegie Corporation of New York
Nathan Cummings Foundation
J. Epstein Foundation
Fetzer Institute
Ford Foundation
William and Flora Hewlett Foundation
Christian A. Johnson Endeavor Foundation
Thomas H. Lee
Pew Charitable Trusts
Jesse Phillips Foundation Fund
Louise and Claude Rosenberg Jr. Family Foundation
Ross Family Charitable Foundation
Spencer Foundation
Thrive Foundation
John Templeton Foundation

For useful comments and suggestions on earlier versions of this book, we thank Sissela Bok, Jay Gardner, George Klein, Bill Kovach, Jonathan Levy, Tom Rosenstiel, and Ellen Winner.

We wish to thank our literary agent, John Williams, for his help in conceptualizing this project and for his support throughout the writing process. At Basic Books, we thank Jo Ann Miller, our energetic editor, her able assistant Jessica Callaway, our thoughtful copyeditor Sharon Sharp, our responsive production manager Lori Hobkirk, and our capable production copy editor John Taylor Howard. Lisa Bromer and Alex Chisholm provided exemplary support for Howard Gardner, as did Kathy Davis for William Damon.

We have been blessed with an extraordinary set of researchers who have carried out the brunt of work on this complex project. Our outstanding managers have been Lynn Barendsen, Anne Gregory, Jeremy Hunter, Paula Marshall, Mimi Michaelson, Jeanne Nakamura, Heather Ross, Becca Solomon, Jeff Solomon, David Shernoff, and Susan Verducci. Assisting them over the years have been several excellent researchers: Kim Barberich, Veronica Boix-Mansilla, Jennifer DiBara, Dan Dillon, Greg Feldman, Molly Galloway, Francie Green, Yael Harlap, Jonathan Heller, Mara Krechevsky, Grace Lam, Marcy LeLacheur, Kaley Middlebrooks, Laurinda Morway, Jenna Moskowitz, Liza Percer, Kimberly Powell, Sara Simeone, David Stevens, Bernadette Sibuma, Barbara Tollentino, Evan Zullow, Nicole Brodsky, Lynn Chan, Christopher Csikszentimihalyi, David Gortner, Shelli Greenslade, Charles Hooker, Jeremy Hunter, Eleni Makris, Purvi Patel, Barbara Simeon, Leanne Stahnke and Shonali Tejwani.

Finally, a word about the dedication of our book to John W. Gardner (no relation to Howard). John Gardner has been one of the great leaders of America during the twentieth century. The nation is in his debt for his outstanding service in the 1940s and 1950s at the Carnegie Corporation and in the U.S. Department of Health Education and Welfare during the Johnson Administration; we are all beneficiaries of his founding role in such organizations as the Urban Coalition, Common Cause, Independent Sector, and the White House Fellows. Millions have been inspired by his wisdom as expressed in *Excellence, On Leadership, Self-Renewal,* and other writings. The authors had the privilege of getting to know John Gardner personally during the year that we spent at the Center for the Advanced Study in the Behavioral Sciences. He counseled us about the issues that we wanted to study; he helped us to secure funding; and in our view he continues to exemplify Good Work. It is our honor to be able to dedicate this book to our friend John W. Gardner.

PART ONE

BACKGROUND

1

GOOD WORK
IN DIFFICULT TIMES

IN EVERY HISTORICAL ERA, many people have sought to carry out good work. It has always been true that some people do their work expertly but not very responsibly. People who do good work, in our sense of the term, are clearly skilled in one or more professional realms. At the same time, rather than merely following money or fame alone, or choosing the path of least resistance when in conflict, they are thoughtful about their responsibilities and the implications of their work. At best, they are concerned to act in a responsible fashion with respect toward their personal goals; their family, friends, peers and colleagues; their mission or sense of calling; the institutions with which they are affiliated; and, lastly, the wider world—people they do not know, those who will come afterwards, and, in the grandest sense, to the planet or to God.

To be sure, no one can continually monitor each of these responsibilities. Like the proverbial centipede asked to explain how it walks, a worker would find this impractical and probably counterproductive. Still, a good professional maintains these concerns implicitly and returns to them explicitly from time to time.

Good Work in Uncertain Times

To do good work is a laudable goal, one difficult to achieve even under favorable circumstances. In the modern world scarcely anyone is sealed off from rampant and rapid innovations or from intrusive market forces. Indeed, even in professions that might seem immune, these forces are dramatically evident. In education, charter schools and voucher programs are sprouting up in different corners of the globe. For-profit institutions like the University of Phoenix are roiling traditional liberal arts colleges and universities. In the museum world, where competition rages for bigger-than-ever blockbuster shows, exhibitions are sponsored by corporations that demand an increasing say over *what* is displayed and *how*. Churches are competing for larger congregations, more lavish buildings, and more charismatic religious leaders. And even traditionally secretive philanthropic foundations are hiring publicists to make sure that their "good works" are well known: they are contemplating "strategic alliances" with neighboring institutions and fretting about the challenges posed by new-style venture philanthropy or charitable accounts offered by investment houses. Similarly, there are physicians who cannot prescribe a course of treatment because it will not be underwritten by the HMO, corporate lawyers whose employers engage in shady practices, teachers who believe they should hug unhappy children but are forbidden even to touch them on the shoulder, and museum curators who need money to mount shows but like neither the artists, the policies, nor the restrictions imposed by the most generous arts funders.

Of course, ethical and professional dilemmas are not new. And many would argue, with some justification, that the ways to deal with them have long been known. They would say that the solutions can be found in the great religions, in the Bible and other sacred texts, in long-standing models of behavior contained in the very traditions of the professions, and in the behaviors of well-known exemplars—for instance, physicians such as Albert Schweitzer and Jonas Salk, and journalists such as Edward R. Murrow and I. F. Stone. But religious and professional traditions are not always available to young people, and they are not always credible. Much evil has been carried out in the name of religion, and many once-idolized figures (ranging from politicians such as John F. Kennedy to business titans such as Henry Ford or Walt Disney to athletes such as Ty Cobb) turn out to have had notable character flaws. And even when the idols remain relatively untarnished and the relevant texts have been studied, it is becoming increasingly difficult to know just *how* to draw inspiration from models in vastly changing circumstances. Murrow did not have to compete with the Internet; Salk did not face an environment in which virtually every medical discovery was immediately patented; Abraham Lincoln did not have every element of his private life scrutinized by the media or made into a lurid TV movie while he was attempting to command the Union forces. This is why we speak not just of "good work" but of "good work in difficult times." Not difficult, necessarily, in terms of daily creature comforts, but difficult in terms of people's ability to know the right thing to do and remain in their professions.

Still, there is an important clue as to whether one is carrying out good work. Doing good work *feels* good. Few things in life are as enjoyable as when we concentrate on a difficult task, using all our skills, knowing what has to be done. And, contrary to popular opinion, these highly enjoyable moments—the ones Mihaly Csikszentmihalyi calls "flow experiences"—occur more often on the job than in leisure time.[1*] In flow we feel totally involved, lost in a seemingly effortless performance. Paradoxically, we feel 100 percent alive when we are so committed to the task at hand that we lose track of time, of our interests—even of our own existence. Intense flow can happen anywhere: in making love, in listening to music, in playing a good game of squash or chess. But it also happens surprisingly often at work—as long as the job provides clear goals, immediate feedback, and a level of challenges matching our skills. When these conditions are present, we have a chance to experience work as "good"— that is, as something that allows the full expression of what is best in us, something we experience as rewarding and enjoyable. To be sure, feelings of flow do not always signal that one is performing "good work" in our sense; the robber who is fully engaged in cracking a safe may well undergo comparable engagement. Nor do we want to imply that "good work" is always accompanied by flow; it can be frustrating and discouraging at times. Yet, time and again, we have observed the rewards of flow bestowed on individuals who have become wholly engaged in activities that exhibit the highest sense of responsibility.

---

* All notes are at the end of the book.

Journalism and Genetics:
An Instructive Contrast

Journalism and genetics are textbook examples of professions that must continually face new challenges. As we began to probe how journalists and geneticists carry out their work, we discovered that professionals in these fields differ in a way that we had not anticipated. Geneticists are working at a time in which the profession is tremendously exciting; all of the relevant forces in their universe are well aligned. The general public, the shareholders of genetech corporations, and the scientists themselves are working toward a common goal: ensuring healthier and longer lives for people. In sharp contrast, journalists tell us they are working at a time when their profession is wracked by confusion and doubt—that is, a time when the relevant forces are massively misaligned. Journalists may feel the need to take time to investigate a complex story, but the public is calling instead for gossip and scandal while management is seeking greater profits in the next quarter. At a time of alignment, good work seems relatively unproblematic. During a phase of misalignment, however, it becomes a challenge. (We discuss alignment and misalignment much more in Chapter 2.)

And so, to an extent that we could not have anticipated, genetics and journalism represent sharply contrasting—virtually polar opposite—cases in a study of professional realms. In well-aligned genetics, the pursuit of good work may appear to be relatively unproblematic; in misaligned journalism, the threat to carrying out good work is ubiquitous. Yet, the emerging story is not quite so simple. Apparent alignment may blind workers to troublesome forces, even as significant threats to good work bubble beneath the untroubled surface. There are in genetics today many reasons for concern, ranging from the blurring of the line between disinterested scholarly research and research carried out to ensure profits, to the tendency to deny the risks entailed in genetic therapy or the cloning of organisms. Conversely, blatant misalignment may actually have a beneficent dimension; such disequilibrium clearly exposes the threats to good work and may mobilize people to struggle productively, to confirm the essence of their calling, embrace high standards, and reaffirm their personal identities. Journalism may well become stronger—and better aligned—just because the fault lines in the profession have become obvious.

A Crisis in the Journalism Profession

Time for an example. In 1993 broadcast journalist Ray Suarez found himself in a quandary—the biggest conflict of his professional life. His heart told him to get out of this line of work, while his bank balance told him to swallow his pride and do his assigned job. His head, where he had to sort out the alternatives and make a decision, was swirling.

Suarez, now senior correspondent for the Public Broadcasting Service's *News Hour*, has since 1993 been associated with public broadcasting. Best known for his six-year stint as the host of the two-hour afternoon show *Talk of the Nation*, on National Public Radio (NPR), Suarez has been an innovator, much honored within the profession and widely respected among the listening public. He was one of the first journalists to whom we spoke as part of our study of good work.

Before joining NPR, Suarez had a richly varied but not always palatable life in journalism. Having discovered a love of writing during high school, he had worked as a radio and television reporter both in the United States and abroad. Beginning in the mid-1980s Suarez had a seven-year stint in commercial news with Channel 5, an NBC affiliate in Chicago. While there, he encountered the dilemma that made him consider quitting the profession entirely:

> When video games first started to become hot, a family sued the major makers of video games in the United States for some unbelievable amount of money . . . because their kids would get seizures. And about half-way into the reporting of the story, I realized that we were talking about one-tenth of one one-hundredth of one one-thousandth of the kids who play video games. But TV has a tendency to play everything like, *"Here's a possible danger of video games."*
>
> And I called in, sort of to telegraph my concerns ahead, sort of in advance for this fight that I knew we were going to have, about the way we were going to play this story. And I said . . . it's irresponsible to give people the idea that video games are dangerous, or, in the way that television usually does, it teases "could be dangerous" to your family, making no guarantees but getting you to salivate and listen. I said, we're talking about a tiny number of American

children, a tiny number. And once you find out that your kids have this, which you may have already known before they ever sat down to play one video game, because all kinds of computer and TV monitors shoot impulses to the eye at this number of times per second. . . . If they play anyway, and have seizures, well whose fault is that? We're talking about a story that we're going to play as a hot, big story, that isn't a story. Because we tell stories that have impact with large numbers of people, so what we're trying to do is just cross our fingers, put them behind our back, and we'll tell them at the end, oh, and by the way, your kids probably are okay. I said, I don't want to do that. I think it's cheap, I think it's not true, I think even, no matter how many times we couch it and qualify it, it will leave an untrue residue in the minds of people who watch the story. So what are we really doing? We're just winding people up. We're not telling them good information.

Suarez sadly summed up the battle with the executive of the station: "And that fight went on for a long time, in TV terms, like an hour or an hour and a half. I lost."

He comments ruefully on the outcome: "There's only so much in the way of showboaty integrity that you can afford to have, because if you have a contract and the contract says certain things, and one of the things is, you have to do what you're told." Eventually finding the situation intolerable, Suarez recalled, "At the time that NPR hired me, I was making active plans to get out of the news business. You know, thank God, I had that option."

During the course of their careers, most people find themselves in situations that test their sense of appropriate behavior and challenge them to reassess major aspects of their lives. At this point of crisis, Suarez probably found it helpful to take into account his personal goals, the core values of journalism, the needs of the television station and network that employed him, and, finally, the implication of his actions for those whom he did not know, especially the thousands of individuals influenced by his broadcasts. Sometimes professionals find ways to resolve complex dilemmas without too much stress. But when resolutions are not easily forthcoming, they are faced, as was Suarez, with a sharp set of choices.

What options would you or any other professional have in such situations? To begin with, you could decide simply to take the easiest course and go along with the mandated behavior. In fact, family and financial obligations might leave few other options. Or you could remain in your current position and continue to fight, perhaps even managing to convince your employer of the superiority of your stand. There would also be the risk of your getting fired or becoming exhausted, frustrated, and demoralized. You could band together with others who shared your perspective and begin to protest privately or even publicly. When management's behavior has been flagrantly inappropriate, as occasionally happens in the news media, group action can be effective. But as President Ronald Reagan demonstrated in 1981 when he summarily fired the nation's striking air traffic controllers, it is all too easy to replace a defiant crew with a more compliant one.

Of course, you could always choose to quit—a more viable option if you had marketable skills and other jobs were there for the asking. But abandoning a career altogether, as Suarez considered doing, is an extremely wrenching option.

Finally, you could find or create an organization that would allow you to realize your professional aspirations. This would be the ideal solution—and it is one of particular interest to us in this study of good work. If an institution already existed that embodied your values, you could try to secure a position with it, even at the cost of moving to a new locale or accepting a reduction in pay. Or you could help create or transform an existing institution. Suarez was not the creator of National Public Radio, but he helped turn it into the powerful and intellectually respectable broadcast news outlet that it remains today.

Mission, Standards, and Identity

Stepping back from Ray Suarez's quandary, let's look at how any engaged worker or professional might handle similar situations. Consider, for example, the HMO physician who believes that each patient needs to be seen until that patient has received a proper evaluation and diagnosis, but whose employer insists that she schedule at least six visits an hour and penalizes her when she does not comply. Or a lawyer working for a large multinational who is told that a bribe will be necessary in a third world country and is instructed to pay money under the table in a forthcoming negotiation. Or the teacher who believes that history is best taught by a deep immersion in a limited number of topics, but must abandon his curriculum and "teach to" a newly mandated state test that probes one's memory for disparate facts. Or the craftsman who believes in using only the finest materials, but who is instructed by his contractor to use inferior materials, which are unlikely to be detected by trusting purchasers and which will half the production costs.

At such critical times, we suggest, thoughtful practitioners should consider three basic issues: *mission*—the defining features of the profession in which they are engaged; *standards*—the established "best practices" of a profession; and *identity*—their personal integrity and values.

Mission

Each realm of work has a central mission, which reflects a basic societal need and which the practitioner should feel committed to realizing. The core of the mission of medicine is the healing of the sick and the afflicted. The core mission of the legal profession is the pursuit of justice, through the resolution of conflict or the orderly and civilized righting of wrongs. Teachers pass on the most important knowledge of the past and prepare their students for the future. Craftspersons make objects that are beautiful and useful. All practitioners should be able to state the core traditional mission of their own fields. At best, the mission is part of what draws the practitioner to a chosen profession and remains as a principal sustenance in times of conflict. A good way of clarifying this sense of mission is to ask: "Why should society reward the kind of work that I do with status and certain privileges?"

Standards

Each profession prescribes standards of performance, some permanent, some changing with time and place. The classic example is the Hippocratic oath: the physician is enjoined to do no harm, to respond to calls without attention to personal preferences, to keep confidences, to lead an honorable life, to use medicines only for curative purposes, and to desist from exploiting the patient. There are comparable standards for other professions. Lawyers are expected to be personally ethical, to provide the best possible defense for their clients, not to withhold information from the court, not to use perjured testimony, and to maintain confidences. Teachers are expected to be moral exemplars, to be well informed, to treat all youngsters fairly, and to avoid personal relations with their students. People involved in the crafts are expected to use the finest materials, to pass on their special skills and understandings to apprentices, and to avoid cutting corners in their work.

Professionals should be able to employ, as a standards test, the question, "Which workers in the profession best realize the calling and why?" A list of admired workers, along with their virtues, should reveal the standards embodied in the profession.

Identity

Our third consideration is a person's own background, traits, and values, as these add up to a holistic sense of identity: a person's deeply felt convictions about who she is, and what matters most to her existence as a worker, a citizen, and a human being. A central element of identity is moral—people must determine for themselves *what* lines they will not cross and *why* they will not cross them. But a sense of identity also includes personality traits, motivation, intellectual strengths and weaknesses, and personal likes and dislikes.

As psychologists, we have an enduring interest in issues of identity. (In fact, Howard Gardner and William Damon studied with Erik Erikson, the psychologist who, in the mid-1900s, developed the concept of identity.)[2] Each person's identity is shaped by an amalgam of forces, including family history, religious and ideological beliefs, community membership, and idiosyncratic individual experiences. In the best of circumstances, these complement one another and add up to a coherent and positive attitude, one that makes sense to the person and to the surrounding community. Of course, such an integrated sense of identity remains an ideal: nearly everyone suffers at times from some fragmentation of identity, some diffusion, some confusion. Nor does identity ever completely coalesce. Rich lives include continuing internal conversations about who we are, what we want to achieve, where we are successful, and where we are falling short.

There is a clear-cut gauge for identity, which might be called the "mirror test." The image comes from the story of a German ambassador in London who, as part of a celebration he had to host in honor of Britain's King Edward VII, was asked to provide a bevy of prostitutes. The diplomat felt that he could not do this and instead resigned his position. Asked why, he responded, "I refused to see a pimp in the mirror in the morning when I shave."[3] Only when we can look proudly in the mirror can we be said to have affirmed our identity. Of course, on occasion the hacker who cripples a network or the politician who has no intention of fulfilling his promises may be proud of what he has gotten away with. In such cases, it is necessary to invoke the universal mirror test: "What would it be like to live in a world if everyone were to behave in the way that I have?"

The Psychological Perspective

In framing the situation of the worker in terms of these three considerations, we are drawing on our own professional formations and values. We are psychologists–social scientists who study the mind's capacities and resources—its intelligences, motives, needs, and values. All human beings endeavor to understand what is happening around us, to make sense of our experiences. All human beings also have the capacity to frame experiences in certain ways—to construe them in a way that either motivates or paralyzes action. And most crucially, all human beings are able to choose from a range of actions—as the economist Albert Hirschman memorably phrased it, we may speak, express loyalty, voice concerns, or exit from the scene.[4] The authors' disciplinary backgrounds have shaped our appreciation for the powerful role played by personal capacities and resources in the lives of contemporary professionals.

If we consider Ray Suarez's situation as a representative one, we can better understand how psychological factors can affect choices. When Suarez's employer told him to accentuate the dangers of video games, he could have reflexively followed the orders. Indeed, in a totalitarian society, such blind obedience would probably be the realistic course to ensure that he could wake up and see his family the next morning. Let's say, however, that he decided that he could not comply with the directive. At this point, one's construal of the situation becomes crucial. If Suarez were insecure and pessimistic, he might conclude that he had no future in journalism and should move instead to a less demanding, if also less satisfying, career. But if he were more self-confident and optimistic about the future, he might interpret the boss's words as a wake-up call. At that point he would have to decide whether to cede his sense of personal agency to someone else or to retain control of his own life and of his own sense about the right way to pursue journalism. We have seen how he, in fact, dealt with the dilemma, but others might have responded differently.

Scholars belonging to other disciplines would offer their own interpretations of the Suarez quandary. A classical Marxist economist might point out the excessive power of management and advise Suarez to join a union, be prepared to strike, or even await a revolution. A mainstream economist might speak about the inevitability of market forces and advise Suarez to investigate how the competition succeeds in securing higher ratings. A historian might observe that there have long been oscillations in journalism between periods of responsibility and periods of "yellow journalism," and then counsel Suarez to wait patiently for the pendulum to swing in the opposite direction. A sociologist might underscore that each society must facilitate a certain set of communication and entertainment functions and, in light of that, encourage Suarez to seek out the current roles and institutions that most closely fit his own set of values.

As social scientists, we have been informed by these and analogous perspectives. We are keenly aware of powerful economic, political, social, and cultural forces, and we realize that people often feel powerless to oppose them. But our primary focus in this study of good work is what happens "inside the head" of engaged professionals. We are interested not only in how people make sense of their situations but also which plans and actions they ultimately pursue and why. Adopting this psychological perspective enables us to understand what we see as essential on a personal level for ourselves and everyone else. In our view all of us need to take stock of our own situations, weigh the various alternatives in light of our own values and goals, and make decisions that are optimal under the circumstances and that we can live with in the long run. In the absence of this person-centered perspective, we are merely observers buffeted by the fates.

Beyond the Bottom Line

We are writing about professional work at a particular historical moment, and that moment necessarily colors our observations and interpretations. With the fall of communism at the end of 1980s, a certain view has become increasingly dominant around the world: a democratic approach to government and a market approach to economics.

As advocates of democracy, we are heartened by the decline of totalitarian regimes and the ascendancy of electoral politics. As Winston Churchill correctly observed, democracy may be an imperfect form of government, but all the others are worse. We have no fundamental quarrel with the operations of the market in economic spheres; we recognize the positive role that markets can play, for example, in competition among publications or pharmaceutical companies. And like many others, we have personally benefited from a flexible and relatively laissez-faire economic system. But not all spheres of life are best run on a market model. Major professional spheres—medicine, science, education, art— ought not to operate in the same way as commercial enterprises do, in the way suggested by the Adam Smith–Friederich von Hayek–Milton Fried- man view of the marketplace. Medicine requires financial prudence, but the purpose of this profession should not be to achieve the greatest profit for shareholders of a health maintenance organization. Nor should legal protection, educational opportunities, and other vital human needs and privileges simply be allocated to the highest bidder. In the words of the French prime minister, Lionel Jospin, "We are not against market-based economy, but market-based society."[5]

Of course, the market can be salutary. For instance, the government- funded Human Genome Project was stimulated by competition from the privately funded Celera Corporation. And, as deftly presented in the 1999 movie *The Insider*, about a whistle-blower in the cigarette industry, journalists waste no time in calling attention to the missteps and ethical violations of their rivals. Neither of these situations would occur in a to- talitarian world. We also stress that the market is as much a consequence as a cause of many phenomena. One could argue that technological ad- vances—themselves brought about by scientific breakthroughs—have wrought the cataclysmic changes in many fields and that the markets are reflecting the rise of new technologies. Still, we feel the need to sound an alarm when any valued human sphere threatens to be overwhelmed by the search for profit—when the bottom line becomes the only line that matters.

2

THE CONDITIONS OF
GOOD WORK

ACCORDING TO POPULAR WISDOM, suggested both by the Bible (that describes toil as God's punishment for Adam and Eve's disobedience) and by contemporary comic strips (that depict work as a meaningless charade run by and for morons), work is a burden people must bear out of necessity, even as they long for weekends and holidays. Yet when Americans were asked in the early 1980s whether they would retire from working if they had enough money to live on comfortably, about 80 percent said they would not.[1] Retirement is often accompanied by deep stress and depression. In fact, human beings are programmed twice to be psychologically dependent on being productive: once by the genes and then by the pressure of social expectations. Already in the first year of life, infants show pleasure in causing events, as when turning a tap or a light switch on and off, or knocking a ball suspended over the crib. Children in a reasonably stimulating and structured environment learn to enjoy concentrated effort. Indeed, our species would not have survived if most of us had not developed a taste for work. And, of course, human communities reinforce this innate tendency by shaming and shunning those who do not contribute to the common good.

We are now entering an unprecedented era in which the economy requires people all over the world to become "knowledge workers." Entirely new tasks that require the constant and imaginative manipulation of symbols are providing employment to cohorts of computer programmers, software designers, bio-engineers, and entrepreneurs knowledgeable enough to perceive opportunities in the evolving trends. Even those in professions seemingly remote from the cyber-revolution—say, the ministry or philanthropy—are affected by our computer-drenched society. Entering new territory always involves risk. As the forms of labor change, traditional safeguards for ensuring good work—from professional codes to trade unions—are no longer adequate. New questions arise: What is the responsibility of multinational corporations to the communities in which they operate and to the workers they employ? What is the responsibility of knowledge workers who are increasingly unsupervised and independent of their employers? How should traditional professionals trained to honor ancient codes respond to the opportunities and challenges posed by seismic global changes?

The quality of life in the future will depend on whether we find a way to do good work under these changing conditions. If the fundamentals of good work—excellence and ethics—are in harmony, we lead a personally fulfilling and socially rewarded life. If they are not, either the individual or the community, or both, will suffer. Since most people want to do work that is useful as well as meaningful, one important question for us to begin with is, "What can people do when conditions threaten a harmonious alignment?" To answer that question, however, we need a broader understanding of how professions typically evolve, how they adapt to change, and what factors can lead to misalignment problems. Medicine, the oldest and best-understood profession, provides a rich grounding for such an understanding. Thus, we examine that profession's history to discern general principles we can apply later when discussing genetics and journalism in depth.

How Professional Realms Change

Becoming a professional involves a bargain between a person and the community. People agree to provide needed services; the community agrees to compensate them for the services and recognize their right to perform those. For instance, the realm of medicine involves a social contract whereby someone trained according to agreed-upon specifications has the right to advise patients and treat physical illness, if necessary with surgery or prescribed medicines. Who can be a physician and what level of care patients should expect from this specialist have always been contested issues. The Code of Hammurabi, setting down the laws of Babylon some thirty-seven hundred years ago, prescribed cutting off the hand of any surgeon who killed a patient while removing an abscess. Physicians were unregulated in Europe until Frederick II in 1221 decided that no one should practice medicine unless he was accepted by the doctors of the southern Italian school of Salerno, whose knowledge the emperor trusted.

Medicine is often considered the oldest profession, though some wits might nominate an even older one. A considerable body of scholarly literature has developed about what qualifies as a profession, and medicine clearly falls within the accepted definitions. But we have not selected medicine as a measure against which to judge the other realms of work we discuss later, and our focus is not on evaluating what work meets certain technical criteria for classification as a profession. Therefore, we often use the terms *professional realm* and *practitioners* to allow for broader interpretation.

The relationship between practitioners and the public they serve is always in a delicate balance, with the professionals interested in securing more rights and the public seeking more services. Over time, this built-in tension can either result in a fruitful synergy or degenerate into conflict. Realms change as a result of four factors.

New Tools, Procedures, and Understandings

First are forces that operate in the cultural environment—the most important being developments in science and technology. Whenever new tools, procedures, or ways of understanding arise anywhere in the culture, they produce ripples that can have far-reaching and unexpected consequences. Until about two hundred years ago, for instance, physicians were difficult to distinguish from charlatans. Medicine became a respected profession only after discoveries made in other fields such as physiology, microbiology, and health practices grounded it scientifically. The development of tools like the microscope, the thermometer, and the stethoscope also helped make medicine a more rigorous practice. Chemists such as Louis Pasteur and Robert Koch shaped medical changes when they carried out experiments and identified the microorganisms responsible for diseases like smallpox, tuberculosis, and cholera. Even advances in unrelated fields can have an impact. Leopold Auenbrugger, the son of a nineteenth-century Austrian innkeeper, learned in his father's store how to tell the amount of wine contained in a barrel by tapping its side. Later, as a physician, he applied the technique to the percussion of patients' chests to diagnose the presence of fluids in the lung—a procedure still used by doctors. Thus, new discoveries from unexpected quarters may reconfigure a realm. This is clearly the case for the two professions that are the subjects of this book. Journalism has been transformed by many innovations, such as the telephone, the personal computer, and the Internet. The short history of genetics has depended even more on technological advances in related fields, as we shall see later.

Cultural Values and Beliefs

A second major influence is the changes in a culture's values and beliefs. What a person can or cannot do at work depends on what is considered morally right, or even on what happens to be fashionable at the time. For example, medical knowledge has been hampered by religious injunctions against dissecting the human body. For this reason Indian and Chinese physicians, who had developed sophisticated medical knowledge more than two thousand years ago, never had a chance to study the internal structure and function of organs.[2] Western medicine was also slowed by the prohibition against doing autopsies until well into the fourteenth century, but afterward it became increasingly permissible to analyze the body's internal workings. Thus, Western physicians caught up with and then surpassed their counterparts in Asia.[3]

Realms differ in how central or peripheral they are with respect to the current priorities of a community. In Europe, as in other parts of the world, physical healing was long bound up with spiritual healing. In the Middle Ages, doctors and nurses typically worked in hospitals and infirmaries attached to abbeys and convents, and were members of religious orders expected to combine the care of the soul with that of the body. Physicians took over priestly functions, and vice versa. In this combination, religious knowledge usually took precedence over purely medical knowledge. But when religious beliefs become distinct from science, health and longevity become proportionately more valued by the populace—thus the demand for effective health care increases. Greater expectations, in turn, enhance the status and power of physicians, whose claims to treatment are based on scientific knowledge. This shift begins to be obvious in Europe after the Renaissance, with Girolamo Fracastoro's first scientific explanation of how diseases are transmitted, written in 1530. By the end of the seventeenth century, a number of systematic observations helped clarify the mystery of how the body worked and set medicine on a purely physical course.

A telling example illustrates how quickly the context of cultural knowledge can change a realm. Phrenology—the study of the relation between the size and shape of the cranium and the manifest traits of the individual—was accepted as a branch of medicine until quite recently. The ninth edition of the *Encyclopaedia Britannica*, presumably an authoritative source in the 1880s, described people with a pronounced bump on the occipital lobe of the skull as being high on "philoprogenitiveness . . . the organ for the love of children because this part of the skull is usually more prominent in apes and in women, in whom the love of children is supposed to be stronger than in men." Right above this area was the part of the skull that the phrenologist Johann Kaspar Spurzheim thought to be diagnostic of "inhabitiveness," because he found it large in cats and in a clergyman fond of his home. Clearly, what counts as credible medical knowledge can change dramatically in less than a century.

Changing Social Environments

Realms often change because of developments in the social environment. A realm must always be responsive to the demand for its services, which determines its market value. Between roughly the fifth and sixteenth centuries in Europe (as in many other parts of the world) most material surplus was placed in the coffers of religious institutions. During that time, monks and priests were among the most powerful, respected, and wealthy individuals. Hospitals, infirmaries, and medical training were administered by the clergy. At other times societies have put a high value on the performance of military leaders, lawyers, engineers, or entertainers. Lately, scientists and physicians in developed Western nations have enjoyed unprecedented esteem, because people have hoped and expected to benefit from their performances more than from those of leading figures in other realms. In contrast, the status of politicians and journalists has been unenviable at best, especially in the United States.

Concern for health has long guaranteed a demand for physicians. However, depending on the expectations for quality health services, the demand may grow or shrink at any given time. This is clearest in the waxing and waning of different specialties. Until a few decades ago the market value of a degree in one of the more esoteric branches, such as radiology or anesthesiology, was much greater than that for general or internal medicine. Since the 1990s, however, the public demand for family physicians has grown, while that for some previously highly sought-out specialists (e.g., psychoanalysts) has decreased.

Patterns of ownership, control, and other political shifts also affect professional realms. Practitioners acting essentially as freelancers who regulate themselves may be turned into salaried employees responsible to outside authorities and their rules. For instance, physicians currently are in the throes of transformation from professionals into employees of managed-care institutions, which may no longer treat them as professionals. This threat to professional status has prompted some physicians to seek some other form of practice that will restore their former autonomy. The institutional organizations and loyalties of physicians will, in turn, largely determine the quality and kind of health care they can provide.

Contributions by Creator-Leaders

A final source of change is innovation by individual practitioners. In every epoch a few people come up with new ideas or new ways of doing things, and if these innovations are accepted by others, dramatic transformations of the realm may result. In medicine, examples abound. In the mid-1600s William Harvey revolutionized physicians' understanding of the circulation of blood and of embryology. In the late 1700s Edward Jenner successfully experimented with the inoculation of smallpox virus, thus pioneering control over many infectious diseases. And in the 1800s Ignaz Semmelweis propounded the radical doctrine that obstetricians inadvertently killed many women by neglecting to wash their hands before assisting during childbirth.

Creative people are usually driven by curiosity and tend to be more intrinsically motivated—more interested in the rewards of intellectual discovery than in financial or status rewards. Therefore, they are often considered odd both by the general public and by fellow practitioners. But the reason innovators are less concerned with money and power is that they get their reward directly from their work. They are satisfied by the excitement and wonder involved in the process of discovery—a fulfillment no amount of money can buy.

Like everyone else, potentially creative individuals will seek to enter careers that promise financial rewards and opportunities for advancement.

But perhaps an even more important element in attracting original minds is the amount of flow a profession has to offer. Gifted, often idealistic, young people gravitate to challenging careers. As the historian of science Thomas Kuhn has argued, paradigms change most readily when a discipline attracts highly motivated practitioners who look forward to solving puzzles and making discoveries.[4]

Medicine has traditionally attracted intellectually gifted young people not only because it has paid well and has had high status, but also because it has entailed intrinsic factors—especially the opportunity to help patients, provide personal autonomy, and make novel contributions to knowledge. These intrinsic rewards become scarce, however, when a recognized profession like medicine is transformed into a bureaucratic enterprise. When a career ceases to provide flow, only young people who expect extrinsic rewards will be attracted to it. Hope of financial gain, rather than intellectual challenges, will motivate them. During such periods, professions will become less creative and will tend to stagnate and be susceptible to takeovers from the outside.

The Four Components of Professional Realms

What is necessary for a profession to form and develop? How do we know when a profession can be said to exist? Such questions led us to pinpoint four essential components of professional realms.

Individual Practitioners

People who elect to enter a professional realm, secure training, and pursue their own personal and professional goals must, of course, be available. Professions arise when a group of *individual practitioners* define the specific knowledge, skills, practices, rules, and values that differentiate them from the rest of the culture. For most of prehistory, professional realms did not exist, because knowledge was evenly distributed in the population. In a hunting-gathering tribe, for example, no one knew anything different from anyone else. Or if one person learned more than the others about medicinal plants, for instance, the rest of the tribe valued the knowledge and drew on it, but its possessor still had to continue to hunt and gather like everyone else. It took many thousands of years before hominids had enough material resources to afford supporting specialists such as physicians, who were not directly involved in the daily production of food and shelter.

Today, we readily think in terms of specialized professional activities, and potential practitioners target their choices about training and careers by considering a wide range of factors, from personal interests to societal reward systems. And in certain professions, such as medicine, ways of identifying and rewarding levels of expertise among highly specialized practitioners have become increasingly important aspects of the associated educational, regulatory, and other activities. The subject of hierarchies of professional roles is one we examine more closely later.

Domains

When enough specialized knowledge has been codified for smooth transmission to new practitioners, we call the resulting symbolic system a *domain*. Cultures are made up of hundreds of domains, such as mathematics (which can be further differentiated into subdomains such as calculus, number theory, and so on) or medicine (which can be further differentiated into gastroenterology, pathology, and so on). The domain of gastronomy includes all the foodstuffs and recipes that make it possible for cooks in a given culture to prepare delicious meals, while the domain of religion specifies the rituals and beliefs that allow a person who learns its codes to feel connected with the supernatural. Both journalism and genetics qualify readily as domains.

Domains consist of two main sets of symbolic codes. (The second is the "ethical dimension," discussed below.) The first includes *ideas* (or *memes*) relating to knowledge and practice. How should one pray to the gods? How should one cook chicken? Every domain prescribes sequences of action that lead to some desirable goal. In medicine, the goal is to prevent and alleviate suffering, and to prolong life. The domain of medicine—the knowledge base that a physician must learn before being allowed to practice—grew very slowly at first but accelerated rapidly over the last few centuries, and it presumably will continue to do so for the foreseeable future (no doubt intersecting increasingly with the discoveries of genetics).

The information collected in a domain is coded in symbols—words, catchphrases, graphic notations, and equations that are passed down either by word of mouth or in prose and illustrated texts. Early in human history this information was preserved orally in myths, songs, and verse; later it became codified in written form. Until a few thousand years ago, the domain of medicine consisted largely of magical practices and charms for expelling the demons that were thought to cause diseases. (This was true of other professions, too: Egyptian potters resorted to magical incantations when they came to delicate situations in the process of firing their pots, as protection from evil clay-breaking spirits). After some time, medical specialists began to note and codify the salutary effects of herbs. In the first century, the Indian surgeon Susruta wrote down the medicinal properties of 760 plants, and the Chinese physician Li-Shih-chan in the sixteenth century compiled a great pharmacopeia in fifty-two volumes, based on experience collected by physicians over the preceding centuries and listing the beneficial uses of more than a thousand plants.

In Europe, the domain of medicine remained largely anecdotal well into the eighteenth century. The knowledge of the Salernitan doctors, held in such high esteem by Holy Roman Emperor Frederick II, was expressed in the rhyming couplets of the *Regimen Sanitatis*, which included such pearls of wisdom as *Post prantium stare, post coenam lento paede deambulare*, or "Rest after lunch, and take a slow walk after dinner." Other medical advice from the same source has been translated as "Use three physicians still, first Doctor Quiet, next Doctor Merryman, and Doctor Diet."

Needless to say, over the past ten centuries the knowledge of the medical domain has expanded exponentially. But this has not necessarily been true of every profession. For instance, the equally ancient discipline of the law has not undergone a comparable revolution. New branches have arisen to deal with emerging problems—such as antitrust or intellectual property law—but at least until the advent of the information revolution, scientific and technological advances left the basic principles of the domain relatively unchanged.

A domain needs to contain more than knowledge and skill to be recognized by the rest of society as a profession. In addition, there has to be an *ethical dimension* reassuring people that the skills will not be used against the common interest and solely for the practitioners' advantage. As an example, the oath that Hippocrates formulated in the fourth century B.C. and that graduating medical students still recite, specifies that physicians should refrain from seducing any young man or woman they find in the home of the patients they visit. The Code of Maimonides, written by a Jewish doctor from Cordoba about fifteen hundred years later, and many recent formulations of ethical standards—such as the declaration of Geneva, the International Code of Medical Ethics, and the Canons of the American Medical Association—also spell out the conduct expected of physicians. As we note later, some scientists and journalists are currently engaged in efforts to create codes adequate to our time.

In sum, if a profession cannot convince others that its practices and values are useful, and that its members can be trusted, it will not be given much social support. It will be marginalized in the culture and will not be allocated many resources. The domain, encompassing both the *procedural* and the *ethical* standards of the profession, must be credible enough for the community to pay money and respect for the services of its practitioners.

Fields

As sets of symbols, domains exist only as ideas and values, as words uttered or recorded in some way. To become real, they have to be enacted by people. The third component of a professional realm is what we call *fields*—that is, the men and women who actually practice a domain's procedures. Society is a network made up of hundreds of fields, from mathematicians to farmers, from plumbers to physicians.

What constitutes a field is to a certain extent fluid. For instance, the definition of *physician* differs in the United States and India. In the latter nation, until 1970 anyone could practice medicine without a license, and even today an estimated 500 million patients are still treated by Ayurvedic healers employing techniques based on traditional methods with a combination of diet, herbs, and spiritual exercises. The country with the highest reported number of physicians is Italy, where there are 190 people for each doctor (versus 390 in the United States and more than 30,000 in Ethiopia). But in Italy many physicians do not actually practice after obtaining a medical degree, so the favorable ratio of doctors to patients does not necessarily imply better health care or a stronger medical field.

Individual practitioners in a field occupy one of three major roles. The elite are the *gatekeepers* who preside over the destiny of the professional realm and judge which changes in the domain should be sanctioned.

Some fields formally recognize a hierarchy of gatekeepers, whereas others do not. Gatekeepers emerge as a result of complex interactions among practitioners that involve politics, reputation, respect, and appointment to key institutional positions. In medicine the ranks of gatekeepers include the medical directors of major funding institutions such as the National Institutes of Health (NIH), the deans and department heads of major medical schools, the editors of respected journals such as the *New England Journal of Medicine* and *The Lancet*, and so on.

The great majority of any field is made up of *expert practitioners* who are recognized by the gatekeepers and are authorized to perform within the domain. Without them, the profession would not exist. Finally, a vital field always needs approved *apprentices* or *students*. Although they have little power in the present, they are essential to the continuity of the professional realm. When the knowledge in a domain becomes exhausted or when society is no longer prepared to support a field, the number or the quality of potential recruits diminishes. In the opposite case—as happened with physics in the 1930s and 1940s, and as is happening with molecular biology today—many of the most talented youth will flock to the field. When the opportunities to practice are unevenly distributed, aspiring professionals will move from places that offer fewer rewards to those that offer more. For instance, doctors emigrated in great numbers from Greece to Rome two millennia ago when the latter state became powerful and prosperous; included among their ranks was Galen, the most renowned physician of antiquity. Currently, the United States is attracting promising medical students from around the world, and many American students with meager qualifications are pursuing medical studies in developing countries.

Not all professional realms have equally well-defined domains and fields, and boundaries themselves are fluid and changing. In contrast to medicine, for example, journalism is a much more loosely coupled domain and field. Many of the beliefs and practices that apply to journalism also apply to other kinds of writing, as well as to diverse varieties of scholarship. People who wish to do so can call themselves journalists, while it is illegal for nonphysicians to pass themselves off as doctors. Journalism is less consistently policed at its various levels, and the processes for being a journalist are much less well defined. In the case of genetics, there are clear procedures and standards for receiving a doctoral degree in various branches of biology. However, many of those most actively involved in genetics—including some people who direct highly influential biotechnological companies—do not have such a background.

Other Stakeholders

In addition to individual practitioners, domains, and fields, one must take into account a fourth facet of professional realms—the *other stakeholders*. We use this term to refer to the two groups that are playing increasingly large roles in the operation of genetics, journalism, and other realms today. One group consists of the corporate *shareholders*—the people who in effect own a company (like a media conglomerate or a biotechnology corporation) and have expectations for its performance, especially its profits. The second group consists of the *general public*—the citizens who, as consumers, taxpayers, and voters, indicate their own preferences regarding news stories, medical practices, various kinds of genetic manipulations, and other topics. In the past, these two groups played only a minimal role, but today no professional realm can operate indefinitely if it clashes with the requirements of such stakeholders.

The components of a professional realm can be summarized in the following chart:

Individual Practitioners	Persons who elect to enter a professional realm, secure training, and pursue their own personal and professional goals.
Domain	Knowledge, skills, practices, rules, and values captured in various codes. A culture consists of numerous domains. Domains have ethical dimensions.
Field	The roles that individuals practice when working with symbols of the domain; fields also include institutions. A society consists of numerous fields. Three major roles: elite gatekeepers, expert practitioners, apprentices and students.
Other Stakeholders	1. Corporate shareholders and executives.
	2. General public—consumers and citizens.

A Golden Age—
When Professional Realms Are Aligned

A professional realm is healthiest when the values of the culture are in line with those of the domain, when the expectations of stakeholders match those of the field, and when domain and field are themselves in sync. When these conditions exist, individual practitioners are free to operate at their best, morale is high, and the professional realm flourishes. We term this a situation of *authentic* alignment.

Authentic alignment does not happen often, since domains compete with each other for cultural hegemony. Religion struggles to preserve its predominance over philosophy, political ideology tries to dictate the course of science, and the scientific disciplines vie with each other for premier status. These are not idle academic bickerings, for they bear on the central issue of any culture: Who will formulate the worldview? Depending on the answer to this question, the entire history of a civilization may be set. For example, in China religious and ideological considerations traditionally took precedence over the development of markets, technology, science, and autonomously configured domains.

Fields also compete with each other for societal resources. Physicians' interests often conflict with those of other professionals, such as insurance agents, lawyers, nurses, psychologists, hospital administrators, or politicians. In this case, the issue is, Who controls health care? A certain amount of tension is inevitable and perhaps even beneficial. But society as a whole suffers if there is too much conflict among the various components of the system, and when as a result the interests of either professional realms or of the broader society are ill served.

At different times societies have adopted widely different solutions for arbitrating the competing claims of professionals and other workers. One of the most drastic examples is the Hindu caste system, in which a person's place in the productive (and reproductive) system was fixed at birth as a result of inheritance. Members of the higher castes preserved their status by avoiding the less pure members of lower castes and by not touching impure substances such as blood, flesh, or leather. Since learned physicians until recently were Brahmans, or people of the highest caste who were not supposed to touch impurities, much of their treatment was verbal. Despite the obvious oppressiveness of such a rigid system, castes for several centuries achieved a viable division of labor, perhaps because the Hindu religion—intricate and diverse as it is—made a persuasive enough case for the lower castes to accept their lot without too much complaint.

Societies have developed other means for apportioning productive functions. A guild is essentially a free association of practitioners who set their own standards and compete with rivals for acceptance. Guilds prospered in Europe during the Middle Ages, but with time they developed into increasingly self-serving institutions that approximated the rigidity of castes without the latter's quasi-religious justification. Sometimes, the central authority of the state takes over the regulation of productive work. The corporate state existed in various forms in the nineteenth century and was formally developed in fascist Italy. This solution provided for labor unions, trade unions, and professional associations (rather than political parties) to elect representatives to the legislature. In the socialist system, every worker is legally an employee of the government. These autocratic solutions do not eliminate the basic problems of the competition between fields and the rest of society. In countries where, for ideological reasons, the state paid physicians poorly in comparison with manual workers, patients who wanted good care routinely offered doctors gratuities of money, hams, eggs, sugar, or other gifts in kind. As recently as May 1997, the ethics committee of the Hungarian Medical Association published a position paper in which it warned that accepting gratuities "is demeaning to the physician, because it threatens his sovereignty."[5]

In our society at present, the preferred solution for adjudicating among the various fields is the free market. According to this ideology, the invisible hand of supply and demand—as manifested, for example, by shareholders of major corporations or by the purchasing choices of consumers—automatically adjusts the competing interests of various productive groups. The problem with this solution is evident in the case of medicine, where a substantial proportion of the population cannot afford access to quality health care. Under such conditions, two options arise. One possibility is that humanitarian cultural values will have to be subordinated to the demands of the marketplace, and we will have to concede that health is one of those commodities only the affluent should aspire to having—like a second home or a costly education at a private university. The other option is for us to agree that in this case humanitarian values should take precedence over the unmitigated laws of supply and demand, which requires finding ways for the field to provide its services even to those who cannot pay for them.

In recent years, attempts have been made to develop a global health policy based on humanitarian values. The 1978 Alma-Ata Health Declaration of the World Health Organization stated that health—understood as a state of complete physical, mental, and social well-being, and not merely the absence of disease and infirmity—is a "fundamental human right" that should be accessible to all levels of society. At this point in history, such declarations are still little more than wishful thinking. But perhaps we are approaching a time when common sense will unequivocally converge on the conclusion that individual health and welfare cannot be left to chance, but instead need more broad-based solutions.

A perfect solution is obviously difficult to achieve, and in any case it will be a temporary one. But our model suggests, at least in principle, the conditions necessary to optimize professional contributions to a society—or, in other words, to bring about authentic alignment. In the first place, there should be domains to take care of the major human needs. The goals and values of these domains should support each other and be rationally connected through a common epistemology. Currently in the so-called developed world, the scientific method provides this common ground, although alternative worldviews ranging from humanistic deconstructionism, on the one hand, to religious fundamentalism, on the other, certainly exist. It is possible that the hold of science on popular allegiance will slip unless it is capable of integrating some of the older values, such as a respect for cultural traditions, with newly emerging "green" values, such as environmentalism.

Another condition for alignment is that the fields should be free to practice within the limits of their respective domains and to expand these limits in a reasoned way. Everyone suffers when religious or political authorities try to control the practices of a professional realm by imposing parameters foreign to it. At the same time, fields must take seriously their responsibility to the domain and, ultimately, to the culture and society as a whole. That is, they must apply effective internal standards (sometimes called "policing") within the profession. If members of the field begin to stray from the terms of the implicit contract that authorizes their practice, conflict will inevitably result. In an ideal situation there is a generally accepted relationship among fields, and conflicts are resolved in light of the common good. Members of fields are rewarded in a reasonable approximation of their contributions: merit, rather than other forms of preference, is the basis of advancement.

Finally, harmonious professional realms exist when individual practitioners are attracted to the domains that most suit their interests and abilities, when they are allowed to develop and grow within the parameters of the practice, and when their rewards are commensurate with their skills and contributions. If a profession cannot offer the opportunity for doing good work—in the sense of providing flow experiences and enabling individuals to do their best in meaningful occupations—young people unsuited by talent or temperament will enter whatever field pays better or gives the most prestige. While achieving harmony in a given sphere (that is, cultural, social, or individual) is possible, bringing all dimensions into alignment simultaneously is much more difficult. Ultimately, the judgment of alignment is a subjective one. Practitioners and observers conclude whether the concerns of the practitioner, the domain, the field, and the other stakeholders are being reasonably well met at a historical moment.

Threats to Alignment

Examples of social conflict and chaos are unfortunately all too common in the historical record. It is sobering to realize how even Rome—held up as a model of political stability—was torn for centuries by internal dissension that could have ended the republican experiment at any moment. If we are to trust the historian Livy, almost every year a new war threatened from one of the compass points, and the tribunes tried to dissuade the soldiers from fighting on behalf of their rich compatriots. For centuries the continued existence of society hung in the balance, skirting a fatal crisis from year to year.

When harmony in the social matrix falters, several possible consequences ensue. Occasionally a profession disappears entirely: consider the augurs skilled in reading celestial signs, who in antiquity were consulted by the rulers in matters of public policy. But because most professions address enduring human needs, they seldom fade away completely. Instead, as sociologists remind us, they are threatened by two main forms of dysfunction: *anomie*, which occurs when norms break down to the extent that nobody any longer knows the right thing to do;[6] and *alienation*, when norms become rigid and oppressive and nobody wants to do what has to be done.[7]

Why do such crises occur? In the normal course of events, destructive changes often occur cyclically, either because external conditions destabilize the domain or the field, or because the internal development of the profession takes on pathological forms. One obvious threat to the harmony of a profession is rapid scientific or technological advances. When new knowledge or new procedures arise in adjoining domains, a given field can be overwhelmed by possibilities that throw into question the old practices. Boundaries may shift, so that what once was the province of one field becomes part of another's. Not so long ago it was barbers who did surgery; but as advances in the treatment of pain, infection, and shock made operations more effective, surgery became a branch of medicine. Targeted drugs may someday render surgery unnecessary. If changes are too sudden, practitioners trained in the old methods may start doubting their expertise and eventually may lose faith in the viability of the domain as a whole. At that point, the ethical bonds that justify the profession also begin to weaken. If morale is too severely undermined, the field becomes cynical; instead of seeking rewards in a job well done, practitioners will seek only money, power, or petty distinctions.

Changes in lifestyle that are entirely independent of a domain can also bring disequilibrium. For instance, in the United States, the spread of suburbs after World War II made it increasingly difficult for physicians to make house calls, because too much time was expended in traveling from one home to another. Instead, patients were expected to visit the doctor's office or an outpatient hospital facility. This was just one of many developments that has made health care more impersonal and institutionalized, and that threatens to transform the physician's self-image from community healer to corporate employee. Instead of being immersed in the lives of their patients, physicians now are distanced from the homes and families of those for whom they care. Surrounded in their offices by the tools and paraphernalia of the trade, they often adopt an intimidating professional persona. These changes may make the delivery of health care more efficient, but the potential downside is that, in shedding their traditional image, doctors may also shed those values that made medicine a socially respected and personally rewarding career.

The harmony of professions can also be unsettled by economic and political ties that both support and constrain them from the outside. A field can be co-opted by rulers or by the blandishments of the market: when that happens, it is no longer clear whether the field is serving the function for which it had originally been chartered or is advancing the agenda of special interest groups. Or the field can be compelled to serve the ends of those in power, in which case its original goals and values again become compromised. Currently, the new forms of health-care delivery are forcing physicians to make difficult ethical choices: Should they go ahead and prescribe an expensive treatment that is likely to help their patient or a less effective, cheaper treatment that will benefit their HMO's balance sheet? Divided economic control results in split loyalties, and the old rules no longer apply. But when the function of the domain becomes perverted, the profession loses much of its social mandate and its members become demoralized.

Anomie may result also from the internal development of domains. Changes in values and priorities that seem desirable at first may have hidden costs. Biomedical research is highly desirable. But if, attracted by its glamour, medical schools emphasize research skills over teaching in their curricula, and hospitals stress research over primary care, the nature of the profession can easily change in ways unsettling to the public, at least in the short run. Such a change may also disturb practitioners who were drawn to the domain by traditional values of caring.[8] As the status of basic science increases, physicians are confronted with the temptation of taking on a role from another field—that of the scientist—rather than the venerable role of the healer.

Another threat to the internal harmony of a profession is the exhaustion of the domain's knowledge base. Geographical exploration was a flourishing realm until recently. Now that all the continents have been mapped and no new discoveries are likely to beckon, many young people who want to prove their mettle are moving to more promising frontiers such as outer space or virtual space. Sometimes the drought is only temporary, as it was in physics just before the explosion of quantum mechanics, when leaders of the field had assumed that all the important problems of the domain had been solved. Then suddenly the new theory revitalized physics, attracting some of the best minds who helped usher in the nuclear and the silicon ages. Since the glory days of the mid–twentieth century, the arc of the profession has peaked again and has entered something of a decline. When the flow potential of a domain is exhausted, the risk is that members of the field will become bored and retreat into a rigid orthodoxy in an attempt to protect the relevance of their contribution.

Finally, fields can be corrupted internally, often as a result of access to sudden wealth and power. When a profession yields overwhelming privileges, the temptation is to take advantage of them. Gatekeepers begin to take on political roles at the expense of their expertise, practitioners clamor for ever-larger slices of the economic pie, and recruits turn to the field for extrinsic, rather than intrinsic, reasons. Sometimes, in order to keep the price of their services up, gatekeepers place too many obstacles in the way of certifying practitioners, and thus they reduce the effectiveness of the field. At other times they err in the opposite direction and allow insufficiently prepared or motivated people to practice. Or both excesses may occur simultaneously. For instance, post–World War II Italian medical schools turned out many physicians who had practically no clinical training to speak of. At the same time, if experienced physicians from the United States or from other European countries applied to practice in Italy, they were refused licensure unless they had a good command of ancient Greek and of Latin—a blatantly self-protective measure for the Italian medical establishment.

Thus, alignment can fail because of tension between domains (surgery versus barbering), between fields (physicians versus entrepreneurs),within domains (alternative medicine versus traditional medicine), within fields (family physicians versus specialists), between a domain and the wider culture (disdain for alternative medicine versus a search for more holistic methods of treatment), or between a field and the wider society (clamor for higher incomes versus desire for affordable health care). Domains and fields can clash with the demands of stakeholders. Whenever alignment fragments, both society and the profession are likely to suffer. The long-term needs of society are no longer served, and people lose their professional integrity. At that point, good work becomes rare. It must be revived to restore the balance between the components of the system, and ultimately, new norms of the domains or new institutions of the field may be required as well.

Authentic alignment, which represents an ideal worth striving for, must be differentiated from other conditions with which it might be confused. In a totalitarian state such as Nazi Germany, a professional realm like medicine may seem to be aligned, if practitioners are allowed to carry out their work. However, the alignment is only superficial, since practitioners must pass political litmus tests, refuse aid to certain populations, or ignore some bodies of research while embracing others. As we shall see, *superficial alignment* can also come about when practitioners deliberately or unconsciously ignore potentially troublesome or discrepant situations—for example, the quest for profit overwhelming the execution and publication of quality work. A certain amount of tension may be healthy, for it forces practitioners to examine their own fundamental values. By the same token, the sociological state of alignment should not be confused with personal integrity or a state of flow. Individual practitioners may well be unhappy even if they live in a society where domain, fields, and shareholders are well aligned. Conversely, some practitioners will be personally energized by a situation of nonalignment that they are determined to alter.

Toward a Model of Alignment and Misalignment

Given this sketch of the factors that underlie the vicissitudes of professions, we are now in a better position to resume the main thread of the investigation. By applying these general concepts, we can see more clearly what is happening to the domains that deal with our minds and our bodies, and perhaps hazard a prognosis about the human condition in the near future.

In subsequent chapters we examine the two domains that, in our time, have principal responsibilities for shaping the information inside our bodies and our minds. We do so by portraying journalism and genetics from what anthropologists call an *emic* perspective—that is, as they are described and experienced by leading individual practitioners. In particular, we report how practitioners describe their goals and values, the opportunities they seize, the obstacles they encounter, the ethical dilemmas that arise, the changes (both positive and negative) they observe, the strategies they devise to carry out their work, dreams and nightmares about their occupations, and, in sum, their own sense of the current degree of alignment in their chosen professional realms.

What these professionals say is specific to the domains of genetics and journalism, but the overall perspective applies to knowledge workers in any other domain. The rapid changes in technology and society are destabilizing old occupations, while the newly emerging ones are still in a state of (sometimes beneficent) chaos. "What constitutes good work?" is a question all of us must ask again and again. How can we live up to the demands of our job and the expectations of society without denying the needs of our personal identities? What resources can we draw on, as powerful, often contradictory forces cause stress, doubt, and guilt to creep into the performance of our work?

This study focuses on the United States. Considerations of feasibility, funding, and convenience were all contributing factors to limiting the scope of the investigation. However, the trends observed in the United States are likely to occur in other nations as well, and the model introduced here should ultimately facilitate analysis of professional realms in other parts of the world.

It is proper in such an investigation to begin with the perceptions and testimony of practitioners in their own words, but it is not necessary to end there. Occasionally in parts 2 and 3, and throughout part 4, we adopt a contrasting *etic* view. That is, assuming the perspective of observers trained in the social sciences, we attempt to make sense of the current situation and to lay out future options—benign as well as malignant.

The reason for this long conceptual detour can now be seen more clearly. Genetics at present appears to be well aligned; that is, practitioners feel that they are being true to their domain, that their field is functioning well, that the various stakeholders are being satisfied, and that their future looks most attractive. Under such circumstances it is relatively easy to carry out good work. In contrast, the realm of journalism emerges as poorly aligned; that is, many practitioners feel that it is difficult to honor the precepts of the domain, their field is wracked by tension, the stakeholders are threatening the core values and the principal roles, and the future may well hold even worse tidings. Under such circumstances, good work is but a distant dream.

If this were simply a story of two professional realms—one well aligned, the other poorly aligned—it could be told crisply. However, the case turns out to be more complex. Genetics may well be aligned in a superficial way; but the depth and longevity of the alignment is open to question. In contrast, the very anomie and dis-ease currently observed in the domain of journalism could possibly be the harbinger of a better and firmer alignment in the future.

Which leads to a final point. Alignment is a useful term, but for two reasons, it should not be viewed as an ultimate explanatory one. First, domains and fields are far too complex to be characterized as simply aligned or misaligned; there will always be pockets of relative alignment (for example, Internet journalism today) and pockets of relative misalignment (for example, geneticists and corporations caught in disputes about the possible risks associated with genetically modified foods). Second, all conditions of alignment and misalignment are necessarily temporary. Conditions in the world are always changing, and the alignment of one day almost always contains within it the seeds of at least minor nonalignment, if not major anomie or alienation. This state of affairs may disappoint those who feel that they can find the ultimate profession or practice, but it should stimulate those who are looking for new challenges in unexpected places.

3

EARLY ATTEMPTS TO
SHAPE BODIES AND MINDS

HOW DO WE KNOW whether a person is doing good work? By evaluating the performance in terms of the domain's values, by comparing it to other practitioners' standards, and by assessing the amount of joy it brings to the worker. These steps are unproblematic in occupations with an ancient heritage, such as medicine or bricklaying. It is more difficult in realms of more recent vintage, such as genetics and journalism. Still, we should recognize that the roots of these realms extend as far back as recorded history. To get a better idea about good work in genetics and journalism today, it is useful to look at the origins of these realms, what was expected of them, and how they contributed to the community.

How Bodies Were Shaped

Long before anyone suspected the existence of genes—the molecular strings that, in interaction with a surrounding environment, determine every aspect of humans' physical and mental being—farmers recognized that the traits of parents were passed down to their offspring. So they learned to improve the speed of horses or the size of pigs by selectively breeding the best adult specimens with each other. It took no great leap of reasoning to apply this principle to human beings. Plato devoted a large part of the fifth book of the *Republic* to the question of how to apply the practices used to breed hunting dogs and thereby produce the best "guardians" for the perfect state. In chapter 459, he wrote:

> The best of either sex should be united with the best as often, and the inferior with the inferior as seldom as possible; and that they should rear the offspring of the one sort of union, but not of the other, if the flock is to be maintained in first-rate condition. Now these goings on must be a secret which the rulers only know, or there will be a further danger of . . . rebellion.[1]

Earlier on, Plato had also written: "And God proclaims as a first principle to the rulers . . . that there is nothing which they should so anxiously guard, or of which they should be such good guardians, as of the purity of the race." One problem such policies have always encountered is recognizing "the best of either sex," since that judgment is highly variable and dependent on the a particular culture's beliefs and values. Another problem is that the valued phenotypic (that is, observable) trait might not have any identifiable genetic basis, and thus the parental qualities would not be passed on to the children. As Plato himself noted, "If the son of a golden or silver parent has an admixture of brass and iron, then nature orders a transposition of ranks . . . [and] the child . . . has to descend in the scale and become a husbandman or artisan."[2]

Of course, Plato did not believe only in breeding. Most of the *Republic* deals with the proper ideas and practices to which children should be exposed so that their minds will be strong and harmonious. He devoted more space to discussing the kinds of music they ought to listen to than to what we now call "eugenics." Still, all known societies have practiced some form of eugenics, or what we might now label "genetic engineering." These practices are often justified in terms that have nothing to do with biology—such as religion or custom—but presumably the practices were selected and transmitted over time because they were seen as contributing to the survival of the group. It is useful to remember that the idea of all persons having the right to reproduce is a recent one; previous societies survived by granting that privilege primarily to people who were likely to produce children deemed above average on some valued trait.

Positive practices encouraged the differential reproduction of people with desirable phenotypic traits—physical qualities such as health, strength, and beauty—as well as signs of material success, such as wealth or power. Differential reproduction was achieved by various means: the almost universal practice of obtaining a dowry or brideswealth before marriage ensured that the future parents would have enough resources and kin support to bring up children who would not become a burden to the community. Those who could not secure enough resources to marry might still beget children outside of a socially sanctioned union, but if brought to term, these offspring were more likely to die early because of infanticide or neglect. Thus, by requiring substantial material commitments before marriage, early societies were able to encourage higher reproductive rates among the more wealthy and socially connected class. To the extent that differences in wealth and power may at some point have had a genetic basis, such practices would have resulted indirectly in genetic selection. The effect of tying reproduction to resources was enhanced by the practice of polygyny, which for most of human history was the prevalent form of marriage. Successful males thereby gained disproportionate access to childbearing females.

In contrast, negative practices discouraged the reproduction of people deemed to be undesirable. Some of these practices were simply the mirror images of positive ones: poor, unhealthy individuals were less likely to marry and have children. But other means were more active, ranging from the castration of Icelandic men who had been found drunk outdoors more than three times,[3] to infanticide that differentially affected (and still affects) female children or any children from poor and socially marginal parents. In Asiatic cultures from Outer Mongolia to Thailand, a sizable proportion of the population—as many as one out of five—were encouraged to become celibate monks or nuns. In the Chinese and the Ottoman empires, eunuchs played a significant role in the bureaucracy, and since castration was a precondition for jobs there, impoverished parents had an incentive to emasculate some of their sons.

Attempts to influence the quality and relative distribution of future generations continued more or less haphazardly until the mid-1800s, when Charles Darwin's theory and Gregor Mendel's experiments provided the foundations for a systematic conceptual framework. In 1866 Mendel published the results of his cross-fertilization of peas, which yielded his laws of inheritance—the ratios by which certain phenotypic characteristics of parent plants are transmitted to their offspring through invisible "factors," which the Danish biologist Wilhelm Ludwig Johannsen in 1909 renamed "genes."

The practical implications of this new knowledge were first developed by the nineteenth-century British polymath Sir Francis Galton. In his studies of extraordinary talent, he found that genius was disproportionately represented in a few families. He concluded that arranged marriages between men of distinction and women of wealth would produce a "gifted race."[4] In 1883 he coined the word *eugenics* to designate a so-called science for the improvement of the human race. Putting his money where his science led, Galton left his estate to endow a chair for its study at the University of London. Following his lead, eugenics societies were founded in England (1907) and the United States (1926). These institutions, especially in the United States, directed their efforts in two ways: arguing that the upper classes owed their wealth and privileges to their superior genetic endowment, and lobbying for restricted immigration of "lesser races." A majority of the United States also legalized the sterilization of "undesirables" (mostly, mentally retarded people and criminals), and several thousand people each year were in fact sterilized during the 1920s and 1930s.

As obviously self-serving racial and class interests embraced eugenics, its reputation as an objective scientific endeavor plummeted. The final blow came when some of the most virulent ideologues of Germany's National Socialist Party adopted eugenic principles. These principles embodied in experimental efforts to breed a "pure Aryan" elite, and in parallel policies of sterilization and, eventually, extermination of individuals considered undesirable (including mentally or physically handicapped people and, finally, entire ethnic groups such as Jews and Gypsies).[5]

In a much more benign guise, a new version of genetics arose in the latter half of the twentieth century. By that time molecular biologists had begun to identify single genes responsible for vulnerability to certain physical defects and diseases. Physicians could screen people for such conditions as hemophilia or phenylketonuria, and then advise them as to the likelihood that their offspring would also be affected. In the late 1900s, entire new scientific and medical fields concerned with genetic engineering, counseling, medicine, research, and pharmacology sprang up—and the end is not yet in sight. Whether we like it or not, this enormous spurt in knowledge may force us to face dilemmas that Plato or Galton could scarcely have imagined.

Genetics in the Future

Our ancestors have been practicing crude forms of eugenics as far back as memory reaches. They could determine what was good work in terms of results that revealed themselves slowly, and in small doses: Farmer Joe's cows gave more milk than his neighbor's cows; the family that married shrewdly had healthier and more prosperous children. But now that the potential for more sophisticated ways of reshaping the genetic code is growing each year, the criteria for good work are less clear.

Decisions of this scope cannot be left entirely to specialists, whose personal and financial interests may conflict with those of the community at large, and whose wisdom may be limited to their disciplinary expertise. In fact, most of the geneticists we interviewed denied any privileged knowledge that would allow them to foresee the social implications of their work any better than ordinary citizens could. By and large, they agreed that the decision about the application of genetic knowledge should be made collectively, through communal and political decision making. But how can the public decide about these issues, when most laypeople lack the specialized knowledge necessary to understand—much less evaluate—the anticipated consequences of different courses of action? Information is power, and it is the experts who hold most of the power. Thus, the democratic insistence on collective agenda setting may be no more than an empty gesture.

The first step in resolving this dilemma is to get a better sense of the present reality and the potential of the domain of genetics, especially of consequential practices like genetic engineering. Armed with this knowledge, people outside this rapidly changing field may make informed decisions that the experts expect from the public and that we owe to our own future. Toward this end, we have interviewed several dozen leading geneticists, focusing on those philosophical quandaries about human nature, morality, and social justice that the applications of genetic knowledge raise and that informed laypeople ought to be aware of.

To anticipate our story, we found no unanimity among the experts; indeed, their views were often diametrically opposed. Some of the pioneers in this rapidly expanding field have qualms about what they see ahead. A Nobel Prize–winning molecular geneticist said:

> My greatest worry is as the power of human genetics is vastly extended in the next decade . . . that this science is not misused in society. . . . Should man be involved in genetic engineering of man? . . . I don't think [human] cloning will ever happen so I'm not concerned about that. . . . Should man begin to design man? Or try to? I'm quite cautious about that.

Medical geneticists, whose job includes advising patients about possible applications of biotechnologies to health hazards, are usually even more cautious. Typical is the warning from the president of a health-care foundation who is also a professor at a major medical school:

> Every lecture I give . . . I talk about eugenics, that I don't know what a good gene is. I say you might think that a gene which protects you from malaria is a good gene. But if you [had such a gene], and so did your partner, you have a 1 in 4 chance of having a baby with a debilitating, often fatal disease, sickle cell disease. . . . So a good gene became a bad gene. Same with cystic fibrosis. . . . So I don't know a good gene from a bad gene . . . we need to think these things over very carefully. This is the country that began euthanasia, this is the country that began the eugenics movement, of sterilizing imbeciles. It started here. It was perfected in other places; it started here. We are capable of that here. I don't want to be one of those people.

In contrast, many geneticists display little concern about possible misuses of their work. Scientists employed by biotech companies tend to see benevolent consequences coming from their efforts. The ones involved in basic research usually see their work as too far removed from clinical or social applications to worry about how it could be misused. Many feel that concerns about genetics have been overplayed by a controversy-hungry press. One leading molecular geneticist declared, "Ninety percent of what you hear about . . . are not dangers because it's not going to work . . . so why worry about it . . . almost all the gene fixing-up stuff, none of it works."

If practicing scientists have such widely differing opinions, what are the chances that the untutored public will be able to arrive at enlightened decisions about the uses of new insights and technologies? In fact, this very diversity within the profession is instructive. The public often assumes that the science underlying the technology is far more advanced than it actually is (as in believing that a "gene for madness" has been identified) and that the scientists are unanimous about its practical implications. This gives the public discourse a black-and-white, science-fiction quality that differs from the way scientists look at the situation.

Many of the leading scientists understand full well the distinction between *is* and *ought*; they are aware that just because something can be done, does not mean it *has* to be done. Of course, in practice every new idea, technique, or discovery develops an almost irresistible momentum, and research often resembles a runaway train hurtling toward the end of the tracks. But if we can accept their testimony, most scientists say they would readily subordinate their quest to the oversight of social consensus and change their courses if convinced that their work were leading in an undesirable direction.

How the Mind Was Shaped in the Past

Turning now to the other illustrative domain on which we are focusing, we need, first, to step back from the specifics of news journalism and consider several central, underlying issues related to information processing and the human mind. It is important to realize that the content of our brains is not determined by genetic inheritance. Without information, the human brain is useless. What we call the mind—that literal or metaphoric repository of our thoughts, feelings, experiences, and memories—arises only as a result of information collected from the environment. Indeed, the quality of a person's mind depends, to a large extent, on the information collected and organized in the brain. Long ago, cognitive theorists such as George Miller[6] and Herbert Simon[7] noted that the most precious human resource is information, which is constrained by the brain's processing capacity. Evolutionary psychologists such as John Tooby and Leda Cosmides have extended this notion to all living beings: "Animals subsist on information. The single most limiting resource to reproduction is not food or safety or access to mates, but what makes them each possible: the information required for making adaptive behavioral choices."8

When it comes to human behavior, information is a subjective entity, not an objective one. Cognitive neuroscientists and computer scientists have treated information objectively, as the ratio of signal to noise in the transmission of data. Here, however, we are speaking of information not in this technical sense but in terms of the effects that a signal, message, or stimulus has on the person who receives it—to put it more simply, on the *meanings* gleaned from information.

It is useful to remember that the word *information* has its roots in the Latin *formare*, meaning "to shape"; thus, it refers properly only to data (or "givens") that actually shape the mind. Any objective stimulus that we notice may be said to have a minimum of information value; but how much more it has depends on our goals, interests, and decoding abilities. If a man named Warren were to read a newspaper headline reporting that BankAmerica is contemplating a merger, that information might not evoke any ripple of interest and would be forgotten in a few minutes if he had no dealings with that institution. But if Warren's last name were Buffett and he held stock in the bank or was a potential investor, then the same data might send Warren into a flurry of activity and might make a significant difference to his life and to the lives of the investors he influences.

Information consists in data that modify consciousness either by increasing entropy through producing stress, alarm, worry, or confusion, or by decreasing entropy through creating order, resolving problems, or facilitating an adaptive response. If the data available for decoding have no meaning for a given person, the message contains negligible information for that person. Thus, for instance, the so-called information contained on the Web is no information at all until someone needs it, can decode it, and goes on to use it. An important document written in Mandarin Chinese may convey a great deal of vital information to the 800 million people who can read the language, but very little to those who are not versed in it.

Two boundaries limit how much information each of us can use. One is the brain's capacity to detect and manipulate various kinds of information—what in a broad sense we may call intellectual capacity. In our own view, it is too simpleminded to speak of a single entity called intelligence: human beings possess a spectrum of *intelligences*—ranging from the commonly recognized linguistic and logical-mathematical intelligences to less-widely acknowledged but equally significant interpersonal, spatial, and naturalist intelligences. All of us possess a set of basic intelligences, but we differ from one another on the strength and amalgams of particular intelligences. However defined and however cultivated, intellectual capacities are becoming the traits most rewarded by society and, therefore, most adaptive. In fact, they may be overshadowing previously valued characteristics such as physical strength, manual skill, loyalty, honesty, or cooperation.[9]

The second limit is the data available in the environment. Deprived of meaningful stimulation, even the potentially most intelligent brain cannot make adaptive behavioral choices. In these pages we will focus not on the hardware of the brain but on the external sources of information that provide its contents. In the recent past, the media have become the main source of information for the majority of people in industrialized nations. Thus, if news journalists fail to provide information that is meaningful, our minds are likely to be seriously impoverished—or, to put it differently, to be fed chiefly by rumor and entertainment.

Just as the science of genetics originated in the practices of our farming forebears, so did journalism arise from the ancient practice of exchanging information. In the last few hundred years, *news* has become virtually synonymous with *information,* although this was not always the case. For our ancestors who could not read, the most valuable information concerned the old, rather than the new. Such information had to be passed on by word of mouth, and if people did not listen constantly and carefully to the right speakers, they could miss out on the results of thousands of years of trial-and-error learning. In the absence of written records, a person had to memorize the names of relatives going back several generations and extending to cousins and in-laws far removed. In addition, the person had to recognize and remember edible and poisonous food; medicinal herbs; the lay of the land and the movement of animals; and perhaps most notably, which behaviors were permissible because they enhanced the group's survival and which were forbidden because they had led to undesirable results. To make sure this information was available, constant repetition was necessary. Of course, news about predators' movements was also important to know about, and gossip probably was at a premium. But if we are to judge from the few surviving preliterate societies, the task of recognizing and remembering useful past information may well have taken precedence over interest in current or future events.

Reliance on memory began to change as literacy made it possible to preserve important records tangibly. The easier writing became, the more likely it was for recent and more ephemeral facts, or news, to be recorded; thus, news started to compete with the past for the community's attention. The *Acta Diurna*, published in Rome in 59 B.C., was posted in public places with daily updates; in China, beginning in the eighth century A.D., the imperial court of the Tang dynasty circulated a report on current affairs to government officials, and that practice continued until 1911. Nonetheless, newspapers with any sizable circulation did not make their appearance until the early eighteenth century. Even as recently as the 1930s the news in many Central European villages was provided by a town crier who walked through the streets beating on a drum and stopped occasionally to read a summary of events that the authorities believed the populace should hear.

A storyteller who could be heard by the members of a small, isolated tribe performed the same central function that newspapers and television now provide. Throughout most of history, the media of communication consisted in rituals and rites representing crucial events from the past, graced by songs and myths recalling the origins of the tribe and the ancestors' heroic efforts to survive in a hostile world. Even in classical Greece, the closest equivalent to modern mass media were public choral performances of the epic poems commemorating great battles or victories in the athletic games of Olympia, Pithia, or Nemea. Although these epics dealt with real events, the point of them was not to convey facts, which the audience already knew, but to preserve and interpret epoch-making deeds and to give expression to the universal emotions and values underlying them.

One still sees the remains of this oral media tradition in India. During fairs or festivals storytellers known as *pauranikas* set up tents in the squares and for a modest fee chant uplifting episodes from the ancient Sanskrit epics. The Catholic Mass, among other functions, is also a reminder of the founding events of Catholicism, while Memorial Day, Thanksgiving, and Fourth of July celebrations convey information about the civic virtues of the United States.

Certainly people were always interested in current events, scandals, crimes, celebrities, and the weather. But until recently, the equivalent of the formal mass media dealt primarily with preserving information from the remote past, while the task of relaying the news was left to informal conversation and gossip. Now, potential information is stored in readily accessible form, to be used as needed. We can therefore afford to turn our attention away from the past to what is happening now. Of course, a lot of what is happening—and of what the media report—contributes neither useful knowledge nor a sense of personal or communal harmony. At the same time, while formal education is supposed to transmit the best selection of prior knowledge to every young person, much of that heritage is being lost the world over. So the tremendous increase in the availability of data that technology has made possible has not necessarily resulted in an increase in information in the strict sense—in fact, the opposite may be true.

We also have been turning increasingly to the news because of parallel developments in other areas of society, such as the seemingly inexorable trends toward globalization, mobility, and interdependence. Today, farmers on isolated North Dakota ranches may reasonably expect to be more successful if they keep in touch with the daily fluctuations on the Chicago futures market, ponder the foreign affairs section of the *New York Times* to anticipate changes in the global demand for corn, or read about the latest chemical fertilizers or genetically engineered organisms in *Scientific American*. As informal face-to-face interaction has decreased in communities, the mass media have also taken over the function of over-the-fence gossip and coffee-klatch information, providing ever more details about crimes, scandals, and celebrities, as well as advice about health and cooking.

To borrow concepts from biology, the data provided by the media may be thought of as *memes*, or units of information that, once mastered, condition—indeed constitute!—the way we think and that can be passed along from one person to another. Memes share several interesting characteristics with genes. Indeed, it was to call attention to this similarity that the British biologist Richard Dawkins coined the term in the 1970s, to complement the term *gene*.[10] Derived as it is from the Greek root for "imitation," or *mimesis*, memes encode instructions for action through imitation and learning. In this respect, they differ from genes, which encode instructions chemically.

Pursuing the comparison, Dawkins noted that, once we learn a pattern of action—say, an arithmetic operation, a song, or a cooking recipe—we can reproduce the behavior effortlessly. But because of the limited attentional capacity of our nervous system, we must constantly choose *which* memes to select and *which* to ignore. Memes compete with each other for space in memory, and they are often present as alleles, or alternative possibilities. An example is an election ballot, which consists of a list of paired choices among candidates representing different political positions. Depending on their mental predispositions, people will endorse one or the other candidate, thereby expressing a preference for one set of memes over another. Producers of breakfast cereals, cars, jingles, Web banners, and cruises, all try to create memes that will attract consumers' attention and thereby survive in the marketplace.

The memes one chooses can have long-lasting effects, even life-and-death consequences. For instance, the Serbs inhabiting the former Yugoslavia initially shared the same gene pool and the same culture. After the Ottoman Turks occupied the region more than five hundred years ago, some of the Serbs chose to organize their consciousness in line with the memes of Islam, while others held to Christian memes. They paid attention to different religious symbols, ate different foods, recited different prayers, intermarried within different lineages, and obeyed different chains of command. After all these centuries, the two lines of cultural inheritance have been passed on from parents to children, and those rival traditions made it possible for each group to see members of the other as strangers and enemies. Similar scenarios have been enacted in Ireland between Catholics and Protestants, in the Spanish Civil War by brother who fought brother across the Loyalist versus Republican divide, and in countless other cases. Repeatedly, religion, ideology, or sheer prejudice has resulted in people using memes to exterminate genes. Indeed, just as initially genes make memes possible, memes can then be mobilized to favor, annihilate, or refashion genes.

We can see clearly why the mass media, which now provide so much of the information that shapes our thinking, constitute critical institutions. Those who control the media's contents are significantly determining the future lives of their audiences. When communication channels were controlled by ecclesiastical or secular elites, information served primarily their interests; for this reason, a free press is an essential institution in a democracy. But as a democratic medium strives to serve the interests of the population at large, it finds itself in a paradoxical relationship with the audience. On the one hand, it tries to give readers and viewers what they want; on the other, it feels responsible for telling them what they should know even when that information is neither easy to assimilate nor popular. And as newspaper and broadcast conglomerates have become publicly owned financial operations responsive to escalating shareholder expectations, the tendency has been to compete for the audience's attention by providing the news items that are easiest to assimilate. All too often, these are the ones that make the least difference and therefore have the lowest informational content.

It is not only the content of the media that affects our minds. The medium itself, as the educator Marshall McLuhan famously stressed, is part of the message.[11] Flush with excitement about the new technology of television, McLuhan claimed that while print induces a passive, linear mind-set, TV requires viewers' active, creative participation. Subsequent research about cognitive processing while reading and viewing suggests that McLuhan may have gotten things backwards, in that reading requires more mental involvement and gives more creative freedom in decoding information than TV viewing does. Nevertheless, his insight about the importance of ascertaining the effects wrought by specific media still holds. Currently, the Web is heralded as having miraculous and unique properties leading to entirely new forms of information exchange (or meme transmission) in domains ranging from medicine to higher education. It is too early to tell whether these promises will be fulfilled or broken.

The Future of the Mind

Thanks to technological breakthroughs and new forms of social organization, the mental representations that fill up our consciousness and therefore determine the quality of our lives are changing rapidly. If those involved in the transmission of information find ways of doing their work well, we can face events forewarned; otherwise, useless news will simply confuse our picture of reality. For example, what we learn from the news will determine how we regard the uses of biotechnology. In this sense, it is the memes (thoughts, beliefs, and values) that will control our genes.

For this inquiry, we interviewed leading reporters, editors, broadcast anchors, and others who constitute the field of journalism. Our fundamental question was, How do these people define good work, and how do they manage to do it, given the waning of long-standing traditions and the rapidity of technological change?

The people involved in the delivery of news are generally aware of their task's importance and take that seriously. A prominent newscaster on national radio described his profession as almost an extension of our biological senses, as the eyes and ears of the community:

Reporters . . . are the people who watch things happen in the world
on behalf of everybody else. And try to tell everybody else what was
important about the things they didn't see. . . . So we are there out
in the world, experiencing life on their behalf. . . . I go on the air as
a daily deadline journalist and say: "Here's what happened, these
are the things that I saw and learned and understood, and now I
am going to tell you about them because you were off doing your
life all day, and now I'll tell you what I saw, on your behalf."

Journalists perceive their role as transforming data into information—
by presenting objective facts so that they will have subjective meaning
and, thereby, empowering the public to make adaptive choices. But the
situation in which the purveyors of news find themselves today differs
from that of geneticists. For the latter, each technological advance opens
up new horizons beckoning with the promise of additional excitement
and power. This is not true for journalists, who feel a deep ambivalence
about the impact of technology on their craft. Many believe that current
developments are making it hard for the public to extract intelligently the
information it needs. The Internet is seen as piling up useless, undigested
junk. C-Span has the same drawback: it forces the viewer to confront
hours of unedited events, which could be encapsulated in a few minutes
of telling summary or commentary. Commercial television, in the view of
some, provides mostly "highly engineered lies" for the benefit of the
sponsors and a docile audience. One of our respondents spoke for the
majority of his colleagues:

We really need to have a furious debate in this country about how
we are going to do the news. What we are going to do it for, who
we are going to do it for, how we are going to do it. Everything is
sort of careened along in this licentious, laissez-faire manner, and
we have ended up with a news business which serves its public
poorly.

The Power of Conscious Choice

Both geneticists and journalists agree that public debate should decide the
future of their respective realms. But most people know too little about
these domains to take an informed stance about what kind of good work

the community should expect. Accordingly, in the chapters that follow, we present an insider's view of the worlds of geneticists and journalists today, told by the individuals who can best inform this discussion. These accounts should help raise the level of the debate about the way genetic and journalistic information should be used, and the inevitable choices that will define our future.

But neither our genes nor the informational codes of our culture alone are responsible for how the future will unfold. The crucial final component in the causal chain is the code of consciousness—the use we choose to make of the instructions handed down by biology and culture.[12] The deterministic forces of the past are modified, rejected, or improved upon by ideas and ideals invented by individuals, and then shared by communities. Hence, our vision of the future shapes what happens.

To be sure, this premise that conscious human choice significantly influences events is far from a popular assumption. In the past, most people believed that human intention and effort have but a negligible influence on what happens. Some variant of fatalism is certainly understandable when human control over the environment is slight. It made sense for our ancestors, helpless in the face of inexplicable cosmic forces, to think that their best chances lay in submitting themselves to superhuman powers. Fatalism has also been a convenient stance, removing the burden of responsibility from our shoulders. Whether we look to the stars for advice, believe that ultimately the will of the gods will prevail, or trust in the inevitable unfolding of the materialist dialectic, we then face a restricted range of necessary decisions for which we feel answerable.

In our day, fatalism is still widespread, even though expressed in new forms. In the United States it is manifested most clearly in the belief that the "invisible hand" of the free market will lead us to an ever more prosperous, painless, and peaceful future. The recent upsurge of New Age beliefs in extraterrestrial beings or "Old Age" beliefs in angels further absolves us of personal responsibility. The advantage of these systems of belief is that they provide a meaningful interpretive framework for ordering otherwise chaotic or threatening information. The downside is that if we believe only in them, we may throw up our hands when facing vast problems, since there is no chance for us to do anything about them anyway.

But the reluctance to assume responsibility for the future is dangerous. The powers that technology has put in our hands are too great to be left to chance or to greed. What is the alternative to trying to direct the course of the future? To trust in the benevolent gods or a ubiquitous Gaia, or in an economic system that will miraculously turn waste into well-being? Or is the alternative to become callously selfish and hope that collective disaster will not trample the flowerbeds of our private gardens? Our hope clearly lies in our best individual and collective efforts, imperfect as these might be.

Understanding what makes for good work in genetics and the media is essential to the long-term future of our species. And there is another message in these interviews. The way journalists and geneticists define their own good work has implications for everyone involved in the "knowledge industry," which these days means the majority of us. We can draw from their examples as we reflect on today's pressing questions: What values can help us to do our jobs well? How can we feel proud of what we do for a living, when cutting corners and taking advantage of the public seem to be the surest paths to success? As we peer into the mirror, we must all answer these questions in our own work.

PART TWO

GENETICS

4

GENETICS IN
THE LIMELIGHT

In February 1943, at the height of World War II, Erwin Schroedinger, the winner of the 1933 Nobel Prize in physics for his studies of wave mechanics, delivered a set of lectures to the Institute for Advanced Studies at Trinity College, Dublin. Published a year later under the title *What Is Life?*, these lectures powerfully influenced intellectual life. In subsequent years Schroedinger's book captured the imagination of many aspiring young scientists.

In these lectures Schroedinger asked whether the principles of physics and chemistry could account for events that occurred within the boundaries of a living organism. In the twentieth century, the so-called hard sciences had made tremendous progress in describing events that occurred at the level of atomic particles; statistical laws were indispensable in accounting for the behavior of large numbers of atoms. Yet, Schroedinger claimed, the lawful events that take place within the bodies of living organisms involve relatively small groups of atoms. Indeed, through the mechanisms of heredity, patterns existing in only one "copy" of an organism somehow succeed in producing a uniquely well ordered series of events across countless generations.

Schroedinger described what biologists had established about heredity: the existence of dominant and recessive genes, their arrangement along chromosomes, the occurrence of mutations, and the mechanisms of mitosis and meiosis, by which such traits as the trademark disfigured lip of members of the Hapsburg dynasty were transmitted from one generation to the next. Despite Schroedinger's estimate that gene structure involved only a thousand atoms, these elements of heredity led to "a most regular and lawful activity—with a durability or permanence that borders upon the miraculous."[1]

Schroedinger reached the following conclusions. Genes must have a structure that is stable (so that inheritance occurs reliably) yet has slightly different forms (to allow genetic variation). Genes must consist of a long series of a few different elements that are repeated over and over again; the exact sequence of these elements represents a *code* in which hereditary information is encrypted.[1] Nature has apparently developed two mechanisms by which orderly events can be produced: the statistical mechanism uncovered by physics, which produces order from disorder; and the organic one, probed by biologists, whereby order is produced from order— "the finest masterpiece ever achieved along the lines of the Lord's quantum mechanics."[2]

Schroedinger issued a clear challenge to his scientific contemporaries who were studying the molecules of life. He exhorted them to apply the same degree of precision and explanatory accuracy that had been brought to the study of physical particles by the remarkable cohort of European workers from the early twentieth century, including Niels Bohr, Paul Dirac, Albert Einstein, Werner Heisenberg, Max Planck, and Schroedinger himself.

A Period of Unparalleled Scientific Flux

It would be difficult to find an earlier decade in the history of the sciences that proved to be as apocalyptic as the 1940s. At the very time that Schroedinger was delivering his lectures, many hundreds of scientists in Los Alamos, New Mexico, and affiliated research laboratories were working feverishly on the Manhattan Project—an unprecedented collaborative effort to produce a weapon of mass destruction that, they hoped, would bring a terrible war to an early conclusion. By the summer of 1945 their scientific and technological efforts had been crowned with success, and with the explosion that August of two atomic weapons over Japan, World War II indeed came to an end.

During that same fateful year, Vanevar Bush, a physicist who was the president of the prestigious Carnegie Institute of Washington and the director of the federal Office of Scientific Research and Development, issued an important document. In *Science: The Endless Frontier*, Bush argued that discoveries in the basic sciences constituted an incredible human adventure, that breakthroughs would continue indefinitely, and that forward-looking policy makers needed to ensure sufficient support for scientific work in the United States. Bush called for the unprecedented— a perennial effort to carry out "the best science" even when national defense efforts were not all-encompassing. Ignoring possible destructive applications of science, Bush audaciously declared, "Without scientific progress, no amount of achievement in other directions can insure our health, prosperity, and security as a nation in the modern world."[3]

At the time that Bush wrote, physics was the preeminent science. Atomic physicists basked in the glory of theoretical advances of relativity and quantum mechanics, and the technological windfall of nuclear weapons. However, this exuberance proved short-lived. When physicists such as J. Robert Oppenheimer, the director of the Manhattan Project, questioned the further development and possible deployment of nuclear weapons, their patriotism was called into question. Moreover, physicists soon discovered the limits of their influence; the ultimate decisions about the uses of their science would be made by politicians, for political ends, and not by theorists, experimentalists, or other scientists.

One other event, virtually unheralded at the time, turned out to be of singular consequence for our story. In 1944, at the Rockefeller University in New York City, a team of investigators led by Oswald Avery announced a most important discovery. In the process of demonstrating that a characteristic of the species could be passed from dead bacteria to living ones, and that the future strains of the bacteria would themselves be able to transmit that characteristic (as if they had "learned" how to do so), Avery and his colleagues had isolated and identified the critical material of heredity.[4] Rather than proteins or other cellular components, as most scientists had speculated, an organic molecule called DNA (deoxyribonucleic acid) had proved to be the vehicle of genetic inheritance.

The significance of Avery's discovery was not appreciated at the time, because DNA was thought to be a uniform chemical molecule, one incapable of carrying the "individualizing" code that Schroedinger had specified. But within the next few years, scientists gradually concluded that DNA must be the molecule that encoded information, performed functions, and duplicated itself precisely. In its slightly varying coded information (from one DNA molecule to another) lay the key to heredity.

At this point biological scientists on both sides of the Atlantic engaged in an unprecedented race to discover the actual structure and mechanisms of DNA. This contest was won in 1953 by the young British physicist-turned-biologist Francis Crick and the even younger American molecular biologist James D. Watson. Thanks to their epoch-making work, we now know that DNA is a double helix, composed of four separate repeatable chemical nucleotide bases. The unraveling of the helixes and the subsequent re-creation of their original constituents through a process of complementarity constitute the essence of the once-mysterious hereditary process. Whether or not anyone was aware of it, the torch of dominance in science was passing rapidly from the physicists to the biologists.

The Rise of Biology in Our Time

Once DNA's double helical structure had been determined, work in genetics and microbiology took off—and it has maintained rocketlike thrust ever since. Genetics became a science concerned with the transmission of biological information from cell to cell, from organism to organism. Talented young scientists were attracted to the domain of molecular biology (that is, microbiology) rather than physics, and a number of people who had been trained as physicists (including Schroedinger and Crick) turned their attention to biological processes.

Since then, innumerable major advances have been made, and we can mention but a few here. The 1950s were marked by methods for separating chromosomes from the rest of the cell and by the discovery of the fine structure of the DNA replication mechanisms. During the 1960s the complete genetic code was "cracked" (that is, researchers determined how DNA is transcribed to RNA, RNA is translated to amino acids, and amino acids yield proteins), and cutting and rejoining techniques for the recombining of DNA were developed. The early 1970s ushered in actual "recombinant" efforts to reengineer organisms, for example, by snipping genes from one organism and inserting them into another or splicing together molecules from different DNA strands.

The importance of this work was widely acknowledged, often by the timely awarding of Nobel Prizes to those who carried it out. And, perhaps bearing in mind the mixed blessing of atomic energy, at least some ob servers realized that these discoveries raised ethical issues and harbored social dilemmas. In a surprisingly prescient editorial in 1963, the *New York Times* declared:

> Geneticists are on the threshold of a historical breakthrough in their efforts to probe the secrets of heredity. Is mankind ready for such powers? The moral, economic, and political implications of the possibilities are staggering, yet they receive little organized public attention. The danger exists that scientists will make at least some of these God-like powers available to us in the next few years, well before society—on present evidence—is likely to be even remotely prepared for the ethical and other dilemmas with which we shall be faced.[5]

The conundrum forecast by the *Times* had come to pass by the early 1970s. Biologists in U.S. and European laboratories were isolating genes and creating or remaking organisms in a way that would have smacked of science fiction a few decades earlier. In a much-praised move, without clear precedent (or equivalent follow-up), molecular biologists voluntarily instituted a moratorium on such recombinant research. In February 1975, more than a hundred scientific leaders gathered at a conference center in Asilomar, California, to discuss the risks associated with experiments that involved the manipulation of genes. As a result of this meeting, the scientists postponed certain experiments that involved the recombination of DNA. Alerted by this meeting, citizens and politicians became concerned that one or more of these genetically altered organisms might be toxic and could damage other living organisms or disturb the natural environment. In the following year, the city council in the university community of Cambridge, Massachusetts, held raucous public meetings at which the safety of such research was debated. In yet another event of the period, a group of presidents of major research universities met in Pajaro Dunes, California, in March 1982 to discuss the principles that should govern university participation in the emerging biotechnology industries.

Such activities indicate that leaders in the realm of genetics, and in related areas like university governance and city government, were concerned about possible negative effects of the new research—sufficiently concerned to conduct public discussions of these implications. Apparently this was a domain prepared to police itself, and its leading representatives saw themselves as guardians of the domain. Top geneticists showed a willingness to critique their area of study and to consider restraining their own activities because of possible harmful effects on the wider community or the planet. Even if some of the concerns proved unfounded, little was lost by this exercise in reflection and restraint.

The late 1970s marked the apex of public concern about the course of U.S. biological research. (Concerns about new drugs, techniques, creatures, or cellular manipulations have been more marked in Europe.) One reason for the diminution of widespread public concern stands out: as of this writing, there have been no reports of disasters attendant to genetic engineering—"no Chernobyls or Three Mile Islands," as one of the people we interviewed put it.

Two other factors alleviated popular concern. One was the accelerated pace of changes in genetics—the identification of genes for specific diseases and for specific traits, the production of far more precise drugs, and the launching and completion of the Human Genome Project (an unprecedented effort to identify the total three-billion-base pair genetic sequence of the human being). There were also such dramatic events as the first in vitro (test-tube) human fertilization (1978), injection of genetically engineered cells into a human patient (1989), the cloning of mice and sheep (1996 and 1997), the creation of the first artificial human chromosome (1997), the enhanced capacity to use undifferentiated stem cells to create replacement tissue or organs or even entire organisms (the late 1990s), and the birth of a monkey with a foreign (jellyfish) gene in its cells (2001). With change so rapid, it may be difficult—particularly for Americans, who are enthralled by change—to pause and reflect on possible consequences. There may also be a naive faith that technology in itself can solve problems.

The other contributor was the coming together of basic science, technologically oriented industry, and venture capital. For the first time, it appeared that major human diseases might be controlled, thanks to an understanding of their genetic basis and to the creation of effective treatments. Buoyed by the prospect of tremendous discoveries and possibly commensurate profits, new companies sprang up throughout the United States, as well as in other nations.

Characteristically, these companies were launched by, or at least featured, major biological scientists, preferably ones who had won a Nobel or a Lasker Prize. The companies often selected names featuring some variant of the word *gene*, such as Amgen, Biogen, or Genentech. A company typically focused its efforts on a particular portion of the genetic enterprise, such as foods, drugs, the treatment or cure of specific diseases, or the discovery and transmission of biochemical information. Often located near major universities or research centers, companies hired promising younger scientists as staff, offering them higher salaries, more congenial teamwork, and less of a publish-or-perish atmosphere than they could have expected at the nearby research university. Few of these companies actually turned significant profits during the first years, but enough of them showed sufficient promise to justify an initial public offering and to make many scientists rich (at least on paper) as well as distinguished.

The role played today by venture capital and newly emerging hybrid institutions is unprecedented in the sciences. While the "marketization of genetics" may turn out to be problematic, at this point the members of the field report a euphoric sense of alignment: the pace of discoveries and the possibilities of profit invigorate practitioners as well as investors, yielding experiences of flow. The situation in journalism could not be more different. A recent article in *Newsweek* effectively captured this ecstatic mood: "We will deploy gene therapy and 'nanobiology' (extremely tiny devices and medicines) to cure a number of nasty disorders. We will perfect organic transplants from animals to humans. We will find ways to rewire our brains to repair individual deficiencies."[6]

The Geneticists Interviewed

We and our research assistants interviewed four groups of geneticists. First, there were thirty-nine prominent Ph.D. and M.D. scientists, all of them "creator-leaders" who have made major discoveries and who head significant laboratories at universities or research institutions. A second comparison group consisted of ten midlevel practitioners who work at smaller, less prestigious institutions or who hold nonleadership roles in prominent institutions. We also interviewed seven gatekeepers who are no longer actively involved in research because they now head up leading national institutions. The latter turned out to be virtually indistinguishable in their responses from creator–leaders, presumably because they were drawn from the same ranks. (In this respect, genetics differs from other domains, where a firmer line can be drawn between those conducting basic work and those occupying managerial roles.) As part of other studies that we carried out during the same period, we also interviewed forty other prominent geneticists as well as twenty younger geneticists who were either completing their doctoral studies or pursuing their first jobs. While our major findings emerged from the fifty-six geneticists just enumerated, we also draw on these other interviews as appropriate.

The majority of the people we interviewed worked in universities or in nonprofit research institutions. Fourteen worked exclusively or primarily for biotechnological companies. Most of the university or research institution–based scientists agreed readily to our interviews (though they often took weeks to schedule), but we were almost always turned down when we approached for-profit companies. Granting of interviews, even on topics outside of current work, was apparently seen as a threat to the operation of such companies. Surprisingly, the prohibitions proved strongest for midlevel practitioners. It was easier to gain access to CEOs, who presumably did not have to seek a manager's approval of their remarks or of their time given to such a purpose. We also learned of privately held companies so secretive that their existence is not known to the outside world. Eventually, we gained interviews with a reasonable sample of individuals in industry, though most spoke only under conditions of anonymity. This island of resistance suggests a troubling tendency on the part of the genetics industry to be defensive and secretive about its activities.

This sample is neither random nor systematically structured in a research sense, but no major group or perspective in genetics has been ignored. On the basis of well over a hundred probing interviews, we have gained considerable knowledge about the late–1990s U.S. practice of genetics research.

The core interviews as well as the interviews with people in related studies featured the same structure and topics. We began each interview with a discussion of current work and then asked about the person's central goals and values, and the guiding principles of the work. After asking about formative and training influences, we raised questions about workplace conditions, with a focus on obstacles encountered, opportunities grasped, and strategies devised. We also elicited information about the changes taking place in the domain and the field, and we asked about personal evaluations of these changes. Using both direct and indirect probes, we focused directly on issues of good work: the workers' dreams and nightmares, the people or agencies to which they felt responsible, and their concerns (or lack thereof) about ethical issues. (Further details can be found in Appendixes B, C, and D.)

The Prototypical Creator-Leader in Genetics

The life stories of geneticists have a surprisingly similar ring. Differences appear in research interests and temperament, rather than in biographical data. In an effort to capture the common themes, we have created a prototypical or exemplary geneticist—referred to here as E.G.—who could be a man or a woman. Not every clinician, counselor, and basic scientific researcher resembles this exemplary geneticist, but a few such people can be found at every major research institution. To a surprising extent, we discovered, even those with widely different career histories measured themselves with reference to an image similar to the profile we present. It is as if leading figures in today's computer industry compare themselves to founding figures like Bill Gates or Steve Jobs; or as if journalists a few decades ago thought of themselves with reference to James Reston of the *New York Times* or Edward R. Murrow of *CBS News*.

In 1999 (when the interviews were completed) E.G. was fifty-five years old, and he provided the following picture of his background. He was born in the United States in a middle-sized community to a family that was reasonably comfortable, but not affluent, and that strongly valued education. E.G. was a good student who, by the time of high school, had shown an inclination toward mathematics or science. Neither a wildly popular person nor an outcast, E.G. was seen by classmates as bookish, independent, and a bit weird. By the time he entered college, E.G.'s mathematical interests had cooled; his scientific proclivities were geared more toward chemistry or biology than toward physics or the social sciences. It seemed likely that he would either pursue a medical degree or a doctorate in biology. He did well in college, was encouraged by his professors, and often carried out additional scientific work after classes or during the summer. After he won a fellowship and several prizes, his already ambitious career goals became even clearer.

Growing up in the 1950s and 1960s, E.G. was excited to learn about the discovery of DNA, the cracking of the genetic code, and the first tentative efforts to recombine or even constitute genetic material for research or therapeutic ends. He eagerly anticipated joining this world-changing enterprise at its early stages and, thereby, participating in discoveries of historical consequence, to illuminate the nature of life. Many of the strongest students in E.G.'s cohort of young scientists—those who might

have become physicists in the 1930s or computer scientists or Internet pioneers in the 1990s—deliberately chose to enter the competitive field of
genetics during the Kennedy-Johnson-Nixon eras, or to take a less
parochial perspective, the comparable times of Charles de Gaulle, Leonid
Brezhnev, or Harold Wilson.

In 1970, when E.G. was completing his doctoral degree, the bright future of genetics was already being recognized, and departments of genetics or molecular biology were being created at various places. E.G. had a
strong record as a student, had begun to publish research articles, and was
blessed with an adviser-mentor who was willing to vouch for him to
other gatekeepers. Rather than worry about a first job, as a contemporary
with a doctorate in classics or history might have had to do, E.G. con-
templated the luxury of options: pursue one or more postdoctoral fellow-
ships in a prestigious laboratory, become an assistant professor at a
top-ranking college or university, or take a position as a full-time investigator at a new research institute.

These opportunities did not come without costs. Even in the early
days, molecular biology and genetics were highly competitive fields. Researchers had to work ten or more hours a day, six or seven days a week,
for months on end. A premium was placed on selecting the most promising area for research, pursuing a problem imaginatively and doggedly, being the first to make a consequential scientific finding, and then
presenting that finding at respected conferences or other such forums and
publishing it in the appropriate journals (for example, *Science*, *Nature*,
Cell) or in proceedings of a prestigious national academy of science. As a
single man who thought of marriage and family involvements only as
possibilities in coming years, E.G. was able and eager to focus solely on
his work.

In 1972, E.G. accepted a post at a prestigious research university and
quickly established himself as a rising star. Whatever personal doubts he
may have had about pushing ahead with recombinatorial DNA, he certainly did not want his professional career to be jeopardized by lengthy
moratoria or outright prohibitions on certain lines of research. He was
aware, too, that if he voiced doubts, he would encounter challenges from
his colleagues. Fortunately for E.G., no alarming developments associated with his research area arose, nor did any major controversies.

Just as E.G. was easing into a more senior role as a tenured professor,
the first biotechnology companies were being launched. Still relatively
young and energetic, as well as knowledgeable about future directions of

research, he was offered a senior position in 1984 as a scientific adviser at one of these companies and given an opportunity to invest in it as well. Thus, by age forty, E.G. was in the enviable position of being not only a prominent scientist relatively assured of continued governmental funding for his own priority research and already cited in textbooks but also a frontline participant in commercial enterprises that promised to make him very rich.

No longer required to take the biologists' "vows of poverty" (as one of our informants put it), E.G. could look forward to a comfortable and possibly luxurious lifestyle. Asked about obstacles he faced then and in subsequent years, E.G. was hard-pressed to list those imposed from the outside. Most, he said, came from his own personality (he sometimes procrastinates), his own mind (he cannot remember the details of studies), or the existential limits of life (there is just not enough time to accomplish all he desires while still an active scientist).

E.G. has proven to be one of the new captains of science-industry—a third-millennium equivalent of a sixteenth-century explorer or nineteenth-century capitalist entrepreneur. As the head of a vast and multifaceted enterprise, he spends much of his time writing, or supervising the writing, of grants that ensure the millions of dollars needed to sustain this enterprise. He relies on carefully chosen senior personnel—research or office managers—to select, train, and guide the careers of junior researchers and students, technicians, and support staff. He relies as heavily on a cohort of young research scientists, who hope to emulate his success and who work very hard—with or without sufficient credit—on the laboratory's investigative program. E.G. also spends many hours shuttling back and forth between his research laboratory at the university and the complementary facilities at biotech companies. He is expected to spend "quality time" with venture capitalists, wealthy celebrities, and philanthropists to gain their financial support. He must also attend national and international scientific congresses; serve on national committees that deal with research, ethical, and training issues; and confer regularly with his own students and colleagues.

E.G. has not done regular benchtop science for many years, nor has he had the opportunity to keep up with the copious scientific literature, except in the narrowest of specialties. He relies on word of mouth from his students and close colleagues and, increasingly, on brief summaries posted on the Internet. There is not much time for family, exercise, leisure, or contemplative moments—he regrets this but accepts it as part of life's bargain. Indeed, E.G. seems to thrive on this hectic life, rather than being frustrated or exhausted. His daily routine is imbued with considerable flow and is only rarely scarred by self-doubts. He still feels that he is a frontline participant in one of the singular scientific events of all time. Through many of his comments, he happily affirms that the values of the domain, the current practices of the field, public needs, and his own personal aspirations are well aligned.

Yet the rapid changes in his domain present a significant challenge. E.G. cannot look to those senior to him (let alone to historical paragons like Gregor Mendel or Charles Darwin) for models. The financial, ethical, and even scientific questions are of a scale unprecedented in the annals of research. Flying blind, E.G. and his colleagues are creating new kinds of institutions that cut across biological sciences, information science, and economics.

Variations on a Theme

While our sketch of one exemplary geneticist covers much of the landscape, we need to consider how geneticists may differ from one another. We can best do this by considering two dimensions in which differences often are reflected: the shape of the career trajectory and the nature of institutional affiliations.

Career Ascendancy

A few scientists such as James Watson or Mark Ptashne emerged as stars very early in their careers. Watson codiscovered the structure of DNA when he was twenty-five. He became an influential professor and department head at Harvard in his thirties and was named the head of the prestigious Cold Spring Harbor Laboratory at age forty. Mark Ptashne raced against Walter Gilbert, his older colleague down the hall at the Harvard Biological Laboratories, and first isolated and described the operation of the lambda repressor—that is, the process that shuts off, or represses, genes. This discovery not only solidified his career as a scientific investigator but also placed him in a position to cofound the Genetics Institute, a biotechnology company, around 1980 and to become wealthy in his forties.[7]

The earlier that people stand out in their careers, the more choices they will have. The sociologist Robert Merton dubbed this situation the

"Matthew effect" ("To everyone who has, more will be given"—Matthew 25:29). Watson used his prominence to become a gatekeeper at an early age and, ultimately, to emerge as probably the most authoritative and prestigious figure in genetics. When the time came to select a head of the Human Genome Project, Watson was the obvious and widely praised first choice. Ptashne continued his distinguished scientific work but also explored extrascientific fields; he became a serious student of golf, a significant collector in the visual arts, and a first-rate amateur violinist who now performs internationally. Asked what his money allowed him to do, Ptashne quipped: "Who knows? Maybe one of my chief motivations has been to be in a position to afford a great violin. Going into business . . . founding a genetics company . . . had one big payoff: the violin I now own, which means more to me than I can say. . . . I would still be playing on a cigar box if it hadn't been for that."

It is much more difficult to launch a significant scientific career later in life. One can draw inspiration from the unusual career of Jane Rowley, who in 1998 received the National Medal of Science, the nation's highest scientific award. Trained as a physician, Rowley first took time off to raise her three children. In the early 1960s, in her late thirties, Rowley recommenced studies in cytogenetics at Oxford University. Thereafter, with her children then in school, Rowley approached Leon Jacobson, a distinguished medical researcher at the University of Chicago, and requested a microscope, a desk, and a modest salary for part-time work. Jacobson was able to grant Rowley's requests, and under his guidance, she began an indepth investigation of the causes of leukemia.

This work was crowned with success when, in the early 1970s, Rowley discovered that certain types of leukemia were connected to chromosomal abnormalities called translocations (where chromosomes are broken and the ends of the chromosomes are exchanged). A decade later she was able to clone the translocation breakpoint and identify the controlling genes. Mechanisms of translocation have been observed in many forms of cancer and are now firmly established.

Rowley's success was abetted by several factors. She singles out the support of her husband ("the most important person") and her supervisors, chiefly Jacobson. She was allowed to rise through the professorial ranks while keeping a part-time position, a most unusual pattern at the University of Chicago and elsewhere. She began to work full-time only when her youngest child had gone away to school. Rowley applied for grants during her fifties and sixties, putting in eighty-hour workweeks and gradually, if belatedly, joining the ranks of the scientific elite. Now in her mid-seventies, she continues to conduct research, finding time to inspire young people, and especially women, to enter the field of medical-scientific research.

If an unconventional researcher like Rowley is to attain a leadership role, the institutions of the field may have to tolerate a greater number of exceptions (for example, less-than-full-time work). Nor do those with a late-beginning career have the spectrum of options that exist for early beneficiaries of the Matthew effect. It is unlikely that they will have as much opportunity to affect the knowledge in the domain, as did Watson, or to achieve high levels of mastery outside the domain, as did Ptashne.

Institutional Affiliation

Most of our creator-leaders maintain a primary affiliation with universities or research institutions. Watson retained his Harvard professorship during his first years at Cold Springs Harbor, and Ptashne also remained at Harvard until 1998, when he moved to New York City's Sloan-Kettering Institute for Cancer Research. Nearly all have had at least a modest relation with a biotechnology company (generally, by serving on a board of scientific advisers), and some (like Ptashne) have been heavily involved with such an enterprise for a decade or more.

But other patterns are possible as well, and these diverse trajectories reveal the flexibility of a scientific field that is expanding into various social spheres. For instance, Craig Venter, an influential researcher at NIH for nearly a decade, pioneered in inventing speedier methods for mapping the human genome. Venter's discoveries, and the struggles over how to patent them, placed him increasingly at odds with the NIH administrators. In 1992, he left the government, started the nonprofit Institute for Genetic Research, and helped create the for-profit company Human Genome Sciences.

For several years, Venter's partner at Human Genome Sciences was William Haseltine, who had been a major Harvard Medical School researcher focusing on AIDS. When the possibility arose for creating drugs that made use of newly discovered information about the human genome, Haseltine also elected to move full-time to the private sector.

In a split that received a great deal of press attention, Venter and Haseltine discontinued their collaboration in the late 1990s. Haseltine continued to head Human Genome Sciences, while Venter launched Celera, a for-profit company. Celera played a major role in the decoding of the human genome, essentially completed in late spring 2000, and the company is poised to be the major purveyor of information about the human genome to the corporate sector and the general public. Indeed, Venter and Haseltine became heated competitors with one another and with the federally funded research consortium, each claiming that his company would complete genomic sequencing first and make findings available to the public in the most proper form, and each claiming that his brand of scientific work was more important.

To secure a feeling for what it is like to be a new "captain of science and industry," it is instructive to hear Haseltine on the subject of institutions:

> I do not define myself as a business executive but rather as a scientist who uses tools that society provides to accomplish my primary goal, advancing science in the service of medicine. I have come to understand that a university is a tool that society has created for a special purpose—government research laboratory is also a tool to accomplish a slightly different purpose—so too are pharmaceutical companies. I feel free to use any of those tools to accomplish my ends. As a scientist, I felt free to use either a pipette or a mass spectrometer. If the appropriate tool to accomplish my goal of isolating and characterizing a complete set of human genes for medical purpose is the creation of a new company, I decided that was the tool I should use. The rapid isolation of a complete collection of human genes simply could not be done in a university setting. No pharmaceutical company was willing to invest in the new genomics effort. When I began, the government-sponsored Human Genome Project had just decided to discontinue rapid human gene discovery in favor of a slower, more systematic approach. Consequently, the only tool available . . . for me to accomplish my goal was to create a new company. As it happened that tool was extremely well-suited to the task.

If investigators alter their primary affiliations, the shift tends to take place from the university or a research institution to the corporate sector. Those with primary industrial ties would find it difficult to move to the academy for two reasons: First, scientists from the corporate world typically lack the necessary publication (and teaching) credentials; and second, universities prefer to promote from within the university community rather than to hire at senior ranks from the commercial sphere.

In some cases, however, people have moved back and forth between industry and university settings. Leon Rosenberg, a major research scientist and pioneer in the domain of medical genetics, rose through the professorial ranks and eventually became the dean of the Yale University Medical School. After twenty-six years at that institution, Rosenberg decided to work at the pharmaceutical company Bristol-Myers Squibb. As he explained, "It was very clear to me that someone who headed R&D at a major pharmaceutical company would have a way of affecting medicine in a considerable fashion. Would have a way of defining how major resources, how major financial resources were going to be used in a scientific setting. I thought that would be fascinating."

Rosenberg's stint in industry was instructive but not always easy. He recalled: "There were plenty of near rejection episodes which I can smile about in retrospect but which I didn't spent a lot of time smiling about in the first couple of years that I was there. Or maybe in any of the years." By the end of his tenure at Bristol-Myers Squibb, Rosenberg felt that he had strengthened the scientific side of the company. When he was forced to retire because of age, Rosenberg was able to return to the academy, serving as the head of a new research advocacy facility situated at Princeton University. In this position, tailored for him, Rosenberg has a great deal of freedom: he can teach, launch faculty seminars, and lead policy task forces. Rosenberg attributed his varied career to accident and temperament:

> There certainly hasn't been any grand plan in all of that. I've sort of enjoyed the accidental nature of many of those changes. I suppose I've been willing to take the risks that a lot of other people would not. In becoming a chairman, in becoming a dean, in going to industry—I recognize, and I recognized at the time, that there were enormous risks associated with those career choices. But I think psychologically taking risk . . . suited me.

A final, illuminating career path is described by a thirty-five-year-old man who is the founder, CEO, and president of a start-up biotech company. This person, whom we will call Blake Connor, was a highly promising young biologist at the university. He had been a postdoctoral fellow in a prestigious laboratory and clearly had had the option of pursuing a successful academic career. Indeed, like his mentors, he was on the road to becoming an E.G. But in the spirit of the Silicon Valley hackers of decades past and present, when the opportunity came to start a company, Connor and three of his colleagues (also promising young scientists) could not resist. They assembled a prestigious board of advisers and, with the help of family and friends, raised several million dollars.

Connor is now completely absorbed in the business side of the enterprise. He speaks candidly about the differences between the university and industry. While Connor rejects the label of "serial entrepreneur," he clearly draws excitement from starting businesses and steering them to success. Whereas academics have to spend years on one line of research, which may or may not pay off, the young scientist in the start-up can work more quickly. Resources are readily available and one can see results and payoff much more directly. In his words:

> I was never clear on what my goals were in academics or why I was doing it. I was just doing it for fun. In business, the rules are clear. You have to be honest and ethical, but the goal is to win, crush, dominate, and deliver a long-term shareholder return, maximize cash out for cash in. I like that. It's a clear filter through which to put a question.

There are evident advantages in the plethora of new institutional arrangements and in the potential for working in more than one institution, either serially or simultaneously. As Haseltine indicates, people can use these institutions to achieve varying goals; the flexibility provided by diverse settings is valuable for practitioners bent on making discoveries and seeing that they are put to best use. Still, this approach holds perils. Each domain has its cardinal missions, and these missions are not necessarily shared (or even understood) by the range of institutions that have cropped up in recent years. For example, the biology department at the university may look for discoveries that advance knowledge about the basic mechanisms of organic development, and its measure of success is publication in a prestigious journal. In contrast, a drug company's research department may ignore developmental puzzles in favor of finding the least expensive and most efficient way to cure a disease, and its measure of success is a large share of the commercial market. In times of flux, however, both individuals and institutions may become confused if they attempt to blur functions, flexibility may lead to chaos, and deeper concerns of the domain and wider interests of various stakeholders may become obscured or lost in the ensuing shuffle.

As we examine specific features—the trajectory of career ascendancy, the predominant institutional affiliation, the extent and measure of success—the differences among geneticists come into sharper focus. Yet, although all of the practitioners we interviewed expressed some degree of euphoria: it is difficult to suppress the air of triumphalism. What was once a backwater of inquiry has moved to center stage, not only in the scientific world but also in the arena of public attention. Biology in 2001 is at least as dominant as physics was in 1945. Moreover, as in the days directly after the completion of the Manhattan Project, the science seems to be embarking on a golden age. In Chapter 5 we closely examine the particular goals, values, and practices that mark today's genetics community and that so far have rendered the notion of good work relatively unproblematic. It remains to be seen whether this seeming Golden Age of good work will prove transient—as in the case of atomic physics—or more enduring.

5

A GOLDEN AGE IN A
WELL-ALIGNED DOMAIN

GENETICISTS HOLD A COMMON VIEW of their enterprise and it is a beneficent one. Nearly all of the people we interviewed expressed great excitement about their scientific work. Indeed, when asked about their goals or missions, more than three quarters of the respondents report they are able to carry out the scientific work they cherish and believe that their work will ultimately help others.

The Best of Both Worlds:
Four Main Themes

Four themes ran through our interviews with geneticists. First was *the thrill of scientific inquiry.* One of our respondents, Leroy Hood, has contributed to many different areas of molecular biology. At the time of the interview he had moved from the California Institute of Technology to the University of Seattle so that he could set up an interdisciplinary department of biology. He told us, "I'd rather go create a whole new area that opens up new possibilities in biology. . . . I like the discovery aspects of science, the frontier aspects, the being out there in the uncharted territory." The exciting aura of science is evident early on for many people. David Hirsch, who is completing doctoral work in a combined M.D.-Ph.D. program at MIT and the Harvard Medical School, has been studying how fat enters the body's cells—work that has implications for the treatment of diabetes, heart disease, and obesity. This young investigator reflected: "Scientists work in a very privileged field. . . . Science is a great field because it's one of the very few fields where you sit at your desk and you think, What would I like to learn more about today? . . . Then you get to go and do it."

A second theme is *the pleasure of working with scientific materials.* Hirsch spoke of the work's aesthetic appeal: "I think there's the beautiful science, which is when you put the story together it just has the aesthetics of looking very pleasing . . . you created a work of art." Others connect in a personal, almost visceral way to the specific contours of the entities or processes they are studying. An expert in the genetics of cardiovascular disease rhapsodized:

> Understanding these issues is emotionally driving. . . . I love the heart, I love the function of contractile apparatus, and blood being injected. I love the noises of listening on a person's chest to murmurs and blows and things. It's just what excites me. Understanding how it can go awry is great. I'm not interested in coronary artery disease, that's plumbing.

Enchantment with *the quality of thinking* that goes into the practice of science constitutes a third theme. Mark Ptashne, whose career was launched by his pioneering work on gene repression (as noted in Chapter 4), stressed the importance of certain modes of conceptualization:

> The real payoffs are formulations, analogies, metaphors, ways of looking at the world . . . new language. Imposing a way of talking about things that (paraphrasing a remark of Emerson's) helps turn fact into truth. You are trying to discover the most basic things . . . which means that your eyes are constantly open for what is going on in areas that are only vaguely related, and trying to make the whole thing coherent. This is a dangerous thing of course. . . . I tend to be unable to take in details unless they illuminate the big picture . . . and the trouble with imposing the big picture is that I could be—usually am—wrong.

Finally, there is *the belief that science foregrounds a certain kind of rational thinking*. James D. Watson is ever vigilant for scientifically grounded explanations: "Always you like to see reason prevail over prejudice. To the extent there are real answers or real explanations, you'd like people who do things for real explanations rather than false ones. The desire for rationality."

These are the primary sources of intrinsic satisfaction in science. We frequently encountered people who yoked the practice of science with a commitment to help other individuals. Irene Chow has worked for large pharmaceutical companies and now heads a relatively small biotechnology company on the West Coast. She explained: "What I have really always been interested in was to discover, develop, and eventually commercialize new treatments, new drugs, which can treat severely debilitating and life-threatening diseases which currently have no satisfactory treatment. That was always the thing that inspired me."

Ian Wilmut achieved international acclaim in 1997 as head of the team that cloned the sheep Dolly. Since then, he has been studying how a patient's own cells might be used to treat crippling conditions such as diabetes or Parkinson's disease. The patient's cells will in effect revert to an undeveloped form and then be guided so as to differentiate anew into the desired tissue. Wilmut attributes his own interest in this line of stem-cell investigation to personal experience. He watched helplessly over several decades as his father's health deteriorated from diabetes. Asked about his overarching goal, Wilmut readily responded, "The reality is that the most important thing to me, at present, would be to use the new knowledge and the new opportunities that we've got in the scientific research to produce some new understandings that will ultimately lead to treatments for some of these awful diseases."

Given this broad consensus about goals, are there any significant differences among geneticists who assume different roles within the field? Not surprisingly, the Ph.D. scientists we interviewed unanimously embraced the goal of discovery, while only about 60 percent of physicians, industry workers, and clinicians articulated this mission. In contrast, nearly all clinicians and half of the physicians spoke of the importance of helping others; this altruistic motivation emerged as a goal for only 10 percent of the Ph.D.s. Educating and informing the public were the highest goals among clinical workers. Nearly all of the industry-based scientists cited the need to work toward the goals of their companies, but they differed in the extent to which they saw the achievement of company goals as consistent with the practice of science. A few like Chow described broad congruence: "I feel there's really no conflict. . . . I mean, that if you do good science you will have a good product. And we'll maximize shareholder value eventually."

More commonly, however, the geneticists in our study who worked in for-profit companies reported a tension that required monitoring and negotiation. William Rutter is a West Coast executive in his seventies who started out as an academic researcher. Some years ago he became the head of Chiron, a biotech company of seventy-five hundred employees that specializes in the development of vaccines. He reflected:

> Yes, for sure, . . . this is probably my main function—to achieve a balance which is good. Obviously that's helped a lot if the commercial part is working well, so I do everything I can to make that happen. But at the same time, the commercial part being as it is, we—this organization—spends a lot more than other organizations do, of similar size, on research funding.

And the academic administrator Leon Rosenberg (see Chapter 4), reflecting on his stint in industry, talked about the basic scientist's need to compromise and accept periodic setbacks:

> I had hoped to change the culture of Bristol-Myer's Squibb just as the company hoped to change my behavior. I think I succeeded in convincing the company to be science-driven as well as business-driven. I was appreciated for that, particularly by the R&D organization, and a bit more grudgingly by the business side. I fit in well enough to survive—even to thrive.

This kind of testimony could be a warning. Perhaps there can be a healthy and productive division of labor: basic scientists making the bulk of the discoveries, and applied scientists at corporations ensuring that these discoveries are mined for their health implications. But the rise of corporate interests may threaten central missions of the domain. The perennial need to show profits—ever-higher ones—may undermine the practice of top-quality science; moreover, pursuit of commercial options can even run counter to the health interests of the general public, most of whom may not be able to afford expensive options.

Consider the changes in biology during the twentieth century. Biologically oriented scientists in 1900 or 1950 were propelled primarily by curiosity; most biologists today cannot ignore the public demand for, and the commercial utility of, various discoveries. The scientists of earlier decades had little money available; today's scientists may receive millions of dollars a year from governmental grants, with even larger sums available from nonprofit or commercial sources. Most of the dilemmas scientists faced in the early 1900s were intellectual ones; today, particularly at the forefront of genetics research, the dilemmas are often ethically tinged.

Integrity Above All

The scientists we spoke with agreed about not only broad goals but also standards or guiding principles. They most highly valued honesty, integrity, and scrupulousness. One geneticist said, "I can't imagine that anybody would be a scientist without believing in the importance of truth and integrity." A second declared, "You always want to make sure that your students live and appreciate the highest level of scientific integrity. . . . The worst possible thing is to . . . have a student who cheated." And a third placed this value in broader perspective:

> Science is a very, very social world—standards of excellence, how
> you go about interfacing with your colleagues in terms of scientific
> integrity, in terms of making sure that the people who really did
> come up with the ideas and do the work are the people who get
> credit for it, and that there are certain very important standards as
> to how you actually behave in the field . . . most of it is done by
> example.

Insight into the meaning of honesty in science emerges from a discussion of how researchers should deal with data. A fourth-year graduate student in medical genetics at Harvard stressed her credo:

> Honesty in presenting your data and looking at your data. You can
> try to be honest, mostly, in presenting the data. You can easily over-
> see things, I guess, so being careful to state something and then pro-
> vide the bits of evidence that you say are supporting it . . . People can

either believe a statement, based on the support you've provided. But whereas, if you just say the statement, they might just take it as fact and not think of it otherwise . . . being very critical or evaluating it. Trying not to let your hopes color your vision and honestly questioning people, trying to get other people to be critical.

Honesty and integrity stand as cornerstones in science; only the most dense, disturbed, or corrupt young practitioners fail to grasp this point. We found recognition of these principles so prevalent that we wondered how their centrality is conveyed in the training of scientists: Is there a code equivalent to the Hippocratic oath, or are understandings reached informally, as in journalism? Among the young geneticists we interviewed, much of the learning occurred through observation. Students saw their mentors and lab peers taking great care while formulating problems, and while collecting and interpreting data; thereby, they were inspired to do the same.

This scientific fact of life may help explain one of the most publicized events in biological research in the 1990s. Thereza Imanishi-Kari, a junior scientist collaborating with the Nobel laureate David Baltimore, was accused of fudging data in a series of experiments about how the body creates antibodies against disease. Baltimore strongly defended both the experiments and Imanishi-Kari's reputation. At first, it appeared that she had indeed engaged in fabrication, and the backlash against Baltimore within the discipline of genetics was so severe that he had to resign from the presidency of Rockefeller University. Ultimately, though, both Imanishi-Kari (who may well have been a sloppy researcher) and Baltimore were cleared of scientific wrongdoing, and both were able to resume their careers. Part of the furor seems to have come from a widespread belief among certain scientific colleagues that Baltimore had not monitored (and mentored) his junior collaborators closely enough.

An Openness to Openness

Scientists cannot proceed honestly without a free flow of information and an openness to experience. The geneticists in our study voiced antagonism toward secrecy, close-mindedness, and premature closure. Beatrice Mintz, trained in the 1940s as a developmental biologist, became interested in how normal cells become malignant. In the 1970s she was a leader in the creation of transgenic mice, and she still maintains an active laboratory in her seventies. Mintz talked about the centrality of direct experience in scientific research:

> Receptiveness to the unexpected, without any prejudice about what you think you want to find . . . So I like to do experiments that have reasonable expectations involved in the planning but in which the situation is intrinsically one capable of turning up not merely new answers but even more interestingly, new questions.

Maxine Singer worked for thirty years as a researcher and division head at the National Institutes of Health, where she focused on the biochemistry of nucleic acids. She was one of the organizers of the Asilomar Conference where genetics researchers themselves sanctioned a moratorium on gene-splicing experiments in 1975. She also served as a member of the corporation that oversees Yale University. Now the head of the Carnegie Institution of Washington, Singer describes her reaction, as a young researcher in the 1960s, to learning about secrecy in scientific laboratories: "I was not even aware of people who were secretive, or so driven by their own egos that they were mean to people." We asked Singer whether she was surprised when reading about the ruthless competition among laboratories and the attempts at deception described in James D. Watson's book *The Double Helix*.[1] She replied: "I was astounded. Absolutely astounded. That people would behave that way, yes."

Younger scientists gave us their own perspectives on the *purity* of scientific investigations. Craig Ceol is a fourth-year graduate student at MIT who studies the genes that help cells divide. He hopes this research will illuminate intracellular signaling and the control of cell division, as well as prove applicable to retinoblastoma, a childhood-onset eye cancer. Ceol said: "Whatever experiment it is, I prefer to do it in . . . the cleanest way possible, with lots of experiments. You can do them in a quick and of course dirty way and there'd be lots of caveats to an interpretation." This sentiment was echoed by Laura Attardi, a fourth-year MIT postdoctoral fellow who studies a growth-suppressing protein that causes cells to "commit suicide": "In genomics, there's a tendency for some scientists to jump quickly to thinking something is established by analogy. That is too loose for my liking. They're making what I consider to be a guess and being persuaded that it is a fact. And that bothers me." These observations raise two possibilities. On the one hand, science can benefit from daring leaps. On the other, integrity may be at risk when scientists are too eager to regard a one-time finding or an inspired hunch as proven truth.

Although we do not know whether standards have declined in recent years, changing conditions provide reason for concern. With so much money at stake, scientists such as these have incentives to hide current work or recent findings or to mislead rivals about the nature of their work. Today, nearly everyone takes for granted the patenting of discoveries that, a generation or two ago, might as reflexively have been placed in the public domain. Also, the possibility of receiving large amounts of money for popular causes—eradicating cancer or synthesizing drugs to slow aging—may skew research in that direction. Finally, the changing relationships among institutions may erode the independence of science. Once the possibility arose that institutions might make large amounts of money from discoveries, new pressures encouraged entrepreneurial arrangements. As the lines separating government, independent research institutions, universities, and for-profit commercial ventures have blurred, it has become hard to discern the proper standards for institutions to follow when acting alone and when collaborating or competing with other entities. It is equally problematic for individual investigators to know when to behave like a nonprofit, independent investigator and when to act like a for-profit employee of an institution on a targeted mission.

Dreams

One of our goals was to find out about our informants' domain-related dreams. We quickly learned that in genetics, dreams are not remote aspirations for a dimly sensed future, nor are they rooted in nostalgia for a bygone Golden Age. Several leading geneticists clearly expressed their dreams.

Leroy Hood, much honored for his work in genome sequencing, cancer biology, and cell differentiation, described the ambitious effort at intellectual synthesis he had recently begun: "What excites me is working in systems where you can really unify knowledge . . . I've always been attracted to systems biology. I've always felt that you needed to be able to not only integrate the ideas of science but integrate the disciplines of science." In earlier days, Hood might have had to undertake this visionary work alone, without colleagues or funding. But now he is setting up a self-standing research "Institute for Systems Biology." He explained: "The Institute is in my way a kind of objectivization of a vision that is at the same time going to create new space and resources and bring together the people. . . . We'll be a world leader in this new systems biology. A very exciting place."

Ian Wilmut, who led in the cloning of Dolly, seeks to link his cutting-edge science to major medical discoveries:

> What that will mean is that we will be able to have cells to treat human diseases from the patient. That if you imagine a patient, let's say, with diabetes or Parkinson's disease, you would take a suitable plastic responsive sort of cell from that patient, and treat it in particular ways so that it would go back to the beginning of development without making an embryo and then you would be able to control its redifferentiation, if you like, into the tissue that you needed to put back into the patient. And it's impossible to estimate when that will happen. But it would be my belief that that will be the greatest long-term impact of the Dolly experiment.

A third scientist, at the forefront of work on cancer, imagines a world in which surgical intervention will no longer be necessary. Instead, specific drugs will be fine-tuned or customized to the characteristics of individual cancers in individual patients.

> Can you imagine treating cancer with drugs like that . . . can you imagine a patient comes in and you won't even know what the [cancer is]—you just know that there's a molecule marker and it's gone up. . . . Can you imagine that there are going to be a thousand new companies based on that . . . you're not going to need CAT scans and MRI and ultrasounds. . . . The radiology department's going to shrink.

Perhaps the most all-encompassing dream was articulated by William Haseltine, now one of the chief entrepreneurs of the new biotechnology (see Chapter 4). His company is creating drugs based on emerging knowledge about the human genome:

> We are redefining what it is to be a human—taking a new measure of man. We add to the classical and neo-classical view of human body as a collection of organs, tissues and cells, the notion that human body can also be described as a collection of genes and the

protein each gene specifies. This new definition describes our body in a way that emphasizes human similarity rather than human difference. Our parts, defined as our individual human genes and proteins, are fully interchangeable. The gene or protein from one person can be expected to function and be fully compatible within the body of any other. The concept of an organism built from genes and proteins unites us with all other living species. We recognize that other species too are comprised of genes and proteins which, to a surprising extent, are similar to our own whether they be fruit or fly.

For some, indeed, the dream does not lie in the future—they are living it today. James D. Watson told us:

One of the great things about this job is I can have a meeting on anything that interests me. Because we were given this estate nearby where we have sort of thirty person meetings . . . so I think I've got the best job. . . . The wonderful thing here was that I was the boss and you didn't have to worry whether the Dean felt the department should have balance. . . . I always try and appoint people that I think are . . . brighter than myself. I like to surround myself with bright people.

And Craig Venter, the gene sequencer who is often contrasted to Watson (see Chapter 4), revealed the same euphoria:

I've been accused of trying to have it all ways, and I plead absolutely guilty. It's a fundamental. Intellectually there's no greater joy for me than making fundamental science breakthroughs that can really change the entire spectrum of things. I've been lucky in having at least three major revolutions that have come out of what I've done over the past decade.

Juggling Responsibilities

American author Delmore Schwartz entitled a famous short story "In Dreams Begin Responsibilities." We wondered whether the geneticists in our study would discern a firm connection between their professional dreams and their own sense of responsibility. In contrast with the connections often volunteered by journalists, we found surprisingly little linkage of dreams and responsibilities on the part of our scientists. Accordingly, we elected to probe explicitly about various responsibilities that the participants might feel. We thought that this line of questioning might illuminate aspects of the moral identities of our subjects: the aspirations and anxieties that were closest to their personal value systems. Surprisingly, as we report in the next section of this chapter, it was a responsibility for which we did *not* probe that proved particularly illuminating. We grouped our informants' comments into five broad categories, discussed in turn below.

Responsibility to Society

Responsibility to society means informing the public; minimizing harm to individuals, groups, or the environment; and addressing citizens' concerns. Given the premium that scientists place on independence, we found it surprising that the highest proportion of respondents (82 percent) emphasized their responsibility to the broader society. Sixty-five percent stressed the importance of keeping society informed and educated, 42 percent mentioned helping people in general, and 25 percent spoke about the need to minimize harm. Leon Rosenberg, who has served in both academe and industry, commented:

> I feel a great responsibility and I always have. I have tried to be an educator to the public about my field of medical genetics. I wouldn't say everybody who works in the field of medical genetics had an obligation to do that, because some people would not be good at it. Their efforts would not carry the dialogue forward. But I think the field has an obligation to communicate with the public because it is so new, and it is so important in the way people think about themselves. Therefore, professionals need to be part of the group who try to enlighten the public at large.

Leroy Hood has devoted considerable energy to the education of students in high school:

> I've always been convinced that a fundamental part of the scientist's obligation should be to communicate with society what science is

about. And that's for a lot of reasons. One, you'd like to attract more good people into science, but even more important, you'd like to educate citizens so that they can think about issues of science priority, science regulation, the ethical dimensions and things like that. So our department has gotten very involved in K–12 (precollegiate) science education here and really making very fundamental, very broad change in Seattle in that regard.

Responsibility to a Domain

Responsibility to a domain relates to scientists' calling, or their commitment to the core practices of research and discovery. It also includes prohibitions about work that violates essential tenets of the domain, such as science conducted in secrecy. This type of responsibility was next in prominence. Sixty-nine percent of the geneticists we interviewed felt it important to carry out science of the highest quality. This variety of responsibility takes different forms. For Phyllis Strauss, who investigates the damage and repair of DNA, it is most important to train groups that can carry out science, to create new knowledge, and to monitor the people doing the work. For Robert Tjian, who studies how genetic information is decoded by the cell, it is important for scientists to be precise about their achievements: "Our responsibility is to make sure we're getting the right answers." Thomas Caskey, formerly a university researcher and now a chief scientist at Merck, said: "I really like the primary discovery . . . that's my role. That's what I do. I don't do regulatory, safety. I must make the discovery. That's my responsibility." And graduate student David Hirsch focuses on the daily practice of science: "The highest responsibility I have is that the data be correct. Because if other people are going to do work based on your results, you can't be wrong."

Responsibility to Others

Responsibility to others refers to obligations to students, employees, staff, patients, subjects, family members, or colleagues with whom one comes in regular contact. Sixty-two percent of the geneticists we interviewed underscored the importance of responsibility to others; students or employees were usually singled out for mention. Harry Meade is an inventive industry-based researcher who now works for a subsidiary of Genzyme. He described the working environment that he tried to create while at Biogen:

For the longest time at Biogen, we had to work with radioactivity. I didn't let young fertile women do it because I thought it was just not good. So I think that you have a responsibility to look out for everybody—if everybody takes care of the person who works for them, we'll all get along fine. . . . What I found sometimes is that people would use those people beneath them to take the blame . . . you have to have that kind of communication with them that if things are not working they will tell you.

Hirsch has already discovered the importance of creating and maintaining academic lineages that link the generations: "Which is why I need to teach. Because there's not much I can do for Harvey [Lodish], Sol [Snyder], and Jonathan [Reizer] [his mentors]. Because they're pretty much where they're going to get. So I have to do for other people what they did for me."

Responsibility to Self

Responsibility to self involves an explicit reference to a person's goals or commitments—whether selfish, selfless, or mixed. Forty-two percent of our respondents cited responsibility to self as a high priority. Sandra Nusinoff-Lehrman, a physician who now heads a biotech company, stressed the importance of having a strong internal compass:

I guess at the end of the day my responsibility is to myself. I recognize that there are lots of other people that I'm also responsible to, but in the end I'm responsible to myself and having some consistency. If I do that then I think I provide the best guidance. You make everybody crazy, including yourself, if you're inconsistent.

Responsibility to the Workplace

Responsibility to the workplace means people's concern about their institutions, obligations to shareholders, and efforts to improve the work environment. Thirty-one of our respondents cited this focus. As might be expected, it was the gatekeepers who spoke most eloquently about their responsibilities to the institutions they head. When we asked Singer about her responsibilities at the Carnegie Institution of Washington, she responded:

As a scientist, right. Put aside family, obviously that would always
come first. Well, you know I feel I have tremendous responsibility
because of the nature of this institution. I really think it's an important institution, small as it is, it stands for something that comes
and goes in other research situations . . . so having stewardship of
such an institution is a responsibility to science, it's a responsibility
to the institution. I guess it's really to the advancement of science
and understanding of the natural world in general and I think
that's what drives all these educational things that I'm into as well.

Watson articulated how he, as a gatekeeper presiding over a research institution with hundreds of employees and a budget of about $50 million a
year, thinks about his position:

I want people's respect. I don't want them to think I'm quote a
"good person" because "good persons," it's almost a religious
phrase. Good to whom under what circumstances and did they do
me a favor? Sometimes . . . to do my job, you have to worry about
the best thing you can do for the health of the institution, even
though some person may feel it's not to theirs at all. But if you
don't worry about the institution, no one has a job.

The Hierarchy Among Responsibilities

Since most people wish to appear responsible, it is not surprising that,
when asked, geneticists describe themselves as a highly responsible group.
But we also wanted to know how they differ among themselves in regard
to the hierarchy among responsibilities. In fact, subgroups differed dramatically: for example, 10 percent of Ph.D. researchers, as compared to 75
percent of clinical workers, stressed the responsibility to help people in
general. Clinicians were much less concerned about educating and informing the public (38 percent) as compared to a mean of 70 percent
across the other three professional groups. More than two-thirds of those
in industry stressed responsibility to their workplace, while the institutional dimension was cited by only 20 percent of the Ph.D.s, 17 percent
of the M.D.s, and 13 percent of the clinicians. Comparing the twenty
geneticists still in training with the fifty-six in our core group of
creator-leaders, we found that the young geneticists felt a stronger responsibility to others than to the domain—the reverse of the picture ob-

tained with their seniors. Finally, we noted some sex differences. By a two-to-one margin, women were more likely to stress their responsibilities to self, others, and society, while men were more likely to mention their responsibility to their domain and to cite the general maxim to "minimize harm." Such differences in response profiles across groups confirmed that our interview question elicited genuine information, rather than merely socially appropriate responses.

The Responsibilities of Others

Despite the planning of researchers, sometimes a question can elicit a totally unexpected response across a population. In our case, 58 percent of the geneticists voluntarily brought up the responsibilities of other parties as crucially related to the successful functioning of the professional realm. This response was far more common among midlevel practitioners (80 percent) than among creator-leaders and gatekeepers (40 percent). It was also far more common among young geneticists, 85 percent of whom cited the responsibility of others. We might speculate that midlevel practitioners feel that they have less power with which to bring about change themselves. One university-based researcher confessed that she is "not necessarily satisfied with [her place] in the hierarchy." She explained:

> You know, it's hard to see exactly how you would effect the changes . . . I'm not sure. Scientists have been traditionally reluctant, for example, to get into lobbying in a big way. Although that's changing to some degree. But they're not effective—they're not very effective at that. That's not their interest and they tend not to be very good at it. . . . We clearly need to do a better job at making sure that we have a scientifically literate population. . . . But I don't think that individual scientists can do much. . . . I'm not sure how to see it happening—how to do anything about it now, from where I am . . . you know, sort of a more global education.

An analogous asymmetry emerged across professional groups. Industry workers were more likely to stress the responsibility of other agencies (73 percent), while only 25 percent of clinicians attempted to place responsibility beyond their own institutions. The chief scientific officer for a small company said: "Who's responsible for education? I think [the] community is responsible. I think industry has responsibility but no matter what you do in industry, it's always going to be viewed as an advertisement."

Sometimes, conflicting pulls can be felt within the same person. Rosenberg recalls his struggles as the head of a large pharmaceutical research-and-development enterprise:

> At Bristol-Myers there were situations where my personal views
> about the kind of projects we should be engaged in were not shared
> by the real decision-makers in the company. On a few occasions, I
> felt uncomfortable about the clash between what I thought was my
> responsibility as a physician and my responsibility as the leader of
> R&D. I made the strongest case I possibly could for what I
> believed.

These statements about responsibility suggest that researchers in genetics are trying to carry out their work thoughtfully. Guided by their scientific credo, they strive both to be faithful to the calling of the scientist and to make sure that their work is put to a positive end—or at least not to a harmful one. (In these respects, they resemble journalists, who for the most part are also clear on their values and wary about pressures that may make it difficult to carry out their craft effectively.)

Where the cohorts differ dramatically, of course, is that most geneticists are relatively sanguine about the current course of their specialty: domain, field, stakeholders, shareholders, and individual desires are well aligned. In contrast, as we later document, a majority of journalists are worried about whether the domain of journalism as they know it will survive in the present climate. One would like to believe that the geneticists' missions and responsibilities will prove adequate to the times: we are by no means certain that this is so.

Religion, Calling, and Worldview

Not surprisingly, the subject of religion seldom arose in our interviews with geneticists. Relentless focus on experimental scrupulousness, a belief in rigorous reasoning, and a concern with the worldly implications of their work may be among the reasons that religion does not emerge as an important factor in the working lives of most scientists. It may also explain why, in our survey of values, religious factors ranked near the bottom of the hierarchy.

Still, a life in genetics can certainly coexist with a strong religious orientation. One leading researcher, Francis Collins, has found genes for several hereditary diseases, including cystic fibrosis. Watson's successor as the head of the National Center of Human Genome Research, Collins continues to do research on the genetics of diabetes. Collins had no hesitancy in discussing his beliefs as a practicing Christian:

> I am a person whose religious faith matters to him a good deal, and that's not something that was true when I started into science . . . it happened along the way. It's fair to say that my belief in God accentuates my sense that one of the things that we are supposed to do while we are here is to reach out to other people. This contributes to the motivation to try to see genetic research benefit human beings. In the mandates of the long tradition of Judaism and Christianity, one of the things we are to do is to try to heal the sick.

The power of a religious belief is not easily rivaled, but the mission of a domain—the sense of calling for a profession—can play an analogous role. Judah Folkman has become celebrated in recent years because of his demonstration that tumors can grow only if they have an adequate blood supply and that a promising way to prevent the growth of tumors is to cut off their blood supply. The son of a rabbi, Folkman grew up in Columbus, Ohio. As a young boy, he thought that he, too, would become a rabbi. He used to accompany his father on visits to sick or elderly patients at local hospitals and nursing homes. One day Folkman observed that the physicians were allowed to open the oxygen tent but his father was not. He inferred that the physicians could most directly help the patients, and thereupon he vowed instead to become a doctor.

A well-known physician recalled the dramatic impact made on him and his fellow classmates as they entered the Harvard Medical School in the early 1950s and were addressed by Dean George Packer Berry:

> You'd come, brand new freshmen, right out of college, and he says, "Welcome to Harvard Medical School. Tell me the definition of a profession." None of us had a clue, because we had never thought of it. We're going into this lifelong profession and we didn't have a

clue. So he would call on people and have them stand up. They . . .
usually would drone on about "learned everything." After an hour
. . . he'd slam his hand and he said, "No. A profession is a set of behaviors, a code of behavior above the marketplace. You do not lie to
your patients. You do not deceive them. You do not overcharge
them, and you do not abandon them." And he walked out.

It is not necessary to contrast a belief in science to a belief in religion,
nor is it necessary to contrast responsibility to other people to a responsibility to a divine power or being. We suspect that, among geneticists, it is
not only Collins who manages to find a place for both realms in his personal philosophy. Still, we are tempted by the inference that, at least for
some individuals, involvement in science provides a belief system that is
sufficiently complete and coherent as to leave less need, and less place, for
traditional religious or spiritual concerns.

Genetics emerges at the turn of the millennium as a profession in remarkably good shape. Leaders and midlevel practitioners concur about
the primary missions, the most important standards, and the principal
personal goals and profiles of responsibilities. They look comfortably into
their mirrors and are reassured by the identity they behold. To an extent
that can only generate envy among professionals in less favorable environments, genetics appears to be a beautifully aligned enterprise: the aspirations of the practitioners, the values of the domain, the practices of the
field, and the desires of the shareholders and the stakeholders blend together harmoniously. There is little temptation to think of some past time
as a golden age or to dwell on visions of a more promising future. But no
domain is perfect, just as no practitioner is free of concerns, anxieties,
ambivalences, and nightmares. With a touch of regret, we turn next to
the possible discordant signs in the halcyon domain of genetics.

6

Storm Clouds
in Genetics

At the beginning of this research, one of our informants remarked, "The graduate students in genetics used to sit in the lunchroom of the Bio Labs, reading copies of the journal *Cell*. Nowadays, they still sit there reading, but they're scanning copies of the *Wall Street Journal*." Enormous change has indeed taken place in microbiology since the 1960s and 1970s. In the wake of James Watson and Francis Crick's groundbreaking discovery of the double helix, molecular biology became "hot." And once it became clear that scientists could rearrange genetic material, creating new life forms, the implications for medical research and practice readily suggested themselves. But until the last two decades, few could anticipate the enormous amounts of money that biologically trained scientists could make. Indeed, such opportunities for wealth had never presented themselves in "hard sciences" like physics or chemistry, even when those domains were attracting "the best and the brightest." The closest parallel in recent years has been in computer or information sciences.

The Market Changes Everything

What do we mean when we assert that the "market model" has been adopted in domains such as genetics or journalism? In a word, for-profit enterprises have become major players, competing with one another to make discoveries, figuring out the practical implications of these discoveries, creating products or services with commercial appeal, and then selling those products to maximize return for the owners or shareholders.

Some people (especially in the United States) believe that the mechanisms of the market are sacrosanct: in virtually every sphere of life, say the enthusiasts, progress is most likely to ensue if market forces are given free sway. For others, markets are suspect: too often, they lead to unbridled competition, with large segments of society (indeed, of the planet) losing out. Not surprisingly, the effects of the market in science have been varied and variously interpreted.

Of course "the market" is not a monolithic entity. There are local, national, and global markets; there are customer markets and capital markets; there are the commercial interests of consumers, governments, and profit and nonprofit entities, which may operate under different degrees of regulation. Some enterprises seek immediate returns on investments, while others (in the spirit of Internet start-ups of the late 1990s) are more concerned with building up a loyal customer base or a rich knowledge base than turning large quarterly profits in the short run. Finally, lest Darwinian thinking be given too wide a scope, we must acknowledge that markets are human inventions, and that humans have the power to limit them or to change the rules by which they operate.

According to one recent estimate, there are about thirteen thousand biotech companies in the United States, with $13 billion in annual revenue and approximately a hundred thousand employees.[1] As noted in Chapter 5, many of the scientists we interviewed move back and forth between the campus and the company; and with every passing year, closer ties are being forged among universities, nonprofit research centers and for-profit enterprises. Wearing multiple hats has become a fact of life.

Some differences between academe and the corporation are evident. Businesses need to make a profit; they are responsible to shareholders who expect a return on investments. Technically speaking, universities and research institutions are not permitted to make profits: any surplus of revenue over expenses must be ploughed back into further educational or research purposes. Their "shareholders"—above all, the general public, which grants them tax-free status and underwrites the costs of research—expect that the work will be carried out in exemplary fashion and will redound to the common good.

Our informants help to flesh out this picture. Laura Attardi, an advanced postdoctoral student, stressed different timescales. "My picture of

industry . . . is that they set very immediate goals and a short timescale.
. . . The only timescale [in the university] is that I wish I had done it yesterday." Professor–turned–corporate leader Thomas Caskey described a
division of labor: "I will give you the numbers quickly: 98 percent of all
discoveries come from academics, 2 percent come out of the pharmaceutical industry; 95 percent of all drugs come out of the pharmaceutical industry, 5 percent come out of academics." A corporate executive talked
about the different orders of capital available:

> In an academic setting, except in the genome center, you tend to
> raise your money, 2 or 300,000 dollars [at] a time and in this kind
> of [corporate] setting you tend to raise your money in terms of tens
> of millions of dollars at a time. Just your investors are different.
> . . . I think that the pressures are that companies at some point in
> time have to be profitable . . . that's part of the price of admission.
> . . . Although what I've seen is that the academic world is also being
> increasingly constrained by these boundary conditions [as academic
> centers turn toward corporate resources to meet the increasing costs
> of research].

Strings come attached to such large amounts of money. Mark Osborne,
the youthful leader of a research team studying osteoporosis at Genome
Therapeutics Corporation, reflected:

> Academic-type science, where it's just asking questions for the sake
> of understanding a system. If it's not heading in the direction of
> having a product, that would be discouraged . . . the slow kinds of
> projects, the things that would take a long time to develop, things
> that might be very interesting, it's just not practical to pursue them.
> Industry typically waits for academics to do that. We can then ac-
> cess them by licensing them out.

Such differences in time and resource scale foster diverse cultures. Leon
Rosenberg, who has held influential positions in both industry and academe (see Chapters 4 and 5), contrasted the atmospheres:

> The culture of academia and the culture of the pharmaceutical in-
> dustry have little in common. Many of the characteristics that per-
> mit people to succeed in academe are characteristics which are
> unappreciated, to say the least, in industry: speaking one's mind,

being a "rugged individual," looking for unusual connections, being charismatic. Those are all characteristics I associate with acade-
mia. They are certainly not the characteristics that are looked for in
people who come into industry.

Pluses and Minuses of the Market

We asked our respondents to indicate the pluses and minuses of the
market approach to scientific research. One positive feature many cited is
the possibility of raising far larger amounts of money. James Robl is a
university-based researcher whose team has been genetically modifying
cells so that they can be used in organ transplantation:

> If I go . . . and try to get a $5 million grant as a university faculty
> member, for a research program, companies won't listen to me. If I
> go as, say, an officer in a company, I can go out and talk to them
> and instead of a $5 million deal, it might be a $20 million deal. But
> I can't do it as a university faculty member. I can't put people to-
> gether. I can't put technology together. I can't make the package
> that I can go out to sell.

In addition to bestowing larger budgets, corporations sometimes give
researchers a wider realm in which to pursue their ideas. David Ledbetter, a university-based scientist who has consulted for pharmaceutical
companies and commercial genetic laboratories, described his own experience:

> We went through an early phase where all the academics frowned
> on anybody who worked in industry and thought that was a hor-
> rible thing to do, accepting the money from private sources was
> terrible. We got over that. . . . There's also an interesting trend of
> senior geneticists moving from academics into pharmaceutical in-
> dustries . . . the assumption is it's purely for money, since they
> quadruple their salary when they do that. But in part today, there
> are big pharmaceutical companies who call you up and say, "We
> want to establish a genetics research program and it's going to
> have a research budget of $50 million a year. And we want you to
> be the person to decide how to spend that and who to recruit,"

and that kind of scientific opportunity doesn't happen in an academic setting. . . . And so, some people, I think honestly make the change because their science is at a point where they want to do things on a much larger scale. You just can't write a grant that big. You can *write* it. You won't get it funded. For a grant that big. And so there are certain types of research that you can do now in a pharmaceutical setting that you can't do in an academic setting.

Despite the opportunities in industry, our informants were more likely to stress the disadvantages of a career spent wholly in that sphere. They cited both the lack of autonomy and the questionable means that are sometimes employed, seeming to suggest that the central standards and mission of scientific work—the core of the domain—become vulnerable in an industrial setting.

The researcher Leroy Hood, who has taught at the California Institute of Technology and the University of Washington (see Chapter 5), explained why he has avoided working in the corporate sector:

I started a gazillion biotech companies in my life and I had never gotten directly involved with the biotech companies because I want the freedom of doing what I want to do, and I don't want to be constrained by having to make money. . . . What you do would be very different from what you do in a research institute or in an academic setting.

The quality of life in a corporate setting is also less appealing to independent types. A scientist who has worked both in the university and in a number of biotechnology companies chronicled his observations of the corporate biomedical world:

If you complain and you point out things that are wrong, I think that is not particularly rewarded, because then you are not part of the team . . . they want everyone to stand on the sides and say, "We all believe," instead of saying, "Wait a minute, we got to keep going, there's something wrong here." So that kind of critical analysis of where you are going I think is not particularly rewarded. . . . I think that that happened at Biogen. They got rid of all the people who were, they said, . . . negative, but many people were creative.

Some of our informants who come out of the sheltered atmosphere of the academy are shocked by the seamier side of life in the commercial sphere. Paul Siebert, who works at Clontech on the West Coast, remarked:

> In terms of biotechnology, this whole thing about patents and su-
> ing people is rather distasteful . . . just crazy but I guess in the end
> it's just business. . . . There are some unscrupulous business prac-
> tices that you see. Again like Adidas and this, you just try to kill the
> competition. People suing everybody. Copying other people's stuff,
> even though you can't sue them because it's not patented.

He yearns for a quieter life: "I will probably like to get to the point where I am financially secure enough to stop doing what I'm doing now and do some teaching, some research in a community college, for instance . . . I'd like to have enough money to be able to take a huge cut in salary and still have retirement."

The corporate leader Irene Chow (see Chapter 5) laments the stress of having to keep one's eyes fixed on the bottom line: "This stress comes from where? From Wall Street. It's a public company. If it's a private company, it's ten time easier. . . . [The stress] comes from the shareholder."

We encountered participants who are bothered by the aura of secrecy, which they find inimical to the practice of science. The university researcher Nancy Cox, who has been identifying genes involved in complex disorders like heart disease or diabetes, described her reluctance to become involved with industry:

> I would never think about going into industry now because I feel
> like I have an obligation to keep what I know in the public sector
> and to train students . . . and . . . encourage people to keep things
> as open as possible . . . that's sort of what I mean by feeling an
> obligation to the people who got me into the business . . . the
> American taxpayer.

Thoughtful scientists worry that the institutions of the current field clash with the long-term core principles of the domain. Arno Motulsky is one of the pioneers in medical genetics and now a senior researcher at the University of Washington Medical School. He expressed his concern about the commercial direction of research:

Companies are merging and getting bigger and bigger. . . . Currently life is going well under this system for a large part of the population in this and similar countries, but many people both here and particularly in the third world are much worse off. . . . I think it's going in the wrong direction. The market is winning. We are licensing patents for profits to companies. We are encouraging university professors to start private companies based on their discoveries. Yes, I am concerned but, again, that seems to be the way of doing it. . . . I should not cast stones. I never have been involved directly but I was asked when biotechnology started in 1980, to be on the Scientific Advisory Board of a company called Amgen . . . without the company there probably would be no erythpoietin. We strongly urged that erythpoietin be developed, which was successful and allowed treatment of severe anemia in patients with kidney disease. Without the company, this therapeutic triumph would have been much delayed.

Of course, such worrisome trends do *not* have to be accepted uncritically. Ian Wilmut, the influential Scottish cloning researcher whose methods and presence are in great demand within the corporate sector (see Chapter 5), emphasized that we *do* have a choice with respect to market forces:

There's a misunderstanding here, which, hopefully, is a passing phase in thinking that the market in the United States is all powerful. It isn't and it shouldn't be and it's time you did something about it. . . . If a majority of people in the United States wish to prohibit the technique, it is quite possible for pressure to be brought along those lines and for effective legislation to come through.

Finally, some scientists express an equally cynical view of both realms. Craig Venter, the one-time NIH researcher who moved into the private sector (see Chapter 4), told us:

Well, I see tremendous amounts of hypocrisy in both worlds.
. . . Actually I find the hypocrisy of the academic community slightly more disarming and troublesome than I do in the business

world. . . . I, like other academics, sort of view business as something that was not necessarily positive and assume that businessmen have far lower ethical standards than do most scientists. What I found when money and fame are involved is the standards become remarkably low on all sides. . . . I view the academic rules as being far more duplicit. The biggest clashes I'm having right now [are] because most people in this field want to get economic gain while pretending to be academics. They want to get everything. I'm doing it for free so that they can turn around, sell it, and make money off it, all the while evoking academic rights. Businessmen don't understand that. Frankly, even a year ago if you'd ask me did I think I'd be heading a big corporation in the future, I'd have told you "absolutely no" . . . I was being held back by the system and had to go, the cliché is "outside the box," to make advances.

Changes in the Domain and the Field

How do scientists regard the tremendous advances in genetics, climaxed by the completion of the mapping of the human genome in the spring of 2000? What do they think about the seismic changes in the amount and nature of funding available for research and applications?

Most geneticists are very pleased by the trends they discern. In fact, 89 percent of our respondents cited positive *domain* changes, while only 24 percent mentioned negative ones. Our positively disposed scientists pointed to the tremendous technical advances; the plethora of new institutions devoted to scientific research; the creation of new subfields in which genetics blends with other areas of biology, medicine, information science, and economics; and even the achievement of a higher quality of life.

The explosion of corporate interests produces a much more mixed picture: institutions in rapid and sometimes disturbing flux. Indeed, our respondents divided fairly evenly into those who cited positive changes (45 percent) in the current *field* and those who cited negative ones (40 percent). Scientists-in-training are even less sanguine: of those who mention field changes, 20 percent see those changes as positive, 50 percent as negative. Three changes—competitiveness, the fragility of career paths, and the control of information—were repeatedly cited.

Competitiveness

Some scientists view competition favorably. William Haseltine, the former academic researcher who moved to the private sector (see Chapter 4), attributes America's current overwhelming lead in biotechnology to the "ferocious freedom" and "enormously competitive atmosphere" in the land. William Rutter, the head of a large biotech company (Chapter 5), rhapsodized: "I love competition. Whether it's in science or in anything else, I think that challenge has the effect of focusing your own mind and your own energies around a solution to a problem, you work a little better in competition." And David Hirsch, a scientist-in-training, agreed:

> There is competition but that's not a bad thing. Competition basically means that you're working in a field that other people deem important enough to work in too. So it can't be bad. If you have no competitors, it either means that you're a genius beyond all else— you're the Mozart of what you do—or it's so uninteresting that nobody think it's worth any time to spend doing it.

But clearly this competitiveness has an unattractive dimension. Theodore Friedmann, a pioneer in gene therapy, reflected: "I think it's a very young field. It was populated from the beginning by very ambitious, very bright people. All of whom smelled blood. . . . Not very willing to give credit to each other . . . It's as if they've all discovered things from scratch all for themselves . . . not shining examples of goodhearted people." And a researcher from industry, who works in the area of gene therapy, concurred:

> You have this Darwinian thing in the lab where only two or three of the people, and they're not necessarily the best scientists, but they're probably the best combination of science and ambition, only two or three really succeed. There's a selection for people who are exceptionally aggressive, who will walk over dead bodies.

This competitiveness seems to take an especially severe toll on women, who may be less energized by heads-on competition and more frustrated by lack of support from colleagues. One woman at a leading medical research center lamented:

> I found it sad that you have to win a national award for someone to realize that you've done it for twelve years. . . . So I think I didn't have the personal confidence or strength to feel good about knowing I was doing the right thing. I sort of craved a sense of acknowledgement from the medical community . . . there's never the tiniest bit of acknowledgement from [the major hospital] in that regard, you know, twenty some years of teaching.

Control of Information

There has been a veritable explosion of information in the domain of genetics. One respondent estimated that the amount of information doubles every year, and that if people are cut off from the flow of information for as little as three months, they will have difficulty making up the lost time. Interestingly, the proliferation of information proved more problematic for women than for men, for clinicians than for basic researchers, and for midlevel workers than for leaders. It is possible that the creator-leaders have more ready access to the information and are more likely to be briefed about important scientific breakthroughs immediately after they occur.

This explosion of scientific information provides business opportunities—production, publication, synthesizing, critiquing. Craig Venter has proposed an arrangement whereby his company will make information about genomes available to the public and yet achieve financial viability by providing that information in streamlined and organized forms for paying customers. The availability of information may also have had a democratizing effect on the field. A leader of the biotechnology industry said: "I think the genome project did some very important things . . . And one of the things it did early on was create a notion of democratizing resources . . . the sort of commitment to put certain kinds of data into public spaces."

Information is power, however, and power inheres as well in withholding information. Phyllis Strauss, a university-based researcher (see Chapter 5), lamented that it is possible for people to publish their research results and still hold relevant information secret for up to three years, thereby unconscionably increasing their lead over rival research teams. CEO William Rutter told us:

> Usually, you can make a deal for information that you need. . . . What I do think has happened dramatically in both the academic and nonacademic arena, because value has been more closely related to intellectual property, you find people who have a clearer understanding of that, and therefore they retain more information until they get to the point where they can disclose it in a more formal way.

And Donald Frederickson, the former director of the NIH, expressed his concern: "Entrepreneurs are repressing any information that suggests an unfavorable outcome as 'proprietary' and keep it secret. . . . We need a re-awakening—a moral evaluation."[2]

Some of our informants lamented the loss of a sense of community, of a feeling of common cause. Nancy Wexler, a leading researcher on Huntington's disease, described getting discouraged:

> I think the problem is with these kinds of tensions—with the publish-or-perish mentality—with the popularity contest among scientists. It destroys a community of people who are friends, who hang out and enjoy each other. . . . If you can't talk to each other . . . how do you organize a community to work on problems together? I do think it's up to us . . . but it's a mess. I'm not sure what's going to happen. I really don't know.

Another well-known geneticist was more blunt. Asked if he sees anything negative in the new technologies, he paused for five seconds and then answered:

> It's created chaos in the interface between the public [and] the private spheres. It's created chaos because of patenting and cross-patenting and reach-through patenting and ambiguity of legal regulation and ambiguity of discrimination legislation. . . . Who owns what, what right do individuals have, how do we balance the need to do research in order to continue to make progress with people's fears? There are some malevolent people around, how do we keep them from playing on the fears and really doing damage?

The field is being threatened by the proliferation of information and the increasing pressures for control over ownership and use of that information. Where members of the genetics guild once worked together, in relative obscurity, on issues of scientific consequence, they now warily guard what they've learned, or consult with lawyers, lest someone exploit their hard-earned knowledge.

The Fragile Situation of Younger Scientists

A final area of concern is the recruitment and career paths of the talented young scientists who are attracted to genetics. Those with the most skills and the strongest ambition may well gain early victories and then, consistent with the Matthew effect[3] (see Chapter 4), continue to accrue benefits. For these individuals, to be young and a geneticist is, as the poet William Wordsworth says, "very Heaven." But most are struck by the yawning distance between their own status and that of the future "exemplary geneticists." A senior university-based researcher mused, "This is not a very happy or comforting time to start out being a young scientist . . . the difficulty in securing funded positions . . . and the competitiveness is at an all-time high."

The heart researcher (Chapter 5) talked about the relentless pressures on newcomers:

> It's harder on young people now because you need to put hours in to acquire your experience and to make mistakes. . . . You can't learn something in six months and understand the basic fundamental concepts. Because a hundred percent of the approaches will probably have turned around by the time a year has passed.

And a newcomer poignantly described the view from her vantage point:

> It's difficult knowing that it's such a long hard road . . . seeing the sacrifices that people make with no guaranteed reward, it's difficult to keep motivated. And seeing people that you think are really intelligent and good scientists not have success. And knowing that you have a limited amount of time, in some sense, to have enough success to reach goals. So, the unpredictability of it, I guess.

Most of the younger scientists stressed the importance of absolute integrity in their work. They worked for years, often with little support, and disparaged those tempted to abandon rigor, make use of privileged information, or publish prematurely. But some were also willing to be flexible in their adherence to norms. A promising postdoctoral fellow said:

> If you want to be a good researcher, you want to be a young Turk. You want to be able to say, "Okay, let's start from the first principle." These techniques are designed to achieve certain things. I shouldn't be a slave of techniques . . . I've always tried to cut corners, so to speak. Tried to find ways to improve even just incrementally previously existing techniques . . . I'm a little sloppy. I never follow protocols to the letter. In fact I don't do experiments by protocol. I usually just talk to somebody who's done it and they describe it to me and I just do it. I almost never follow protocol written on a piece of paper.

And a young scientist at a biotech company described psychic struggles that accompany the pursuit of corporate success:

> You have to tread a thin line between being completely honest about something and telling all its shortcomings and just talking only about what's good about it and hope that they spend their money. . . . Approaching business like that is sort of foreign to the scientists. . . . I'm discovering that in business, ethics . . . are a much more complex thing than I ever realized. It gets harder and harder to really decide when something is not quite right.

A newly minted Ph.D. seeking a job discussed her own mixed feelings about being a perfectionist in an imperfect world:

> So in the end if it means that I get a job eventually, then that's fine, you know the process was fine. But if I don't then I'll say, "Well, it was really flawed, I should have gotten those papers out sooner even if they were poorer quality papers in lesser journals." It would have been better to have more publications of lesser quality than to have one publication at the end of high quality.

In this context, it is chastening to encounter a story related by a fifth-year graduate student. He had learned of an organization that was applying computational technology in a way that was yielding faulty data. He told us, "I believe that's it's not fair for the rest of the country to go through using this data and they don't even know if it's error prone. It's horrible." He attempted to contact the organization but was rejected at several levels of the hierarchy. After much frustration, he succeeded in bringing the matter to the attention of a high authority at the National Institutes of Health. At first, the student was relieved that the scientific flaw was being addressed, but then he was shocked to find that the government official had posted the data on the Web without seeking his permission *and* without crediting him. He tried to get an explanation from the official but was "blown off." His own mentor told him: "Listen, this is what it is. This is what it's about. And now you've learned a valuable lesson; don't go [public] before you publish." Other professors concurred: "This is the way it happens. This is science politics." Our respondent reached a disappointing conclusion: "I don't understand it. I'm not sure I agree with it. But if I'm going to stay in this field, that's the way; you've got to abide by these rules."

Another young scientist at a large university realized that exactly the same research projects were being supported by the NIH at taxpayers' expense and also by a for-profit pharmaceutical firm. This was not cofunding; neither source knew that its studies were being double-billed. This geneticist feared being silenced if he brought this issue up with his department head. Steeling himself, he decided to present his concerns directly to the dean of the medical school. The dean listened carefully and thanked the young man for his information. But the whistle-blower soon realized that he was being moved to less and less sensitive positions on the research team and that nothing was being done to correct the situation. It gradually dawned on the researcher that it was the dean, rather than the department head, who had devised the ingenious system of double billing and that the dean had no intention of parting with what had become a substantial part of his budget. The geneticist decided to leave the university for different employment—thus injuring his career and leaving the scam untouched.

Science is vulnerable to the egos of ambitious researchers and the pressures of the marketplace. As long as the work of science is of interest chiefly to scientists alone and there are enough positions for competent researchers, pursuit of the mission and principles of the domain is unproblematic. But once a profession becomes highly competitive and highly remunerative, workers—and particularly young ones—are subjected to unprecedented pressures. Those who are especially aggressive and competitive are at an advantage. Those who do not have strong ethical moorings or a firm identification with the mission are especially susceptible to the marketplace. Currently, science risks becoming a domain that is practiced like an unregulated commercial undertaking. Indeed, in comparison to our veteran geneticists, we found a much less rosy picture of the profession among our younger subjects. Fully half mentioned at least one negative change in the domain and most of them lamented problems in the field. From their perspective, the greatest dangers loomed around the race for profit. As one young scientist put it:

> I think the field is getting much more like sort of "business-y." . . . It seems like scientists now, successful scientists, now are a lot more like successful businessmen or women. They sell their stuff and they have a certain slant and, they, like I said, accentuate the positive and minimize the negative and get people to believe in their system by overloading them with talks and papers and stuff. . . . I think you have to sell yourself more.

We found few young geneticists who were actively contemplating leaving the field. In part, this is because they had already devoted so many years to training. Even those who planned to remain in the domain of genetics, however, often spoke about the harsh personal demands made on them: in particular, they cited the risks of placing so much power in the hands of their academic adviser, the lack of permanent positions in the university (still the position-of-choice for the most talented young geneticists), and not surprisingly, the difficulty of having a balanced personal and family life.

A Casualty of the System

In more than a hundred interviews with geneticists of different ages and statuses, we heard very few horror stories. But one career portrait was sufficiently disturbing that it is worth relating in some detail. This story of a forty-year-old scientist working full-time at a major nonprofit biological research laboratory reveals some of the pressures that can beset a talented

scientist. This promising geneticist made a discovery about the causes of
cancer. However, his discovery and the implications for therapeutic drugs
went against orthodox accounts of the causes of cancer and the ways in
which carcinomas might be countered. By his account, the direction in
which his work was proceeding made him persona non grata among peers
and elders and has embittered him about the entire grant-securing business. He recounted:

> A peer review system breaks down in an atmosphere of extreme com-
> petition. . . . You send in a grant application to the NIH. And it's
> judged by a committee of fifteen to twenty "peers." Okay. Now what
> the "peers" actually means in practice is, some of the guys are your
> direct competitors. And so if your grant application is reviewed by
> them, the last thing in the world they want is to see you funded. And
> it's extremely easy to kill any grant. It doesn't take any skill whatso-
> ever to kill any grant. . . . It takes only one person on the committee
> of twenty to kill a grant . . . the system is corrupt. I mean, blatantly
> corrupt. I mean the NIH is the most corrupt organization this side
> of the Mexico border. Because, literally, you hear these conversations
> where people essentially say, "Hey, man, when you send your grant
> to the NIH, direct it to my study section and I'll help you out."
> . . . It really disfavors people who prefer to keep a low profile and just
> sort of be very scholarly and really favors people who are outgoing,
> exploitative-type people. Opportunists. So what's happening is that
> work that gets funded gets more and more mediocre, really.

This person was also extremely critical about the procedures scientists
have to follow even when funding has been secured:

> I simply refuse to be a businessman. . . . We're supposed to literally
> look at sort of accounting statements every month. . . . I just throw
> it in the garbage . . . I just refuse to be a businessman. . . . Think of
> how much administration would be cut out if instead of begging
> NIH for years to give you money . . . why not . . . send an e-mail
> to the NIH and say, "I need this and this equipment."

In his opinion, the atmosphere of chronic competitiveness has destroyed the quality of life for him and his peers and perhaps even diminished the opportunity for creative work:

I'd like to see a system where the NIH places security guards at the door of each lab that's NIH funded and only allows people to work from 9 to 5, five days a week. . . . Now I'm being a bit facetious. But I think that if everyone ultimately just sort of mellowed out a little bit, that they would have more time to think, they would be more creative, they would exchange ideas and synergize with each other more. . . . Ultimately, biology would move ahead faster and in a more interesting and historically important way.

The costs have been so severe at his own institution that even this business-averse researcher has been reflecting more about advantages of working in the commercial sphere.

It's a very cruel system. They don't at our institute really care fundamentally about the quality of your science. All they care about is the bottom line, in dollars . . . they exert that pressure, if you lose your grant, you lose your job . . . it's a very exploitative system. . . . It's incredibly competitive as much as any business. Even worse because at least if you succeed in business you get rich and you can have some fun with your money. But if you succeed in biology, you just get the chance to keep on struggling.

Such embittered individuals were a tiny minority. Even those young professionals who would never speak of a "charmed life" at least acknowledged an acceptable mode of living and did not muse about going into other lines of work. Our findings are supported by recent statistics documenting remarkably little unemployment or underemployment among biological scientists trained at the doctoral level.[4]

Ethical Dilemmas

We explored the senior geneticists' concerns about issues of control, ownership, and threats to the scientific enterprise by posing ethical dilemmas and by probing for their own worst fears. We presented them with a hypothetical development as related to ten situations: the latter situations tended to be more dramatic.

Hypothetical situation: Suppose that a scientist of your acquaintance discovered the gene for a monogenic disease (a disease caused by a single gene, like Huntington's chorea) from publicly funded research. Which of the following would raise an ethical issue or be a cause for moral concern, and why?

We also asked our informants to categorize their responses: "no concern," "some concern," or "great concern."

1. Withholding information relating to the gene from the scientific community and public until the gene is patented
2. Patenting the gene
3. Licensing the patent for profit to a pharmaceutical company or starting one's own product based on the discovery
4. Developing a genetic screen to detect susceptibility to getting the disease, and sharing the results with the patient's family, employer, and/or provider of health insurance
5. Creating categories of "genetic acceptability" among workers and job applicants, even when carriers of the disease are predominantly from ethnic or minority groups
6. Amniocentesis and genetic counseling of pregnant women or couples, informing them of the likelihood of having offspring with the disease and sharing (in some cases, encouraging) options to divert such a possibility, including sterilization and abortion
7. Developing gene therapy to counteract effects of the defective gene in somatic (bodily) tissue
8. Developing drug therapies for the disease, which may pose certain unknown side effects
9. Germ-line gene therapy (that is, therapy that will affect not only the patients but all of their descendants)
10. Large-scale genetic engineering on human populations for purposes of eugenics or "genetic farming"

The geneticists responded thoughtfully. Often, they pointed out inconsistencies or multiple ways of interpreting the question, and they provided an informative and detailed discussion of alternative stances. These were scientists at their reflective best; indeed, a year-long academic seminar could profitably be dedicated to a review of the rich responses they gave.

We were surprised that respondents did not register "great concern" about most of the issues. Since they often displayed passionate reactions in the interviews, a muted response did not suggest indifference to the questions. Nor were the respondents dismissive or glib. The scientists seemed to have thought through these vexing issues and for the most part concluded that they can live with the consequences.

Had this survey been administered one or two decades ago, geneticists would likely have shown far greater concern. In the ensuing years geneticists have become used to issues such as patenting, genetic screening, and genetic therapy. For example, when ordinary citizens hear about cloning, they have strong visceral reactions. For most scientists, cloning is a simple technique of cellular duplication that has been used for decades; to them, cloning in the biological sphere is no more problematic than photocopying a message or forwarding a copy of an e-mail.

Furthermore, in the two decades scientists have had to examine the impact of this research, there have not been any dramatic setbacks—as we've noted before, no biological Three Mile Islands or Chernobyls. No terrible creatures have been unleashed to the world, no disease has been propagated. Scientists feel that, as a community they have behaved responsibly, most notably in the Asilomar Conference, which endorsed a voluntary moratorium on experiments involving recombinant DNA.

Two-thirds of our subjects did express "great concern" on two topics: "large-scale eugenics experiments" (sometimes called "genetic farming") and "genetic screening." In light of the Nazi experiments, and dystopias like *Brave New World*, the response to "eugenics experiments" was scarcely surprising; we had included "eugenics experiments" as an option primarily to provide a baseline measure of "great concern."

The reaction to "genetic screening" was somewhat more surprising. Many subjects were troubled that information about genetic heritage would be shared and that it could be used prejudicially, for example, in hiring. Subjects called for strong safeguards to prevent such misuse of genetic information. There was less concern about the creation of categories of "genetic acceptability" for certain jobs—for example, those that involved specific stresses or risks. Respondents seemed to feel that once such screening had occurred, it made sense for employees and employers to have access to the information so that they could make informed vocational decisions.

It should be noted that genetic screening is one of the few ethical areas in which the scientists are *not* themselves actively involved and which stands apart from their own research or commercial interests. In a sense, then, this is a topic about which it is easy to express concern. In fact, the finding about genetic screening suggests a third reason for our subjects' muted reactions to the range of dilemmas: they may hesitate to critique practices that fuel much of the current popular interest in, and financial support for, research on genetics.

At the other end of the "concern spectrum," respondents showed very little concern about somatic therapy. Indeed, a full 79 percent voiced "no concern"—the largest consensus obtained. As one scientist put it, "I think that's a great idea, terrific idea, wish I could do it." Said another:

> Who would be against that? In my paper . . . I pointed out that somatic gene therapy is a sophisticated form of medical therapy. Instead of using a drug, you use a gene as a type of drug that is inserted in a somatic cell. You are not changing the eggs or the sperm. You are not doing anything to affect the next generation. Somatic gene therapy is conceptually similar to our current medical therapy.

Respondents proved to be far more ambivalent about germ-line therapy, dividing equally between those who expressed "great concern" (44 percent) and those who voiced "some" (47 percent). Some subjects volunteered that their own viewpoint on this practice had changed as a result of personal experiences. William Haseltine recalled a talk he had delivered:

> Several years ago, during a lecture to a group of graphical and industrial designers, I stated that the current consensus of the scientific and medical community was against changing the inheritance of any human. The reaction was fiery. I remember one woman's response very clearly. She said, "There's a cancer gene in my family. My grandfather died because of this gene, so did my father. I am a carrier of the gene and have cancer myself. My children are also carriers and I'm afraid that my grandchildren will be also. How can you tell me that it may be possible to interrupt this chain of suffering and death, but that you won't do it?"
>
> That response changed my view. I no longer believe it is unthinkable to change inheritance by eliminating genes that cause se-

rious disease. On the contrary, I believe that our job as medical scientists is to make such procedures as safe as possible and then to inform a public debate on the topic. The decision of whether or not to implement this new technology is an issue for a democratic society as a whole to decide, not for the medical professional alone.

Arno Motulsky, one of the most thoughtful respondents, echoed this sentiment:

> I used to be very strongly against germ-line gene therapy. . . . I have changed my mind a little. . . . Once you remove a disease-producing gene by germ-line gene therapy, the descendants would no longer have this gene and the disease would no longer occur in future generations. In addition, we know that somatic gene therapy will not work at all in certain diseases.

James Watson, who has spoken publicly about the pain caused by mental disease in his own family, also endorses germ-line therapy and places his faith in the wisdom of the wider society:

> You shouldn't let the government make genetic decisions. . . . So when people ask me now about—and they're somewhat surprised—should you have germline changes? And I say, "If you can make better human beings and have virile lives I'm in favor if it."
> . . . You always have to trust that there's more good in society or good feelings than bad. Because anything can be misused.

As nonbiologists, we were struck by the geneticists' lack of serious concern about withholding information, making patents, and licensing patents for profit. Since the question stipulates that the research had been funded publicly, we had thought that more subjects would speak out against profit making and secretive activities. Indeed, we recalled Jonas Salk's words in the 1950s after he had created the polio vaccine: In response to the journalist Edward R. Murrow's question, "Who owns the patent on this vaccine?" Salk replied, "Well, the people, I would say. There is no patent. Could you patent the sun?"[5] In fact, however, "great concern" was expressed by only 25 percent of the geneticists about withholding information, by only 22 percent about patenting genes, and by a mere 8 percent about licensing the patent for profit. The remaining divided about 5:3 between those who voiced "some concern" and those who voiced "no concern."

Since those findings surprised us, we pondered the thinking that might have been at play. From an outsider's perspective, the government and private foundations underwrite basic research, not its translation into medical or surgical procedures, drugs, or other kinds of therapeutic interventions. Perhaps in an ideal world, the government would go on to fund applications of basic science; or entrepreneurs would simply pore over the scientific literature, launch companies, and trust that they and their competitors could somehow make a profit on the fruits of scientific breakthroughs. In practice, however, the transition from discovery to application is a lengthy, uncertain, and extremely costly undertaking. It may cost several hundred million dollars to take a drug through trials to the open market, and many promising interventions end up never reaching the marketplace or failing commercially once they do so. One scientist recently estimated that out of studies involving two thousand proteins, about ten blockbuster drugs will emerge.[6]

If a society wishes to encourage—rather than thwart—these attempts to apply medical knowledge, it must provide some protection for those willing to undertake such ventures. In the current world, securing patents or licensing these patents to others for profit-making enterprises may be necessary. It is also possible that, when confronting such issues, scientists have come to be blinded by their own financial self-interest. In a revealing comment on the socialization of geneticists, David Ledbetter, a leading clinician, contrasted incoming students to seasoned professionals:

> Very few [incoming students] have any knowledge or motivation of
> the degree to which biotechnology-pharmaceutical is interwoven
> with genetics research and the commercial implications of genetics.
> . . . So I think the first-year graduate students are still almost as
> naive as they were twenty years ago. . . . They get exposed to that
> during the first couple years of graduate school . . . Harvard, MIT,
> Stanford, UCSF, where there's not a single faculty member who
> doesn't own a company or have multiple patents and gets more
> money from . . . the commercial profits than from their salary.

The question of patenting reveals the deep fault lines in genetics today. To some authorities, like the scientist-entrepreneur Haseltine, it is self-evident that neither basic science nor scientific applications can advance in the absence of the protection provided by patents. To an equally ardent and articulate group—the Huntington's researcher Nancy Wexler, the genetics counselor Susan Pauker, and the physician-researcher Stanley Nelson, for instance—the capacity to patent knowledge, particularly when it has been publicly funded, undercuts science's central mission. Yet a third group—including, for example, the Human Genome project director, Francis Collins, and the Nobel laureate Philip Sharp—tries carefully to distinguish those situations where patenting is appropriate and those where it should be avoided. What strikes an outside observer is how far in the direction of patenting the field of genetics has moved in barely a generation. While patenting of genes is not permitted in France, it is taken for granted in the United States. Indeed, in the year 2000, the Cambridge-based company Millennium Pharmaceuticals had fifteen hundred applications pending at the U.S. Patent and Trademark Office.[7] As with the less rigorous criteria in journalism on what counts as "news," the temperature may be rising one degree at a time—too slowly for anyone to notice, but sufficiently cumulative that the water gradually comes to a boil . . . and the proverbial frog gets cooked.

We had expected that the nightmares of scientists would feature the misuses of biology that we see on television or in the movies: bizarre organisms, dangerous hybrids, tyrants bent on germ warfare, nations or companies having a monopoly on future genomes. Instead, the geneticists we interviewed were, on the whole, far more concerned about threats to the practice of science—the sanctity of the domain and misuses of its findings.

One primordial fear our respondents expressed was that the standards and principles that have long guided their domain will be undermined. Leroy Hood described an experience with a student who plagiarized as "the most traumatic year of my life"—he even used the term "nightmare" to characterize his fears about a lawsuit that threatened to drag on for years. One university-based researcher discovered that a colleague had committed fraud—"a deliberate decision made to publish some things that were absolutely nonsense." She described the experience as "profoundly disillusioning" and continued:

> What do you do then in later years, if you ever have to review a grant from this person? . . . I mean, when you review something, you . . . take it on faith that this person will honestly do what they say they're going to do. I mean that's a given. . . . What happens

when you know that they haven't been honest and—are you justified in saying to other scientists, "I know this person has been dis-
honest. I don't know if they still are, but they have been in the
past."

In the wake of greater competitiveness and higher financial stakes, we
have reason to worry that such threats to good scientific practice may become more widespread. Cho-Yau Yeung is a biomedical researcher who
studies how the same genetic information is manipulated in different cell
types. He voiced his fears that unethical practices are becoming more
frequent:

> I think that [cases of fraud and plagiarism] are more widespread
> than people would admit, because we know of things that don't hit
> the print, and don't come out. . . . By fraud, I mean people that fal-
> sify data, people who just copy other people's work, totally plagia-
> rize their work and publish it as their own. There have been a few
> very well publicized cases, but they're not quite that infrequent. All
> people who are in science are generally very bright and some of
> them are lazy and they want to take a shortcut.

Even in the absence of blatant unscientific behaviors, geneticists worry
that their work will be misunderstood and that legislation will complicate
or block the paths of inquiry. Hood proposed an important distinction:
"To the discovery aspects, there should be nothing closed. To how society
uses that knowledge, there has to be very thoughtful analysis and constraints and restraints and things like that."

Might there be scientific discoveries, or applications of those discoveries, that could be directly damaging to the wider society? Geneticists are
aware of the comparisons with the Manhattan Project and with the
dystopias imagined by science fiction. They tend to be defensive about
these comparisons, as reflected in one respondent's comments:

> Physicists look back and say, "You know, all of our atomic physics
> led to the atomic bomb. Maybe it would have been better if we
> hadn't done it." . . . I just reject that kind of thinking totally . . . in
> genetic research. I mean, there is no question that you can produce
> scenarios that are horror scenarios of how genetic knowledge will in

fact be detrimental or deleterious to both people, society, the way we live. . . . A large part of what I've done before and done, still do, is try to promote the way society deals with discovery or new knowledge, developing essentially the wisdom or the tools for managing its effective use without bringing down the negative qualities of it.

It's not like we're trying to build a nuclear bomb. We're trying to answer some basic biological questions. And I don't see how that would even remotely translate into something that would definitely harm the society at large rather than benefit it.

While the analogy to atomic bombs may be far-fetched, it is possible to envision less fanciful negative consequences of current work. Yeung reflected on possible abuses of work on cloning:

The fact that we can now actually make clonal copies certainly opens the entire Pandora's box of being able to generate organisms that are clones of yourself, that can provide a replacement organ for you if one of your organs fails. . . . And these [cloning technologies] are things that industry has already honed in on and are providing big bucks to do outside, because government really would not support that. But there's tremendous industrial money behind these endeavors. . . . I think scientists should be aware that there are certain things . . . probably not in the best interest of the human race to do. . . . I certainly would have reservations if somebody pays me to clone him so that he can have a heart to replace his, because that would mean that you'll have to take a heart from whatever being that you've cloned.

Ian Wilmut also voiced concerns about possible abuses of his work. When we asked what his greatest fear was about where his pioneering technology might lead, he replied:

Well, I suppose that's got to be the idea that people would use it to copy people, which I think would be very sad because I think that each child should be wanted and treated as an individual. And if you've produced a copy, I think that's much, much more difficult. . . . I don't like the idea of copying people . . . but it is not equivalent to the threat to mankind of, for example, the atomic bombs, which is a comparison which is sometimes made. So it's bad enough, but not quite so bad as people might think.

What Is Said and What Is Not Said

Just as we were surprised by the lack of great concern about issues like patenting, cloning, and germ-line therapy, we were also surprised at the relative lack of attention to topics that often loom large in the popular accounts of genetics research. Jeremy Rifkin, a vociferous, well-known and articulate critic of genetics research, has issued provocative challenges to the Human Genome Project, the prospects of genetic engineering for the less able, the patenting of any organism, the military uses of new biotechnology, reseeding of the biosphere with artificial creatures, and the possible invasions of privacy. In *The Biotech Century* he noted:

> A handful of global corporations could hold patents on virtually all 100,000 genes that make up the blueprints of the human race, as well as the cells, organs, and tissues that comprise the human body. They may also own similar patents of thousands of micro-organisms, plants, and animals, allowing them unprecedented power to dictate the terms by which we and future generations will live our lives.[8]

Interestingly, we heard Rifkin's name mentioned only once or twice—and then, dismissively, as if he were an ideologue. Nor, except for those scientists directly involved, was there mention of the work of the Council for Responsible Genetics or the American Society for Bioethics and Humanities, two "watchdog" organizations. The frightening scenarios presented in 1990 by the British genetics researcher and critic Mae-Wan Ho about the creation of virulent new pathogens, or the release of destructive transgenic organisms, or the rapid demise of entire species received nary a mention in thousands of pages of transcripts.[9]

The issue of genetically modified foods is headline news in Europe and increasingly is garnering U.S. coverage as well. Speaking in 1998 and 1999, our respondents never touched on the topic. The question of whether experiments in plant cultivation or in the laboratory might upset the ecological balance or lessen the diversity on the planet never came up in the interviews. A few scientists spoke of "playing God" with information about a person's genetic fate, and a few raised the analogy to the creation of the atomic bomb. Those who mentioned these examples, however, quickly dismissed them as unrealistic or used them merely as a segue to statements about faith in the fundamental good sense of human beings. One scientist raised the possibility that interventions initially undertaken to wipe out disease might evolve into ill-advised efforts to create "gene-designed" babies, but again there was virtually unanimous faith that this is unlikely to happen on a large scale. There was little concern that "choosy parents" would try to specify the intellect, talents, and physical appearance of their offspring. And no one raised the question of the moral propriety of experimenting with human stem cells or, more speculatively, the human evolutionary process.

Finally, hardly anyone alluded to secret work on biological warfare, either by companies whose existence is hidden from the public or by "rogue states." One of our respondents, Jonathan King, a long-time professor of biology at MIT, did say that he became uncomfortable while doing consulting for a biotechnology company. King found that his work on the basic structure of genes and proteins was being put to genetic therapy uses of which he did not approve. For a while, King debated about what to do, and, questioning whether he could be of use to the company, he finally removed himself from the position. He did not feel that it was appropriate to challenge the company publicly, though he has often spoken out elsewhere about his misgivings with respect to certain uses of basic biological research.

A Continuing Golden Age?

Except for the few disgruntled geneticists we spoke with, most of our respondents clearly believe that they are living in a golden age, in which forces impinging on their work lives are well aligned. There is surprising harmony across their personal goals of discovering the laws governing the biological world, the values of the domain of science, the current institutions and reward systems, the general public's desires, and the shareholders' specific demands. They responded to criticisms by charging that the bad scenarios are inflated; by contending that the broader community must, in fact, impose regulations; and by reminding us that in any case scientists have shown good faith, for example, by calling for the 1975 Asilomar Conference (see Chapter 5).

As George Klein, a noted Swedish tumor biologist and an informal adviser to our study, wrote to us:

> Geneticists are not less fallible, more humane and more ethical than other people, they have documented that many times in the past. They are not less stupid either, sometimes more stupid (because of their blinders). *But they are not stupid in their profession.* Those who are, don't have the respect of their colleagues and cannot prevail for long. The way the dangers of what is called "genetic manipulation" of human beings have been and are being presented to the public are, to a large extent, unrealistic fantasies, *because they are not based on a solid understanding of the way genes work. There are real dangers in the future use of genetics information . . .* these dangers do not involve the manipulative alteration of the human genome. There is neither person nor motivation, nor, indeed, any *reason* for this (because there are much simpler and faster methods for totalitarian regimes to use if they want to), this is just science fiction.[10]

This line of reasoning could, however, be naive. Scientists' faith in their own judgments is by no means beyond question, as evidenced in some recent examples. Only a few years ago many scientists viewed the cloning of higher organisms as impossible.[11] American tobacco companies have never lacked scientists willing to testify that smoking is not harmful. Many European scientists minimized the risks from "mad cow disease" before fatalities began to accrue in Great Britain and then spread to Western Europe.

It may also be naive of scientists to posit a distance between themselves and the rest of society. In the United States early in the twentieth century, and in Nazi Germany during the 1930s and 1940s, scientists found themselves willing (or unwitting) partners in widespread eugenic practices aimed at eliminating unwanted groups of people. More recently, in the Soviet Union and Iraq, arsenals of weapons of biological warfare were accumulated for either defensive or offensive purposes.[12]

Most geneticists deplore the public's poor understanding of science, and many also criticize the coverage by the media. At the same time, most—and especially the young—admit that they are too busy to devote much time to educating laypeople. But if avaricious entrepreneurs or political leaders are willing to put biology to dubious uses, and the public is ignorant about biology, and the scientists themselves are "otherwise engaged," what safeguards are there against flagrant misapplications of the knowledge being accumulated at warp speed by geneticists? In our view, senior scientists significantly underestimate the threat to their profession of two complementary but related factors—either of which could lead to a misalignment of their domain.

Experiments Gone Awry

We see the first underestimated factor—one intrinsic to the practice of science—as the occurrence of genetic experiments with catastrophic results. The nature of genes and their interaction may prove far more complex than hitherto believed, and efforts to cure or alleviate disease through experiments with gene insertion or manipulation are fraught with peril. Already, well-publicized cases of genetic therapy have resulted in patient illness or even death. Most notoriously, in 1999, eighteen-year-old Jesse Gelsinger, who had a mild form of an inherited disease that could ultimately have been fatal, was given a heavy dosage of gene therapy, and he died shortly thereafter. The decision to treat this particular patient with a high dosage was clearly ill advised. Investigations revealed a number of other irregularities: the questionable scientific rationale of the trial, the degree of oversight by the U.S. Recombinant DNA Advisory Committee, and certain administrative aspects of the conduct of the trial. Most troublingly, both the principal investigator and the university had stocks in the company that was supporting the research. In the aftermath of this and other similar episodes, genetic therapy experiments were temporarily halted at the University of Pennsylvania Medical Center and a few other research sites.[13] Should such trends or practices continue, one of the chief promissory notes of the new biology will fail to be redeemed.

The Profit Motive's Sway

The second underestimated factor is the increasing dominance of the profit motive within biology. So far, scientists and corporate managers have had common interests: they are both looking for promising drugs and treatments, and they need one another's expertise. But what happens if the corporate sector overwhelms the nonprofit (and, presumably, more disinterested) lines of research, or if the scientists themselves recede in importance and become interchangeable units in a corporate machine? What happens if the Princeton University biologist Lee Silver is correct in stating that "The growing power of molecular genetics confronts us with future prospects of being able to change *the nature of our species* [his italics] . . . for better *and* worse, a new age is upon us . . . and whether we like it or not, the global marketplace will reign supreme"?[14]

A conference on integrity in biotechnology research held in the summer of 2000 in Bethesda, Maryland, addressed some of these threats.[15] The participants noted that until a few years before the conference, research had been funded largely by the federal government and carried out primarily at universities; in contrast, the most recent trend had been toward research experiments being supported by the private sector and often pursued under cloaks of secrecy. Indeed, of more than sixty thousand human experiments being carried out in 2000, 60 percent were conducted by for-profit companies; in 1991, about 80 percent of such studies were under the aegis of academic medical centers. Among the dubious practices reported were cash payments or stock options to doctors who recruited patients into experiments, biases in the design and reporting of studies to favor the projects' funders (statistical studies confirmed these biases), published articles favoring new treatments that were ghostwritten by company employees but appeared under the name of hired academic shills, and institutional review boards in private companies that were made up of the managers' cronies. Experts noted that it is often impossible to obtain impartial reviews of new work because everyone in the specialty area is working for one or another biotechnology company. Greg Kroski, the newly named director of the federal Office for Human Research Protection, concluded: "Conflicts of interest are very, very serious and a threat to our entire endeavor. During the last five years they may have gotten out of control. Public trust has been eroded."[16]

We cannot know whether such cases of misconduct are isolated ones or whether they are the tip of the iceberg, poised to wreck the domain of genetics and eviscerate the field. Geneticists may soon have to grapple with changes similar to those faced by today's physicians, many of whom feel like expendable cogs in massive health maintenance organizations. If genetics should go in this direction, genetics researchers will face a stark choice between joining large corporate bureaucracies or working in the monastic backwaters of universities or research institutions.

There may also be an arrogance among scientific and medical workers that deserves to be noted. One articulate commentator is Robert Pollack, an architect of the current revolution in genetics. In his 1999 book *The Missing Moment*, Pollack conceded the appeal of germ-line modification, which, in his words, has "the elegance of a complete solution." Yet, as he pointed out, it is a solution that sacrifices the current generation for the next, and in the process it subtly undermines the purpose of medicine: to alleviate or cure patients' suffering. We conclude with Pollack's voice:

The creation of any child with a changed genome would be a Promethean grasp at the human germ line. It would also be an act of enormous hubris, risking inadvertent chromosomal damage that might not show itself in the growing child for many years. This line of research has already raised some new social and legal problems. It has obliged us to decide if we are willing to pay the price of converting kinship and childhood into commodities in order to find out whether these techniques will work properly; it has given us the task—as yet unfulfilled—of setting a proper boundary on the freedom to initiate genetic novelties in our own species.[17]

PART THREE

JOURNALISM

7

Power Gained and Debased
in the News Media

THE MEDIA HAVE ACQUIRED unprecedented power over our lives, a power to shape our culture and our minds. Today, we rely on the media for almost all facets of the outside world—updates on the weather and the traffic, information about the stock market and home finance, the latest word on national and international events, and titillation and entertainment. For a majority of the world's population, news media reports are more informative and more interesting than most of what they encounter firsthand. It is not quite true that the media have replaced real life; but they have become a predominant determiner of what people attend to, how they interpret it, and how they experience it.

Indeed, our very memes, as described in the opening chapters, are profoundly transformed by the media. Depending on the quality of the coverage, the media either will enhance or adulterate the memes that we rely on daily and transmit to future generations. The dangers are obvious. What will happen to our minds and our culture if our most essential memes become contaminated with viral bits of misinformation? News coverage that provides truthful and comprehensive accounts of events fosters the conditions that societies need to thrive economically and politically. And accurate media coverage enables individuals to make sound judgments and gain control over their lives. However, news coverage that is biased, distorted, or incomplete undermines the capacities of societies to flourish and robs individuals of the capacity to adapt purposively to changing conditions.

Workers in the news industry have the power—and the special responsibility—to preserve, protect, and nourish the informational heritage of a populace grown highly dependent on them for its intellectual and social sustenance. Along with such responsibility has come increased attention, scrutiny, and, for the owners and stars of the industry, enormous celebrity and financial gain. Given the power that today's media workers have been accorded, we might expect to see them enjoying many privileges and high morale, akin to that experienced by many of the geneticists portrayed in the previous chapters. We might expect another Golden Age, in which the needs of society seem to be perfectly aligned with the incentives and reward conditions of the field, the traditions of the domain, and the noble aspirations of the individual workers.

Nothing could be further from the truth, our respondents told us. The consensus among our respondents about journalism's current problems was so overwhelming that we felt compelled to discuss those perspectives in this chapter before moving on, in Chapter 8, to their views about answers—ones based on the traditions of the past, methods of the present, and technologies of the future.

Today's journalists see their nightmare as already having arrived. Joe Birch, a Tennessee-based broadcast journalist, speaking for many, summed up his distress:

> I see the country drifting in this mindless direction and I see it has invaded television news, and it's here. And only the people with the intestinal fortitude to stand up to it and to reject it are going to save us from it. Because the temptation, see, is to get an audience by having all these lurid stories and some celebrities. And say to yourself, "Well see, look at our ratings. Isn't that wonderful?" And that is an abdication of our responsibility. While news can be entertaining, that's not our job, to be entertainers. Our job is to be informers. . . . And that's a tremendous challenge today because these forces of infotainment . . . are crashing through the door. And the ratings are imperative, you have to have them or you don't survive, generally. Or if you do survive, you survive at a very meager level.

We found many other news journalists who despair of being allowed to pursue the mission that inspired them to enter the field. If there ever was a Golden Age in journalism—a topic we consider in Chapter 8—it has begun to tarnish. Of course, there are still some journalists who fight on to preserve journalism's mission, either doggedly in the trenches or brilliantly and creatively at the top of the field. But too common are less successful workers who resign themselves to compromise and mediocrity. And then there are the outright catastrophes: workers who succumb to illegitimate pressures and temptations and are drummed out of the field in the wake of blatant and career-disrupting scandals.

Writing in the *Utne Reader,* a periodical digest of the alternative press, the Canadian editor Kalle Lasn declared:

> The next revolution . . . will be in your head. . . . It will be a dirty no-holds-barred propaganda war of competing worldviews and alternative visions of the future. How could it be won? We must build our own meme factory, put out a better product, and beat the corporations at their own game. We must identify macromemes and metamemes—the core ideas without which a sustainable future is unthinkable—and deploy them.[1]

Being locked in a closet of misinformation, unaware of alternatives, manipulated by powerful forces that control the memes—this is the ultimate nightmare that men and women of the future face in the absence of independent media sources. For the individual, it means being consigned to a life of irrelevance, exploitation, or worse. For the society, it means rule by the few rather than by the many—at best, a charade of democratic motions (such as voting without reason) by citizens lacking the accurate information needed for autonomous judgments. In Kalle Lasn's view, we are perilously close to this condition already: "A society whose members spend a great deal of their time in the irrelevant worlds of sport and soap opera, or mythology and metaphysical fantasy, will find it hard to resist the encroachments of those who would manipulate and control it."[2]

Much has been written in recent years about the demise of ethical standards and reportorial quality in journalism and about the "dumbing down" of work in the field. For example, writing in the *Columbia School of Journalism Review*, Paul Starobin recently called the profession "a generation of vipers."[3] In a widely reported speech, Don Hewitt, the long-time producer of CBS's landmark *60 Minutes*, complained that most television shows have become "little more than cesspools overflowing into our nation's living rooms." Hewitt compared the media ethic that he encountered as a young producer thirty years ago ("Make us proud") with the ethic that, he said, has become dominant today: "Make us money!"[4] These views are not confined to insiders or elite social critics. Repeatedly in opinion surveys and polls, the public has expressed skepticism and distaste for the way the news media are now operating. We sought firsthand perspectives on why such changes have occurred and how journalists are being affected.

What Has Gone Wrong and Why

Journalists feel that forces of the field have intruded on their domain's integrity, obstructing their capacity to pursue the mission of good reporting. Our participants were twice as likely to characterize recent news media changes as negative than as positive. In striking contrast to the geneticists, 51 percent of our informants felt that changes in the news media were negative, while only 24 percent characterized the changes as positive. (The rest viewed them as neutral.) They tended to be pessimistic about the state of journalism as a whole, because they see these changes as a threat to quality journalism. Two main points of pessimism were the growing demands to comply with the business goals of the industry (noted by 64 percent of all participants) and a perceived decline in values and ethics within the field (noted by 63 percent of all participants). Those in management or ownership positions were significantly more likely to mention positive changes in the field and less likely to note negative ones. In comparison with front-line reporters, they felt more in control, more shielded from the market model's capricious pressures—and indeed, some of them may have been energized by journalistic and financial opportunities that have opened up in recent years. (Unlike the case in genetics, the journalistic creators, or the reporters, and the journalistic gatekeepers, or the managers, do seem to be drawn from rather different populations.)

Regardless of whether our participants conceived of the changes as positive or negative, there was a marked intensity in their attitudes. Some members of the news industry are thriving, at least for now, on the glamour and power of today's mass media, whereas others are finding it harder and harder to accomplish what they set out to do when they entered the professional realm.

The Impact of New Technologies

Among those who see the recent changes in the field as positive, the main point of optimism was the new technologies, which are said to have improved news-gathering capacities and extended the reach and quality of news reporting. In fact, even those who were discouraged by the other changes often put technology on the plus side of the ledger. In the sample as a whole, 46 percent judged new technology to be a positive force, as opposed to 25 percent who judged it negatively and 29 percent who judged it as a neutral force. But, as we discuss later in this chapter, many among the 25 percent who had reservations felt strongly that the new technologies have presented a serious challenge to quality journalism—a challenge that must be met by bold and creative strategies.

The dizzying technological innovations of recent times have been a wild card. On the one hand, they have added incessant time pressures, reducing reporters' ability to check facts and to establish a meaningful context for a fast-breaking story. On the other, the new technologies present opportunities to magnify the scope, quality, speed, and accuracy of news coverage, as well as the immediacy and accessibility of reporting. Foreign stories can be readily transmitted into the living rooms of the audience, if there is the editorial will to do so. Whether the traditional standards of the domain are upheld or undercut will be determined by the intentions of those who control the field and do the work.

The Push for Market Share

Most prominent among the field forces is the desperate clawing for market share that, journalists believe, is eroding their domain's integrity. The Chicago journalist Bill Kurtis said:

> Fewer people are watching local television news, and networks for that matter. So in a desperate attempt to hold onto the viewers, why, they're doing sensational things, tabloid, bringing [controversial talk-show host] Jerry Springer in and, consequently, creating a newscast that is far more interested in spiking ratings than it is in communicating. It's a very unpleasant place to work and some

managers are stupid enough to literally force people of integrity to leave.

The frenetic market mentality, some say, is producing a herd of un-thinking journalists who do little more than chase after the public whims of the moment. The result has been overattention to trivia such as celebri-ties and their personalities, underattention to news that counts in people's lives, and a destructive cynicism masquerading as toughness:

> And I think in a peculiar way, we are far more destructive than
> we've been, because we betray a pervasive cynicism about every-
> thing, particularly those who serve the public. At the same time,
> we're not tough enough. It's amazing, amazing. We want to be
> much tougher about everything, about life and so forth. We don't
> spend enough time looking up the greater problems. Washington
> journalism, in particular, focuses on the presidency and personali-
> ties. We don't really report on the government the way it actually
> works. We don't report on the country in the way it's really happen-
> ing. We don't talk about the larger burdens of the incredible divi-
> sions in American life, this have-and-have-not world that is
> explosively rising around us. We don't even begin to explain that.
> We allow ourselves to be driven by polls, focus groups, rather than
> doing our own independent thinking.

In the news media today, ferocious competition has created pressures that are strongly felt throughout the field. Nearly every editor feels im-pelled to lean more toward entertaining coverage and less toward more serious probing. Dazzling video techniques that capture the public's eye have led producers to forego the thoughtful effort needed to prepare care-ful or profound presentations. All this has thrown the basic question of "What is news?" up for debate. Material deemed obscure, difficult, or dis-tant has lost out to local "human interest" stories. One prominent exam-ple has been foreign affairs. The former CNN correspondent Peter Arnett pointed out in a 1999 article:

> International news coverage in most [of] America's mainstream pa-
> pers has almost reached the vanishing point. Today, a foreign story
> that doesn't involve bombs, natural disasters, or financial calamity
> has little chance of entering the American consciousness. This is at

a time when the United States has become the world's lone super-power and "news" has so many venues—papers, magazines, broad-cast and cable TV, radio, newsletters, the Internet—that it seems inescapable. So how is it that Americans have never been less in-formed about what's going on in the rest of the world? Because we, the media, have stopped telling them.[5]

In our interviews, we asked journalists how their domain is changing and what, if any, new opportunities or obstacles have been created by the changes. Some of our participants noted that within a short period the priorities have changed dramatically: journalists have been wondering aloud how long they can survive in this professional realm. The most telling of the changes have been the market incentives that now drive per-formance. Our participants told us that, as news companies have merged into ever-larger corporate megaliths, the pursuit of mass audiences and bottom-line results has become increasingly more aggressive and one-sided. As the newsroom becomes but one of many profit centers in a complex corporate structure, it becomes increasingly evaluated on a fiscal dimension. One reporter for a large national newspaper said: "We are be-coming more and more aware as journalists of the business dimensions of our work. Not to suggest that the business office comes into the news-room, that is not what I mean, but we're becoming more and more aware of the importance of selling newspapers." Speaking directly to the effect of this change on journalistic standards, a veteran radio and television news analyst said, "Ethics has now been caught up in something so much bigger than any of us ever dreamed we would have to face, and that is the interests of the vast conglomerate that we now end up working for."

The danger is that the increased focus on business ends will lead to a loss of focus on the journalistic ends, the noble purposes or mission that workers entered the field to pursue. According to Harold Evans, the long-time newspaper editor of the *London Times*, first, and then of the *New York Daily News*, "The problem many organizations face is not to stay in business, but to stay in journalism."[6]

Pressures to cut costs, raise revenues, and enhance productivity become more intense when the goal to maximize profits is pursued so single-mindedly that it drives out the goals stemming from the enterprise's so-cial contribution. According to the journalists we interviewed, many news organizations have become so preoccupied with profits, ratings, and bottom-line financial results that they have downsized, cut their newsroom resources, raised their demands for productivity, and directed their content and coverage to selected advertisers and audiences. Garrick Utley, a leading broadcast journalist, told us:

> News has to make a profit or at least pay for itself. That was the order coming down from G.E. [General Electric, the owner of NBC]. Well, that meant you had to have major cuts. And what you started to do was to cut back on trips, cut back on personnel, cut back on the size of your overseas bureaus, and the same thing happened at CBS. What the bosses said was, "Oh, don't worry. We'll just be leaner and meaner. We can still cover it." [Then they said,] "We don't have to send a somebody to Nicaragua or some other place. We will get news agency tape or film. And we can voice over it here and who's gonna know the difference?" From a broadcasting point of view that may well have been true. You could get away with that at a much lower cost. For those of us who were the working journalists, of course, it was suspect because it wasn't real journalism. You didn't have your reporter on the scene: You were writing captions to pictures that came in through some other means. So this was both an ethical and a professional change of the first order caused by budgetary pressures. Then you get to the question of the cutback in foreign news for editorial and audience reasons.

Single-minded bottom-line pressures can frustrate the work of journalists in many ways. A producer for a TV news magazine show explained that, because of limited resources and the constant pursuit of higher ratings, there is now "a lot of copycat, a lot of recycling of stories." A print journalist explained that productivity enhancement and cost cutting have led to the slashing of travel budgets and increased time pressures. He believes that these types of cuts undermine his creativity as a journalist, because "[traveling,] that's the first philosophical act, to go and see something and think about it." He referred to the serendipity involved in older, more time-consuming means of retrieving information: "There's less time to take the detour and learn something else that might prove to be interesting and productive down the line." He further noted, "There isn't a lot of time for reflection." The changes lead to "living off [intellectual] investments," which in turn creates pressure to "borrow what look like creative ideas from elsewhere," instead of generating one's own. The pressure to copy tried-and-true formulas engenders an aversion to creative risk taking and, inevitably, to pat and superficial coverage of news events.

In effect, budgets predetermine which stories get pursued and which ones eventually get printed or aired. According to many journalists whom we interviewed, it has become increasingly difficult to obtain financial support for stories that have little entertainment appeal, whatever the social significance of the story. The most profound influence has been felt on efforts that require significant resources, such as investigative reporting. As a journalist who had recently worked under managers with a bottom-line orientation put it, the investigative reporting she so values "was not appreciated. And it can wear you down after a while." Another said:

> The investment in daily stories is much smaller than the investment in some explanatory series. I spent six months on one series and produced very few daily stories in that time. For some papers that is an unaffordable luxury. Some papers are committed to doing that kind of story. But I think it is becoming harder for papers to be committed to that kind of work, simply because of the bottom-line pressures that are being felt by people in the field.

On March 19, 2001, the friction between escalating business pressures and journalism's mission became so intense at the San Jose *Mercury News* that it led to an explosion that rocked that newsroom and reverberated throughout the industry. Jay Harris, the paper's distinguished publisher, abruptly resigned in exasperation over what he called "the tyranny of the markets." He complained about impending budget targets that would reduce the *Mercury News*'s staff to a point where it could no longer do top-notch reporting. Pointing out that avaricious budget targets, built on open-ended expectations of higher and higher profit margins, have become an industry-wide norm, Harris said, "I neither believe nor will accept that the current trend can't be changed, that the unwise is somehow unavoidable."

In fairness to the *Mercury News*, the paper continues to have a stellar reputation in the field. CEO Tony Ridder wrote that he was surprised by Harris's resignation and denied mandating higher profit margins for the year 2001. In fact, Ridder declared, he was not at all certain that layoffs at the paper were necessary. The *Mercury News* was "extremely" well staffed and would continue to be so. "It is unthinkable that we would preside over the diminution of the *Mercury News*'s quality," Ridder wrote.

But whatever the precise facts in this important case, it is clear that the relationship between profits and standards in journalism is no longer a "healthy tension," as in journalism's "Golden Age," but rather has become a corrosive conflict. At the *Mercury News*, the destructive climate led to a miscommunication that deprived that newspaper of a fine editor. As Jay Harris said in a speech to the American Society of Newspaper Editors, such contention need not be the case, even now. With commitment and creativity, the "moral, social, and business dimensions" of journalism can go hand-in-hand. We concur completely—this is practically a definition of how one can achieve good work.

The Retreat from In-depth Coverage of Serious Stories

Compounding the budget-driven pressures on quality, there is a widespread perception among news owners and reporters alike that the public has become unprepared to understand serious news coverage. In 1999, the *New York Times* reported that "relatively few people paid attention when the impeachment vote was televised, but [Barbara Walters's] Lewinsky interview drew an incredible audience of 70 million."[7] One journalist noted that her editor screens out stories that seem too "complicated" for their readership. According to a prominent television journalist, the audience often is not only obtuse but also uninterested in serious stories.

> I think now, people, their interest isn't held very well. So, the
> dilemma with modern news directors is, let's give them something
> that's going to hold their interest. So, now we've gotta come up
> with these stories that sometimes are a little more entertainment
> oriented, because they say, well, people are really into Rosie
> O'Donnell these days, and that's a little more entertainment. So
> maybe we ought to do some more entertainment. . . . I think
> people can't hold their interest like they used to.

This journalist punctuated the next remarks with snapping fingers: "We're a lot more bored—bored with that, bored with that, bored, bored, bored. You know. Let's go, let's go, let's go, go, go."

The audience's distaste for in-depth treatments has led to another market-oriented conclusion: if a news story is to garner a large audience, it must play to the most vulgar interests of the public. As for what it takes to grab people's attention, the stakes are always being raised. Sensationalism is like a drug that people habituate to, always needing more and more to trigger the same level of thrill. One anchorman told us: "Well, I think our eyes are calloused, now, in a way that they weren't before. The ambient level of horror is higher, so that to goose people, you have to ratchet it up, higher than you used to have to before."

Meanwhile, issues that are fundamental to our civil life but too complex to lend themselves to light or flashy treatments go neglected. *Washington Post* reporter Bob Woodward complained:

> Instead of worrying about the educational system and the District of Columbia, for instance, all the reporters are worried about whether the mayor (Marion Berry) has a new girlfriend, or is buying cocaine, relevant questions, but the city services, as you know them, collapse . . . schools don't work, and the police aren't there. What effort—how many reporter hours are going to those subjects? . . . There is a scandal press corps.

The frustration that journalists express concerning their audiences has a special edge to it, because they feel an obligation to serve the audience by reporting all the truth that the audience needs—whether or not the audience *thinks* it needs it. One of our participants spoke for a majority of her colleagues: "The ethical question is, Do we cover what people want to watch, or do we cover what we think they should be watching and what we want them to know? That is where you have to make that type of decision and that is where a lot of debate has come in about whether news is more ethical or less ethical."

Is the media's perception of the audience's tawdry tastes real or imagined? Or is this, rather, a self-serving perception? There have been enough success stories in serious news coverage to question whether standards must be lowered to capture market share. Without doubt, audiences can rise to enjoy the most difficult programming if they find good reason: witness the success of Ted Koppel, Mike Wallace, and others who provide in-depth news analyses in a popular format. And even if we were to accept that audience preference has coarsened in recent years, we would ask another, more pointed question: Is this a cause or an effect of dumbed-down media performances? Who is the victim of debased memes—the news media or the public that they serve?

Today's journalists feel caught in the middle, squeezed between two avaricious stakeholders: a corporation single-mindedly intent on expanding market share and an audience on the lookout for entertainment rather than "hard" news. The corporation's overriding profit motive, its aggressive solicitation of mass audiences, and the feeling that today's audiences want to be entertained with superficial stories rather than informed through in-depth coverage, all reinforce one another's effects.

In fact, the combination of these trends amounts to an unholy combination in today's media world, because it has created a set of corporate incentives that many journalists see as pulling them away from their primary mission. One television anchorwoman described the pull of market forces in this way:

> The primary mission is always to get ratings, to get the viewers to watch. And how you do that all depends upon what the viewers in the particular market want to see. If they want to see violence, then you do a lot of crime stories. A shooting here, a homicide there, a child abuse case . . . this is a business, just like any other business, and what do businesses do? They make money.

And she discussed an all-too common decision-making pattern:

> For example, you have a story about a shot, an influenza shot, a new shot that's come out. But then you also have a story about the new Corvette that's coming out. The reporter in me wants to do the story about the shots and why they're important and where they're available. Because that's news that people can use. But they might say, "Well, it's Friday and the viewer at home might want something a little bit lighter, because it's Friday and they're gearing up for the weekend. So go do the story about the Corvette." . . . It just means that sometimes you do the stories that you want and sometimes you don't. Your first choice—sometimes you don't do your first choice.

A number of our respondents mentioned news from the health and education fields that they believed had been underreported because their editors had seen the topics as too obscure or ponderous to gain the attention of a broad audience. In such cases, the result was either noncoverage or a warped presentation of the truth, sometimes bordering on deception. As described in Chapter 1, Ray Suarez's dilemma regarding a report on the risks of video games involved pressures to take an event out of context, exaggerate its importance, and sensationalize it by suggesting that it constitutes a direct threat to the viewing audience.

Why Has the Field Changed for the Worse?

Many of the influential newspapers that flourished in the first half of the twentieth century were owned and controlled by wealthy families who felt close ties with their communities and who believed that journalistic integrity was good for business. When network radio and television news departments came into being, their mode of operating was initially modeled after the standards and practices of the great newspapers. The mission of informing the public about everything important for life in a democratic society was generally clear, and codes of conduct that helped journalists pursue this mission gradually emerged.

In the last few decades, the business climate has changed rapidly. Our informants pointed to several problematic trends in the field. Each trend in itself is worrisome; taken together, they have subjected journalists to a powerful combination of forces that are hard to control, let alone counter.

The Waning of Family Control

By the late 1990s, family control of news outlets mostly had passed to corporate control; the ultimate accountability now lies with a faceless body of shareholders. The most audible voice is one crying out for ever-higher profits, quarter by quarter. It is hard to imagine a group of media stockholders lobbying, say, for more thorough coverage of global warming or of food riots in Pakistan. Whatever the shortcomings of the wealthy old families, they had a broader view of what their business was about. Katharine Graham, the owner of the *Washington Post*, told us:

> I worry some, I guess, about the loss of influence of family on newspapers because the *Globe* (since purchased by the *New York Times*) and the *Times* and ourselves and the *Wall Street Journal* are all still family influenced. That means they can probably pay more attention to the editorial product. We certainly couldn't have made some of the decisions that we made, especially in the Pentagon Pa-

pers case where we risked a lot. I suspect that [a corporate paper] would not have been able to do that, because it was a terribly big risk. It would have been in a business sense too great a risk for a corporate manager.

Discussing the recent acceleration toward corporate control throughout the publishing world, Irving Kristol, a leading conservative writer, told us:

Now when they ran [a publishing company] as a family firm, or as an individually owned firm, they had to meet the market, contend with the market forces. But they were satisfied with a modest return. First of all, they didn't see themselves as part of a growth company. They didn't think they had to do better every year. So long as they got enough to pay their salary and cover all the expenses, with a little extra for development. So it was 9 or 10 percent return on your investment, as it were. Not so bad. Not acceptable if you're in the market, not if you're a publicly owned company, because you're not doing anything for your stockholders. . . . And that has been an awful development . . . clearly, the emphasis becomes, every year, on selling more. . . . You can't just sit back and say, OK, we had a pretty good year. It's not good enough.

An Insatiable Quest for Profits

A little-known fact about the news business is that, compared to other businesses, it has been quite profitable. Twenty percent to twenty-two percent profit margins are the norm, in an economic world where anything in the double digits is usually considered a success. When a newspaper is integrated into a larger corporation, it is often the most profitable unit in the company. Television news shows have been known to carry entire networks with their earnings.

When news outlets operated independently, under the control of a private owner, their considerable earnings potential allowed them leeway. They could forgo short-term profits for the sake of their more enduring reputations, or even for the sake of their broader journalistic missions such as extensive investigative reporting. In short, they could balance their business stake with concerns that were closely linked to the most entrenched values of the domain. When news outlets become part of a larger, publicly owned corporation, expectations change. The corporation hopes to improve upon the 22 percent profit margins. And if the news outlets' profitability should weaken—as might well happen if the public's interest in the news were to continue declining—the pressure ratchets up. The financial issues become not just one part of the mix but the primary, nerve-wracking concern of everyone in the news outlet.

Market pressures do not often result in the actual suppression of news stories. This is a line that has not yet been crossed on any significant scale, at least in the experience of the prominent journalists we interviewed. Rather, the pressures are more subtle. Commercial interests influence the choices of stories that managers wish them to cover, with an eye toward garnering higher ratings (as with "in-your-face" news), capturing a valuable market segment (as with "issues of women aged twenty to thirty-five"), satisfying advertisers or a community relations department (as with promotional activities), and not angering viewers. One journalist we interviewed described her feelings about the effects of business interests on content:

> Someone's got to run a newsroom. And invariably, those are people who are mindful of the concerns of the corporation for whom they work. So there are always questions of what will the viewers think? And the recognition that critical stories generate critical responses, i.e., "Oh God, you just pissed off the Spanish community," or, "Oh, God, a church group is angry because you reported the scandal involving the minister." For some newsrooms that's enough to pull a story. But not for all. Good newsrooms understand corporate tension and community pressure and fight it off. Weak newsrooms don't even try.

The choices made are not viewed as illegal or flagrantly unethical, but the cumulative effect is to weaken reporters' and audience's belief that journalism is a disinterested pursuit of truth.

The Diminishing Returns of Increased Speed

Of all the resources in a newsroom, it is *time* that is coveted most frequently by journalists. "Too little time" was by far the most common complaint mentioned by our informants. Journalists speak of time pressure as a barrier to reflection, in-depth reporting, and accuracy of coverage. There is now an acute sense, shared by most journalists, that modern technology has escalated deadline demands to the point where even the most rapidly executed work can no longer fare adequately. And the Internet has sped up the news cycle beyond even the hurried pace brought on by the last great media invention, television. Consider this lament by a television news writer:

> The game is actually what is going on. This is how I know who is up and who is down, and which ideas are winning and which ideas are not. Because the game is what is practiced and the players are who I cover. So that is part of my job. But to explain then, the issue, and what led to a position and how a position has evolved over time is a challenge for a storyteller, and it is a challenge that is very difficult to meet on deadline. . . . The thing that television has taken away is the luxury of my time, the time that I would have for that. . . . You are moving on, as the reader or viewer, to something else.

The news industry has always placed a premium on speed. The question is not whether it is desirable in general for the news industry to hold workers to a standard of timeliness but rather whether recent changes in the profession have added a corrosive element to this perennial source of journalistic pride and pressure.

How quickly does the public need to find out about a news event? within the same day that it occurs? Within the hour? Within minutes or seconds? Should the media aim to have the public on the spot as an event unfolds? With the advent of worldwide communications, instant coverage is now possible. Electronic media—television, radio, the Internet— are setting the pace, and print journalism is pressed to follow. In the words of one print journalist: "TV . . . offers what we cannot duplicate. You try to go to more analysis and more sort of features about—what we call news magazine style about an event—a position, a pronouncement, a law, what these mean. So very often your reflection is called for . . . I would want more time to reflect."

Today's technology has bolstered the news industry's capacity to broadcast live events of the most flamboyant sort: shootings and arrests, fires and floods, accidents and rescues, warfare and peacemaking. The visual and emotional appeal of such coverage is obvious. But at what cost? Tom Brokaw, the news anchor for NBC, recounted the following story:

Technology is changing at warp speed. And it affects the opportunity to be reflective. I'm going to go to Asia in June. I'm going to try to do it in the old style by doing some stories and having them shipped to Hong Kong and transmitted back. That was routine when film was the medium and there were no satellites. . . . I wouldn't have to be on the air from Jo-burg. I would go overseas, take a couple of days, put some stories together. But now I have to be on the air. Because you can get on the air, you do get on the air. And sometimes we carry that to extremes. That's what's wearing.

The difficulty of producing insightful and accurate news stories in the face of demands for instant coverage makes some journalists question whether the news profession is still the right field for them. We interviewed several who were on the verge of quitting the profession out of frustration with such demands. Many of the talented young journalists we spoke with expressed doubts about the viability of their chosen profession or of their place within it. The number of young journalists considering alternative careers dwarfed the number in genetics who even mentioned the possibility. When a professional realm loses some of its most thoughtful people because of constraints that they see as endemic, it has ventured into dangerous territory. Many in our study echoed the sentiments of one well-known journalist who has turned to writing books rather than news stories: "I am no longer interested in assembling the best view of the world I can by midnight. If I can't assemble an interesting and compelling and meaningful view of the world, I don't want to do it."

Technology and Short-range Perspectives

For many journalists, technology seems a mixed blessing at best. They worry that today's speedier technologies have crippled the profession's mission of truth telling beyond recognition, since finding and conveying the truth means placing events *in perspective*—that is, showing them in the context of the other events that give them meaning. The more urgent the rush for instantaneous reporting, the stronger the press to "cut to the chase" (a phrase borrowed from action entertainment that has now become part of the argot of the newsroom).

Past events in particular are easily (some say eagerly) ignored, since they bog down and complicate the presentation. The eradication of historical awareness is made complete by cost-cutting pressures so short-sighted that they could only reflect a direct intention *not* to take the long view. For example, TV newsrooms now routinely destroy their videotape archives, ostensibly so that they can save money by reusing the tapes. Nick Clooney, a long-time journalist who has worked as a TV news director, explained:

> The assumption is that this moment in time is the pinnacle of all human experience. That's television's view, because television has no history. Television news I'm talking about. Television destroys its history. . . . When newsrooms are taken over by another new news director, sometimes, one of the first things he does, in order to just get more room, more physical room, is destroy all of his files. . . . Well that's your memory. I mean, without that, you can offer no perspective on the story you are about to deliver.

In like vein, a print journalist complained about the "pseudo-information" prevalent in today's television news shows: lacking context, the stories seem to her little more than "a bewildering barrage of facts." One television journalist, who believes that good journalism should be "storytelling," worries that the "instant rush of climaxes, happenings, all the flashy images" in her news shows "crowds out" the narrative elements necessary for a good story—the prior events, characterizations, and surrounding details that make up a compelling sequence.

Violation of the Newsroom Culture

Corporate ownership has consolidated news media outlets into vast companies that may include several other industries, often ones unrelated to information. The head of the corporation may have a better feel for consumer products than for news stories. Tom Brokaw told us about the cultural mismatch between his news team and the General Electric corporate officers who, through GE's ownership of NBC, have legal control over his team's work. In his own experience, there has not been interference, but the potential certainly is there, and newscasters with less influence than Brokaw are no doubt more exposed than he. Brokaw recalled:

The people at the top of GE came up as engineers and scientists, for the most part. When they took over NBC it was an awkward fit at first, especially for those of us in the news division who were much more the product of social sciences. But we learned from each other. And they've never interfered. I've never had a call or even a comment like, "Damn, why would you do that?" I know they've been frustrated by our coverage of some issues from time to time, but it's always been hands off. It's not surprising, I suppose, that the people who run a company such as GE, which relies primarily on manufacturing and financial services, would have a different plane of intellectual interests than those attracted to journalism and entertainment.

A recent event at the *Los Angeles Times* is a textbook example of what happens when the culture of the newsroom and the line between news and marketing are grossly violated. Long considered one of America's best papers, the *Los Angeles Times* began to shift its procedures in the mid-1990s. Under the leadership of an energetic publisher, Mark Willes, the paper became much more aggressive in seeking readers. Willes, whose background was in the cereal business, spoke dramatically about the need to "knock down the wall . . . to use a bazooka if necessary" between the news/editorial and the market/business sectors. Willes's successor as a publisher, Kathryn Downing, continued this policy.

On October 10, 1999, the *Los Angeles Times* published a special 168-page issue of its Sunday magazine, devoted entirely to a new downtown sports and convention venue, the Staples Center. The section was filled with information about the facility, its tenants, its attractions, its appearance; it was also loaded with advertisements. What readers—and most individuals associated with the *Times*—did not know was that the *Times* was dividing the proceeds from advertising in the section with the Staples Center. When word of this arrangement broke out and received nationwide press coverage, a firestorm erupted. Journalists around the country were sharply critical of the decision to share profits with Staples without conveying that information in a timely fashion to the paper's editor and staff. On October 28, Publisher Kathryn Downing met with the newspaper staff. She confessed to a "fundamental misunderstanding of basic journalistic principles"—in our terms, the standards of the domain. And she stated her intention to become better informed about these principles and to try to adhere to them in the future. On Sunday, December 19, the

Times published an apology to its readers, signed by both Downing and editor Michael Parks. They pledged to remain free of compromising activities and stated that "decisions on coverage will be made solely by editors based on newsworthiness and value to readers."

Then, on the following day, Monday, December 20, the *Times* published a fourteen-page section in which the Pulitzer Prize–winning media critic David Shaw presented an exhaustive account and analysis of what had led to the Staples incident, why it happened, and what the likely fallout would be. To ensure complete independence, none of the principals of the paper—not even the editor, the publisher, or the CEO—had seen its content prior to publication. And Shaw pulled no punches. As he declared in the preface to the piece: "Many in the *Times* newsroom see the Staples affair as the very visible and ugly tip of an ethical iceberg of ominous proportions—a boost-the-profits, drive-the-stock-price imperative that threatens to undermine the paper's journalistic quality, integrity, and reputation. . . . Why should *Times* readers trust anything *The Times* wrote about Staples Center, or any of its tenants or attractions, anywhere in the paper, now or in the future, if *The Times* and Staples Center were business partners? More important, how many other such improper arrangements, formal or informal, might also exist or be created in the future with other entities, agencies, and individuals covered by *The Times?*"[8]

While the *Los Angeles Times* served as the flashpoint of this uproar, these problems are clearly not restricted to a single publication. In a trenchant piece called "The Wall Vindicated," *New York Times* columnist Max Frankel chronicled the blurring of distinctions across the profession. In his words:

> Many newspapers, too, now blur the line between news and commerce. They accept or create special sections that guarantee advertisers a friendly "environment." Under the cover of good citizenship, many also collaborate in promotions and community activities with the same politicians and business people they claim to be covering at arm's length. And most media companies have barely begun to confront the ethical quandaries posed by their new Web sites: how to insulate their information services from the on-line merchandising and advertising they conduct in all corners of the site.[9]

Frankel went on to quote a former Los Angeles Times editor, William F. Thomas, who commented "When you take down a wall, you'd better understand why it was there in the first place."

The Times event claimed many victims. In the spring of 2000, the long-time Los Angeles–owned paper was sold to the Chicago Tribune—and many of the key players in the Staples incident have disappeared from its masthead.

Editors' Altered Roles

The unrestrained market model has diminished the authority of news editors, once the guardians of quality, the domain's bulwarks against illegitimate pressures exerted by the owners, the public, or other stakeholders. The editors, in a sense, were newsrooms' superegos, the disinterested enforcers of standards. Most editors are now firmly embedded in the corporate hierarchy, directly answerable for fiscal matters. They are paid like executives—a big change from the recent past—and are expected to conform to corporate fiscal priorities. The legendary, independent, iconoclastic, often grouchy lion of *The Front Page* is gone. In his place is a manager who follows, or at least consults, market research before deciding which stories to cover, who practices "management by objective" (with the foremost objective being to maximize profits), and who receives sizable bonuses through an incentive system geared tightly to corporate earnings. In 1999, Geneva Overholser, the former editor of the *Des Moines Register*, wrote:

> Walk into any sizable newsroom in the country, ask where you can find the editor, and the chances are good the answer will be: In the Marketing Committee. It's the place today where key decisions affecting newsrooms are made—how to boost circulation, how to create new sections, how to structure zoned coverage, how to define the paper's target audience. Editors spend long hours plotting strategy with their counterparts from advertising, marketing and circulation, and they are being pushed to turn news coverage toward the most profitable territory: the interests of women, younger readers, suburbanites and the affluent.[10]

All this, Overholser said, has the "practical effect of changing the shape of the editor's job. . . . Corporate officers are insisting that editors spend much more of their time on personnel and budgetary management, much less on the news." With the loss of editors' traditional role, the domain is all the more seriously imperiled.

How Talented Workers Can Go Astray:
Two Troubling Cases

Matt Drudge: Trading Accuracy for Speed

The Internet is a uniquely democratic news medium, with nothing—not time, not money, not editorial supervision—standing in between Internet newscasters and the material they wish to post. Nothing, that is, but the scruples of the person who does the posting. Hence the unique importance of journalistic standards in the Internet age.

If all Internet newscasters interpreted the standard of truth in the same manner as the leading journalists whom we quote in Chapter 8, this new medium would pose little challenge to the domain. But many Internet newscasters have little journalism training and little respect for the domain's codes and traditions. The most prominent of this new breed is Matt Drudge, a "one-man gossip and news agency," according to one recent account.[11] Drudge managed to first break the Clinton–Lewinsky scandal, because he was willing to go with a story that *Newsweek*, among others, considered not yet adequately confirmed. In subsequent months, Drudge continued to scoop the established media on many juicy components of the story, including the telling proof of semen stains on Monica's blue dress. Drudge turned out to be right about most of the material that he posted, but he also made errors. His fame and notoriety grew with every scoop, and his *Drudgereport.com* gained a multimillion "circulation" that outnumbered every newspaper's in the land.

In a rare appearance before the National Press Club, Drudge repeated a statement that had scandalized the mainstream press corps when *Newsweek* first quoted it: "Oh, I guess I'm 80 percent accurate, the body of my work." Earlier, Doug Harbrecht of the Press Club had asked Drudge, "Could you succeed as a journalist if you worked for an organization which required an accuracy rate of 100 percent, instead of 70 or 80 percent." Drudge was having none of it. "I'd rather stay in my dirty Hollywood apartment," he quipped.

Drudge painted a picture of an entrenched mainstream press that, prior to the Internet, monopolized the news and kept important information from the public. Editors have biases, as do the corporate chieftains that editors work for. "Clearly there is a hunger for unedited information, absent corporate considerations." What about the role of editors in making sure that a news story consists of confirmed facts rather than gossip? Drudge replied: "Well, all truths begin as hearsay, as far as I'm concerned. And some of the best news stories start in gossip. Monica Lewinsky certainly was gossip in the beginning. . . . At what point does it become news? This is the undefinable thing in this current atmosphere, where every reporter will be operating out of their homes with Web sites for free, as I do."

In the supercharged world of today's electronic media, Drudge may be winning the argument. And his influence is by no means confined to the Internet alone. According to the 1999 book *Warp Speed,* written by two journalists,[12] Drudge and his ilk have spawned a "journalism of assertion" that is forcing other mass media outlets to air sensational rumors before they can be properly verified, all in the name of keeping up with the competition.

The authors of *Warp Speed* believe that the "journalism of assertion" is eating away at the foundations of public trust for the press—a trust necessary for the survival of the extraordinary freedoms and privileges that the press requires in order to serve a democracy. Other journalists concur. In a *Brill's Content* cover story on Drudge, Jules Witcover of the *Baltimore Sun* was quoted as calling Drudge "a reckless trader in rumor and gossip—[an] abomination of the Internet."[13] And Joan Konner, the former publisher of the *Columbia Journalism Review,* asserted that "by no reasonable measure [is Drudge] working in the public interest."[14]

In the same piece, *Brill's Content* estimated that, of thirty-one exclusive stories broken by Drudge in 1998, ten (or 32 percent) were untrue or never happened, eleven (36 percent) were true, and the accuracy of the rest was in doubt.[15] These figures make Drudge's claim to 80 percent accuracy look wildly exaggerated, and no reputable journalist would accept even that percentage as an adequate standard. The *Brill's Content* article concluded that "in Drudge's case, he must achieve a higher level of accuracy in his reporting to gain genuine credibility." To which Drudge replied: "Screw journalism! The whole thing's a fraud anyway."[16]

Yet Drudge's work has not been entirely without value. He has shown us the potential of an astonishing technology—the Internet—to open up vast informational territories. Drudge is right when he claims that the "balanced" accounts provided by a small circle of mass media powerhouses can be a narrow balance indeed: in fact, it has sometimes led to an *im*balance fostered by a closed set of unexamined establishment assumptions.

But Internet reporting, like any other news source, needs both internal standards and editorial monitoring if it is to become a moral force in its own right. The universal standard of truthfulness cannot be slighted in any sustained news endeavor, not for the sake of speed, nor for the sake of any other marketplace advantage. And news reporters will not be able to dismiss the editorial function without eventually suffering a ruinous loss of credibility, because the editorial function is the primary means the domain has evolved for checking its work against its accepted standards. In the end, if the Drudges of the world are to succeed in expanding journalism's capacity to accomplish its noble purposes, they will do so only by arming themselves with the best traditions of the domain.

Patricia Smith: Blending Genres into an Incendiary Mix

One of our participants, the *Boston Globe* columnist Patricia Smith, was fired from her post as a *Globe* columnist after she admitted inventing fictional sources and making up quotes from them for some of her columns. The controversy became a cause célèbre in the Boston area, where Smith had both prominent defenders and detractors once word of her firing became public.

In her interview with us, some months before the controversy, Smith expressed a vision of her work that departed significantly from the notion of objective journalism. In fact, she proudly advocated "genre blending," a mix of journalism and literary license that mainstream journalists have long viewed as deviating from the domain's core standards. Smith told us:

> It's blurring genres, yeah. That's actually—when you were talking before about what I see as a reason for being successful, that has a lot to do with it. And, when we were talking about journalism school, and would I be a different writer, that's where I wouldn't put myself in a box. That's where teachers would have said, "No, don't put yourself in the story. That creative element doesn't belong there. No, no, no, no."

And she described her own approach more fully:

> If you want to be a good journalist, you have to be a creative writer when you get home, you know, lock yourself in a room and say, "Okay, now I can write my poetry . . ." because the things in

my writing that attracted editors, that even got them thinking
about giving me this column with no straight news experience,
that would not dare say the "P" word, but it was the fact that I
was a poet. And they wanted that different voice. They're not sure
where the voice comes from, but they know that they like the
effects of it.

Smith was dismissed from the *Globe* for fabricating material for some of
her columns: for example, she invented poignant characters (a brain-tu-
mor victim, a little girl who pressed her hair) and put comments about
topical news stories in the mouths of "ordinary folks" who did not really
exist. In an open letter after her firing, Smith apologized to her readers for
breaking "one of the cardinal sins of journalism: Thou shalt not fabricate."
  But she had been right about at least one thing in her interview with
us: her skillful writing within a genre-blending style had indeed met with
warm approval from the journalism establishment. She had recently won
a coveted American Society of Newspaper Editors (ASNE) Distinguished
Writing Award, and at the time of the firing incident she had been nominated for a Pulitzer Prize. We will never know the kind of implicit or explicit guidance she was given at the *Globe*, but it is certainly clear that the
newspaper was happy to print her columns, with all of their poetic flourishes. After she won the ASNE award, *Globe* editor Matthew Storin said,
"It's great to see Patricia's enormous talent recognized."[17]
  When Smith was seen as a writer who flirted with the line between fact
and fiction, between objectivity and subjectivity, she was lavishly rewarded. When it became undeniable that she had leaped across the line,
Smith was dismissed. Storin was then compelled to say, "Each of the fab-
rications violates the sacred trust that the *Globe* has with its readers." But
his protestations at that point rang a bit hollow. Where was the editorial
filter during the first eight years of Smith's tenure at the *Globe*? And where
was it in relation to the other popular *Globe* columnist Mike Barnicle,
who also was widely suspected of having fabricated material throughout
the years? In fact, the Smith incident turned a spotlight on Barnicle, who
also soon left the paper over accusations of ethical shortcomings. The
question then becomes not what was wrong with Smith's work but rather
what sorts of journalism standards the *Globe* had been allowing—or, very
possibly, encouraging.
  The *Boston Globe's* difficulties resonated with other newspapers across
the country. A week after the Smith incident, the *New York Times* re-

ported intense "self-examination at other newspapers," including the *Chicago Tribune*, the *Washington Post*, the *Los Angeles Times*, and the *Wall Street Journal*. But few gave much thought to examining what had gone wrong. Whenever the problem was discussed, the coverage tended to vilify Smith and Barnicle. We would look, instead, to the emerging climate of the field, a climate in which the search for truth is seen as ultimately futile and the faith in objectivity considered naive.

In the midst of the controversy, a Boston-based radio talk show called "The Connection" devoted an hour to the Smith incident. The show was hosted by Christopher Lydon, himself trained as a journalist: Lydon once wrote for the *Globe* and then, for a while, anchored a Public Broadcasting Service news show. Lydon's comments about the affair are telling. They reveal the ambiguous moral climate that Smith was thrown into as a rising young journalist. Lydon began the show by framing the controversy as an opposition between two legitimate positions: "[Some say] fabricating items in a column is a betrayal of the public trust, others said it's just 'shaving' a quote and is done all the time. Some say Patty Smith made a burlesque out of journalism, others that she's a tremendously creative, talented writer who enhanced her pieces to make strong points stronger."[18]

The appeal that Lydon finds in the "creative shaving" position leads him to ask, pointedly, "Should all the news that's fit to print be verifiably true?" He kept his own views contained during the first few minutes of the show, but before long he burst out with the following conviction:

> There's a huge over-reaction here. I definitely wouldn't have fired her. . . . This is the stereotypical reaction of a lot of scared white older guys going by the rulebook, against a black woman, and is something—there's a lot of stuff wrong with it. I also just want to say as a former practitioner of daily newspaper journalism, the whole business of a winging quotes, piping a quote, or as I was taught at the *Boston Globe* when I first got there, "Whomp it up a little bit Lydon, let's spice it," is part of the game. You're not supposed to get caught.[19]

With defenders like this, Smith hardly needed accusers. But Lydon is clearly not alone: he spoke for a local media establishment that stood by and applauded while the cherished standards of its domain dissolved in a sea of cynicism ("everyone does it") and moral relativism (standards can be different from group to group, the rulebook is for only the "scared white older guys"). The cynicism and relativism create a climate of uncertainty about the very purpose of the work; for, as we have shown throughout this chapter, the domain's informational mission is wholly dependent on the standard of absolute fidelity to truthfulness.

Stepping Back from the Brink

In such a climate of uncertainty, journalists may be tempted to play fast and loose with the facts. If we choose to reward unrestrained subjectivity in the press, we can hardly be shocked when journalists stretch subjectivity to the point of invention. But at such a time, one must then pose a fundamental set of questions: In the wake of undeniable cultural and technological change, is it proper to search for a new form of alignment, organized around a new set of standards? Or is it more appropriate to dig in one's heels, to look back to the most basic values of the professional realm, and, defying popularity and trendiness, defend a more traditional approach to journalism? And if one chooses the latter path, how will this square with the demands of stakeholders?

The changes discussed in this chapter have thrown the news profession into what many observers are describing as a "state of crisis." High-level commissions with titles such as the Committee of Concerned Journalists and the Project for Excellence in Journalism have been established to explore what has gone wrong and how it may be fixed. The head of the Committee of Concerned Journalists, Bill Kovach, contends that "the signs of crisis are clear." Rebecca Rimel, the director of the philanthropic foundation that supports the commissions, worries about the "blurring lines between news and entertainment" that are tempting too many news professionals to "sacrifice their journalistic integrity for the sake of sensationalism." As Rimel notes, and as many participants in our study sensed, "the public's faith in the press" is at stake.

For a profession that relies heavily on its credibility for both its market and its mission, this could be a fatal condition. It also poses a grave risk for a society that needs accurate, widely distributed information in order to function as a free democracy. And it poses a personal risk for individuals, now and in the future, who will always need trustworthy information to make judicious choices and exercise independent control over their lives.

Is it the worst of times in the news media? Not yet. Rather, this is a pivotal moment in which the scales are hanging in a precarious balance. We do not know whether quality journalism or schlock sensationalism will prevail. What we do know is that the outcome of the struggle will have monumental effects far beyond the news media. As one prescient informant told us, "The media are an early warning sign. What happens there forecasts what will happen elsewhere before too long."

8

SOURCES OF STRENGTH
IN JOURNALISM

THE PREDICAMENT WITH WHICH we concluded Chapter 7—the depths to which some sectors of journalism have sunk—has led much of the public to become cynical about the entire realm. Especially in intellectual circles, conventional wisdom has it that journalism was never a true profession, that journalists can never be trusted, that the field was never more than a money-grubbing enterprise, and that the domain is barren of anything but self-serving values. We get this response virtually every time we discuss the topic in a public forum.

This bleak assessment could become a self-fulfilling prophecy if left to fester for too long, but for now it fails to capture the truth about journalism's proud legacy of moral standards and practices. This legacy, still existing as a living tradition, guides the finest work in the field, inspiring those who struggle to pursue journalism's true mission in the face of deteriorating workplace conditions.

Journalists today have three sources of strength they can draw on in their efforts to do high-quality work: the living tradition of standards and practices that the domain has evolved over years, their own personal sense of journalistic mission, and the pockets within the field that still support good work (such as colleagues, employers, institutions, organizations, and awards).

Historical Traditions of the American Press

In its earliest days, the American press was little more than a printing business. The adage that "freedom of the press belongs to those who own one" was the rule of the day: printers rented news space to those who were willing pay the going rate, much as newspapers sell advertising space today. Readers gleaned what was paid for by those with the means and the interest to buy space in one of the local periodicals.

Yet owners of colonial-era printing businesses were not entirely blind to their responsibilities as controllers of essential public information. The leading printer of the day, Ben Franklin, wrote astutely about the ethical obligations of printers. Franklin's ethic was passive: printers should not turn away business, even from those whose opinions they abhor. (For the eminently practical Franklin, this ethic no doubt also seemed sensible, if not self-serving, from a business perspective as well: an early case of alignment, we might say.) But whatever its limitations, Franklin's ethical formulation laid the foundations for the framework of free speech, open debate, and the never-ending search for truth that would later come to define the highest standards of the American press. Franklin said:

> Printers are educated in the Belief that when Men differ in Opinion, both Sides ought equally to have the Advantage of being heard by the Publick; and that when Truth and Error have fair Play, the former is always an overmatch for the latter: Hence they cheerfully serve all contending Writers that pay them well, without regarding on which side they are of the Dispute.[1]

When journalism was little more than passive printing, Franklin's ethic was a fragile one, lacking the seasoned practices of a craft that could help sustain it. Without a known method and capacity for investigative reporting, how could a printer verify a story or check on the reliability of a source? Without a set of conventions, how could a printer allocate space in a manner proportional to its importance? Without the capacity to sample and interview broadly, how could a printer represent all significant points of view? Plus, of course, printers of the Franklin era were publishing only the views of "Writers that pa[id] them well," a limitation that would strike us today as undemocratic. An operative principle of "news space for sale" would never be so baldly stated. At least from a comparative perspective, journalism today emerges as more of a profession, with implicit values endorsed by the mainstream players.

The passive neutrality and almost innocent commercialism of colonial news printing vanished in the heated passion of the American Revolution. Once the war began, no one tried to be the least bit fair to the other side. In particular, the Tory perspective never saw the light of day in the dominant Patriot press. Both during and after the Revolutionary War, the tradition of press partisanship flourished with a vengeance. At one point, Federalists went so far as to launch boycotts (successfully) against the few newspapers that tried to present a balanced account of the Constitutional Convention.

After their military and political victories, the Federalists institutionalized their fondness for a controlled press in the Sedition Act of 1798. This act resulted in the only truly oppressive period in American journalism. Editors by the dozens were rounded up and sent to trial simply for criticizing Federalist policies. There was governmental dominance of the press, analogous in a way to the market monopoly of today.

Mercifully, this brief and uncharacteristic phase was undone in the early 1800s by President Thomas Jefferson, who believed that democracy could not function without a press that invited open debate and a government that allowed unfettered exchanges. Jefferson advanced the strictest possible interpretation of the First Amendment: no constraints on a free press. The Jeffersonian legacy of a broadly protected press remains within the United States today and is admired in many other parts of the world.

The immediate fruits borne by the Jeffersonian legacy included a press that was free, far from monopolistic, and equally far from objective. In the great urban centers of the early nineteenth century—New York, Boston, and Philadelphia—hundreds of bulletins, journals, "penny papers," and other dispatches of all kinds were hawked side by side on city streets. Some of these were attractively designed newspapers of style and substance, complete with artwork. Others were one-page sheets of poorly set type. Most were written in English, but by no means all: German, Celtic, Spanish, Dutch, Hebrew, Swahili, Russian, and Greek were among the languages represented. Each paper catered, consciously and without the slightest reservation, to its own clearly defined constituency. For instance, the *Irish Times* ran stories about fellow members of the

Irish-American community who were succeeding, cooking recipes that used New World ingredients to satisfy Old World tastes, the weather, and the latest election results from County Cork.

Virtually all news sources of the day were blatantly and shamelessly partisan, consistently taking only one side on every controversial issue. A newspaper with sympathies to one political candidate would barely cover the rival candidates except to criticize them in an editorial (often printed on the front page, alongside the reporting). If there was objectivity to be had, it was only through balancing out a host of disparate and clamoring presses. And, of course, even in this pre-Internet era, this balance was secured only through readers' willingness to sample many disparate publications critically. The contentious battle for public opinion took place on the streets rather than in the newsrooms, and all was fair in the noisy war.

The Advent of Professionalism

The movement toward a higher standard of journalism was triggered by the initial steps of a market-driven process. In the economic expansion of the late nineteenth century, as newspapers gathered commercial strength, owners saw opportunities to spur their growth by increasing the quality of their coverage. Adolph Ochs Sulzberger, the brilliant and ambitious owner of the *New York Times*, instituted a rule that would set his paper apart from the scandal sheets of the day: "All the news that's fit to print." This was niche marketing at its finest. It promised readers exposure to everything important, including complete political coverage, as well as merciful relief from the foul language and seamy gossip that was saturating the competitions' rags. In strictly a business sense, the strategy was a winner: the *Times* was positioned to dominate the rapidly expanding market of New York's educated and often progressively oriented classes.

The big business mentality of late–1800s journalism brought another benefit to the quality of news reporting: it freed reporters from their servitude to the single party lines to which newspapers of the prior era had been bound. The job of a reporter was now to present new and possibly surprising information to as broad an audience as possible, rather than merely to confirm the preconceptions of a narrow, predetermined, captive audience. Differing ideas could compete with one another within the same newspaper. Accuracy became the standard, replacing predictability and pandering.

From the late 1800s through the early 1900s, scores of American papers followed in the path of the *New York Times*. Integrity became the first selling point of the mainstream press, craftsmanship its second. Even the William Randolph Hearsts and the Joseph Pulitzers, who had competed for readership by peddling sensationalistic "yellow journalism," finally came around. For example, Pulitzer turned his *New York World* toward meticulous and extensive reportage, muckraking exposés, and crusades against political corruption. Furthermore, his dying bequest established both the Columbia School of Journalism and the standard-bearing Pulitzer Prizes for journalistic excellence.

So good practice—good work—came to mean good business for the mainstream modern press, and good business in turn created the conditions that freed journalists to pursue their craft skillfully and honorably. Enlightened owners of the day saw that they had a financial stake in promoting professionalism among their employees. This sensibility made possible much of the daring reporting (including the so-called muckraking) that ushered in the Progressive Era in American politics.

During the early-to-mid-twentieth century, major newspaper businesses ran on a "build-to-last" ethic. Practices that might have helped the bottom line but damaged the company's reputation in the long run (such as using screaming headlines that turned out to be spurious) were ruled out. For some, the ethic went even further. Many publishers were content to make a modest profit if they could do their jobs and get important stories out to the people. These were very different characters than today's corporate CEOs who lust over another half-point of ratings because these may raise their quarterly profit margins from 22 percent to 24 percent. Then as now, the priorities of gatekeepers exerted powerful effects on the standards and practices of the domain.

In the days when the founding families—the Ochs and Sulzbergers in New York (*New York Times*), the Blethens in Seattle (*Seattle Times*), the Binghams in Louisville (*Post-Gazette*), the Taylors in Boston (*Boston Globe*), the Chandlers in Los Angeles (*Los Angeles Times*)—owned the premier newspapers of their respective hometowns, the priorities of journalistic integrity may have been easier to sustain. The wealthy families were accountable mainly to their own values and beliefs. Within limits of law and economic reality, they could use their investments any way they saw fit. Many of the founding families sincerely valued the goal of providing accurate and honorable news reporting, which they saw as entirely consistent with the goal of maintaining their businesses. In addition, while not altruistic saints, the families lived in, and felt committed to, the communities that their papers served.

The Hutchins Report

In 1947, a blue-ribbon commission headed by the University of Chicago's chancellor, Robert Maynard Hutchins, and comprised mainly of distinguished academics, published a report called *A Free and Responsible Press*.[2] The slim volume began with the provocative question, "Is the freedom of the press in danger?" and responded with an even more provocative yes.

Hutchins's report warned of a trend that had largely escaped public attention. All across the land, proud newspaper companies were disappearing, absorbed by their competition or going out of business. Most places in the United States had once been served by several lively papers, each with its own loyal readership. By the time of the report, even the "greatest cities" were down to three or four; "smaller cities . . . two, but most places . . . only one." The report noted that, from 1910 to 1947, daily newspapers in the United States had dwindled from about 2,600 to 1,750, and weeklies from about 16,000 to 10,500.

Hutchins envisioned—and feared—the day when every community might be left with only a single major newspaper, creating a virtual monopoly on local coverage. He worried also about the nationwide chains of newspapers that were growing in size and power: in 1947, seventy-six chains owned 375 dailies, almost 25 percent of the country's total. Wealthy conglomerates were scooping up print, radio, and television outlets, integrating them "vertically" into huge corporations. It was not hard for Hutchins to imagine the day when a powerful corporation might insist that its many media outlets speak with a single voice. Here lay the danger of letting unrestrained market forces rule the fate of a country's news media: a small group of media moguls could shape the coverage of key public affairs such as whom to vote for in a national election or whether to enter a distant war.

Could journalism of the sort that our society had come to value survive such monopolistic trends? Would voices of dissent continue to be represented? Could the open channels of democratic discourse that Jefferson considered the product of a free and pluralistic press be sustained? Would truth continue to be the bedrock standard of the news profession, and would journalists still aim to "speak truth to power?" Or would corporate powers inevitably bend all reporting toward their own commercially driven wills? Such were the questions examined by the Hutchins Commission.

In its probing report, the commission explained why every democratic society needs a free and diversified press. It expressed its concerns about the trends that were changing the face of the news media during the midtwentieth century. And it issued a warning to fellow citizens: If we allow our cherished institutions to diminish, it may not always be possible to reinvigorate them. In the case of a free and independent press, there is a special craft that must be kept alive. Without nourishment and use, the very craft of reporting—almost like the blowing of glass flowers, the building of intricate stone fences, and other lost arts—could disappear with the passing of generations.

The heart of the Hutchins Commission's report was a nine-page manifesto, forceful and concise, buried about a quarter of the way through the monograph. In this section, which the report called "the requirements," Hutchins and his colleagues laid out the essential standards and purposes of the journalistic tradition, the definition and meaning of good work in a free press. The statement was, in effect, a charter of the responsibilities that journalism as an enterprise—in our terms, a domain and a field responsible to the citizenry—must assume if it is to make its crucial contribution to democracy.

The Hutchins charter explicated a key mission: journalism creates a forum for the free exchange of information, ideas, and opinions. A news outlet should aim to become a common ground in society, welcoming to all, where citizens can find out everything of public interest that has occurred, learn what others are thinking about these events, and discover how they can participate in shaping their society. Such is democracy in action, made possible by open and universal access to information.

To accomplish such a mission, it is necessary for the press to abide by certain standards of conduct. First, journalists must not lie: they must pass on truthful rather than false information, avoid conflicts of interest that distort their perceptions, and master the craft of investigating and verifying the facts. Second, journalists must place facts in a context where they can be properly understood. (As the commission commented, "It is no longer enough to report the fact truthfully. It is now necessary to report the truth about the fact."[3]) But the journalist must do so objectively, by giving a comprehensive and proportional account rather than by editorializing or combining fact and opinion. Third, the journalist must represent all segments of the public without perpetuating stereotypes. (For example, the commission noted: "If the Negro appears in stories published in magazines of national circulation only as a servant; if children figure constantly . . . as ungovernable brats—[then] the image of the Negro and the American child is distorted.[4])" Finally, just as the press must fairly represent all groups in society, it also must represent the whole spectrum of ideas, including the least popular ones. Hutchins wished to advance these hallmarks as de facto standards of the professional realm, much as, say, the medical profession long had announced standards (for example, use only well-tested cures, do no harm, do not misuse your power) that distinguished it from quackery (see Chapter 2).

The report also identified several instances of irresponsible journalism. These included telling stories from the perspective of the newspaper's owner, reporting premature "scoops" that turn out to be mere gossip, attracting readers' attention with sensational headlines and exaggerated accounts of trivial events, mixing facts and opinion, advertising products in the context of a news story, and refusing to cover stories that could make influential sectors of the public uncomfortable. In pointing to shoddy practices such as these, the Hutchins report anticipated a lowest-common denominator approach to journalism that by now has become an all-too-familiar part of the media terrain.[5] In Hutchins's day, however, these practices seemed the exception more than the rule: hence the indifference, and even hostility, that first greeted the Hutchins report.

The Hutchins report noted recent technological innovations like radio and television that raised the stakes of journalistic conduct considerably. With prescience, the report declared: "The form, color, and sound of events will sooner or later be re-enacted by television before enormous household audiences all over the world. People in remote parts of the globe will be permitted the same face-to-face observation of each other that is now limited to citizens of small communities."[6] In retrospect, it is clear that the Hutchins Commission was ahead of its time—and that, lamentably, it went unheard.

Few in 1947 read the report as sage. Despite all its grand intentions, its dramatic warnings, its compelling sense of the future, the Hutchins report fell with a dull thud. Reporters in the trenches rejected the report as the starry-eyed work of academics who knew nothing about the grimy task of ferreting out a story. Some owners saw it as just another version of the trendy leftish socialism that was always complaining about growth and progress. Other owners (namely, William Paley and David Sarnoff, in broadcast; the several old families who remained in charge of important newspapers; and the media magnate Henry Luce, who had sponsored the Hutchins investigation to begin with) had confidence in their abilities to keep the ship of press on an ethically steady course. As for the public, it had no particular reason to take notice, since for the most part it still felt well served by a press imbued with the professionalism developed in the Progressive Era.

More recently, defenders of journalism's noble tradition have heeded the trends highlighted by the commission. The threats to the news mission became so apparent that concerned journalists and their professional associations finally mobilized themselves to action—or at least to energetic reflection in the 1990s. As a result, the news media became increasingly self-conscious about their standards and practices, and symposia and public debates on journalistic ethics cropped up everywhere. In our terms, many members of the field resisted the less palatable demands of stakeholders and corporate shareholders and catalyzed a renewed focus on the social mission of the domain.

Also, often unaware of the Hutchins report, professional organizations began codifying their ethical reflections. For example, in 1950 the Radio-Television News Directors Association (RTNDA) published a formal "Code of Standards" that was widely disseminated throughout broadcast journalism. The RTNDA code articulated "standards of practice" that discouraged bias, sensationalism, stereotyping, and the use of news to promote commercial interests. It emphasized journalists' responsibility to provide the public with true information in context, so it could gain a balanced understanding of the information. The 1950 RTNDA standards included the following points:

- The news director, as a key figure in the broadcasting industry, has the public interests as his foremost responsibility. His principal purpose is to keep the public well-informed.
- Complete coverage of the news is the news director's prime objective, and the emphasis should be on scope and understanding, particularly as it concerns the news within his own listening area.
- Material selected for newscasts must be judged on its news merit alone.

- News presentation must be accurate, factual, in good taste and without bias. Writer and newscaster should co-operate to avoid sensationalism in reporting, writing, editing and broadcasting.
- The use of the word "Bulletin" should be limited to label only those reports of such transcendent interest that they warrant interrupting the regular broadcasting schedule. The word "Flash" must not be used contrary to its historic meaning in news usage.
- Commentary and analysis must be clearly identified in all news broadcasts.
- Editorial material must not be mixed with factual news reporting, and when it is used, it must be clearly labeled.
- The race, creed, color or previous status of an individual in the news should not be mentioned unless it is necessary to the understanding of the story.

The RTNDA code was revised in 1966, 1973, and 1987. In these later versions, the language was made more assertive (for example, "The primary purpose of broadcast newsmen—to inform the public of events of importance and appropriate interest in a manner that is accurate and comprehensive—shall override all other purposes"). Direct statements about conflict of interest were added ("Broadcast newsmen shall govern their personal lives . . . in a manner that will protect them from conflict of interest"). Also added were codes insisting that journalists protect the rights of all their sources, as well as the rights of the accused in legal proceedings. Most interesting was a final code from the 1973 revision, an honor code of sorts, that placed the responsibility for ethical journalism squarely on the shoulders of every individual journalist: "Broadcast journalists shall actively censure and seek to prevent violations of these standards, and shall actively encourage their observance by all journalists, whether of the Radio-Television News Directors Association or not."

By century's end, at the time of our study, both the threats and the solutions buried in the once-obscure Hutchins report had come sharply into focus. In the decades following the commission's work, the trends identified in the report continued unabated. The number of independently owned dailies dropped from 1,750 (a number that, in 1947, Hutchins worried about) to 700 in 1980, and to approximately 300 in the 1990s. By the beginning of the twenty-first century, Westinghouse owned CBS, G.E. owned NBC, AOL Time/Warner owned Turner Broadcasting (including CNN), Disney owned ABC, and Rupert Murdoch or Bill

Gates seemed to own just about everything else. The once-noble journal-istic mission had become endangered—as Hutchins anticipated—by fur-ther corporate consolidation, ever-faster and more far-reaching media technology, and the crass market appeal of cheap sensationalism and other shoddy practices.

The public had begun to pay attention. Media stories about field-related practices proliferated, and at least one wide-circulation magazine, *Brill's Content*, was devoted to examining the quality and ethics of press coverage. That the news media had a responsibility to advance the public good was widely accepted. That something had gone awry in recent times was widely recognized. That the forces behind the missteps might be too powerful to control was widely feared.

The good news is that energetic efforts at affirming journalism's core mission and at codifying high journalistic standards had arisen from within the field. These efforts draw upon the noblest chapters in journal-ism's proud tradition. The diversity of opinion celebrated by Franklin, the open forum for debate promoted by Jefferson, the dedication to craft, in-tegrity, and objectivity endorsed by the great news organizations that arose at the end of the century—all have been revived in the formal codes written by the RTNDA and similar professional groups. These codes re-call formulations of standards in medicine (such as those of Hippocrates and Maimonides, noted in Chapter 2) that have created a centuries-old ethical framework. The codes, and the professional organizations that promote them, stand as a key source of strength for the present and future good workers in journalism: they mesh with the personal sources of strength that these practitioners bring to the workplace.

Personal Sources of Good Work: The Calling, the Mission, and the Sense of Moral Identity

The word *calling* may sound antiquated today, but the notion still lies at the heart of what having a meaningful vocation signifies. Indeed, the Latin root of *vocation* means "to be called," and the suggestion has long prevailed that a good worker is "called" to a task set by God especially for that worker. A contemporary way of framing this ancient notion is through the psychological concept of *moral identity*.[7] When a person thinks about the self, or the self's occupations, in moral terms, the person experiences a sense of moral identity. A journalist whose major motivation is to pursue the moral mission of the journalistic domain is acting out of a sense of moral identity. That journalist will have little trouble passing the mirror test, as described in Chapter 1. That is, if the journalist has strived to do the right thing—to pursue the mission of providing the public with true and useful information—she will be able to look in the mirror and like what she sees. If the sense of calling degenerates into just another job, a way of keeping food on the plate (or the BMW in the garage), the moral identity slips away and the mirror sends back a less attractive image.

Do journalists today still hear the calling that brought them into the field? Do they draw a sense of moral identity from their work? If so, what is the domain mission that inspires them and keeps them going in the face of pressures and temptations to compromise? Our answers to these questions will seem surprising to those who believe that a sophisticated take on journalists today can yield nothing beyond pure cynicism.

Half of the journalists expressed a primary commitment to informing the public about the events important for their lives. Another third said that their primary commitment was to supporting democracy by reporting all the news necessary for open, free, and well-informed debates. The remaining ones expressed purposes such as empowering disenfranchised minorities, airing unorthodox points of view, and creating social change—all of which are closely related to the larger missions of informing the public and supporting democracy. In *none* of the interviews was entertainment, commercial advantage, or higher market ratings noted as a primary purpose of the work.

Were the participants in our study simply telling us what we wanted to hear? Or were the missions they identified truly part of their moral identities, their inner sense of self? We do not claim the ability to read the minds of participants in interviews, but our procedure was designed to test the full extent and veracity of participants' belief systems. The interviews were open-ended, deep, and probing, filled with countersuggestions. They were *not* surveys, in which a participant makes a forced choice and the answer is left at that (as, for example, "As a reporter, do you believe that you can capture the truth—yes or no?"). Rather, we took nothing at face value. We challenged our participants' statements, explored the reasons behind statements, and asked the participants to give examples that demonstrated their own real-life commitments to the ideals that they had espoused. Our participants knew little about the conceptual framework and the principal

ideas driving our study, so they were not "primed" to respond in a certain
way (as if, in any case, it would have been possible to feed seasoned journalists primed responses). Perhaps it is possible to fake beliefs on such an
interview, but it is highly implausible that more than one hundred rookie
and veteran journalists did so, independently, for the entire length of their
two- to three-hour interviews. Also, we note the contrast between the
journalists' stated beliefs and those of the geneticists in our study. Such
contrasts would not exist if the uniform tendency of people being interviewed were to fake claims of moral belief.

The Mission of Informing the Public

Most still embrace the traditional mission of informing the public accurately about all the important events of the day. Their guiding assumption is that those who work in the news are charged with the duty of
discovering and revealing any and all important facts—facts that would
otherwise remain out of reach of most people. Some portray themselves
much like hunters who bring back food to a hungry tribe. Recall that one
broadcast journalist's ambition is to tell people: "Here's what happened,
these are the things that I saw and learned and understood, and now I'm
going to tell you about them because you were off doing your life all day,
and now I'll tell you what I saw, on your behalf."

Carol Marin, a television journalist, said:

> News is a kind of quest for as much of the truth as you can find.
> It's a search. People have an absolute right to know what is going
> on and to not be kept from things. My view of news is that it is the
> release of information that might not otherwise be available. It is
> telling people things they need to know but may not know how to
> ask for.

Similarly, Ben Bradlee, the long-time editor of the *Washington Post*, told
us:

> I really do believe that if you shed light in dark corners you make
> the world more understandable, you catch people lying, dissem-
> bling, committing some offense against humankind. If you can
> put one miscreant into jail or if you can take one innocent per-

son out of jail, those are the two, sort of, dramatic extremes. But
in between those two extremes, if you can persuade through
good reporting a legislator or just a reader or a business person
that this is fair and this is not fair, you have made the world a
better place.

Finding important new information and airing it openly is the most
fundamental mission of the news business, according to the majority of
its workers. News reporting to them means gaining access to the events of
the day—great or small, overt or hidden—and then disclosing, to all who
will read or listen, the most enlightening facts and insights they have
gathered. Reporters believe that these facts and insights help people lead
good lives. Bill Kurtis, for example, said he always tries "[to] find a story
that no one knows of, that can be helpful to people out there, and then
. . . communicate it." And William Whitaker, a California-based television journalist, spoke of searching for "information that can help [people]
in their daily lives or when they are making decisions about who to vote
for or what to be outraged about."

The Mission of Empowering the Powerless

Beyond revealing important new information for its use in people's lives
generally, some journalists pay special attention to people who otherwise
would be ill informed and invisible in our money-and-status-oriented society. One reporter spoke about "looking out for the little guy . . . giving
a voice to the people who don't have a voice." Another said, "I want to
give voices to people who need the voice, like write a lot about immi-
grants, people who are powerless. Expose what's wrong, how people get
screwed."

This purpose is consistent with the journalistic tradition of monitoring
the powerful, of "afflicting the comfortable and comforting the afflicted,"
of "speaking truth to power," in the ringing phrases known to all journalists. It is part of the watchdog role of the journalist, the Jeffersonian ideal
that an independent press constitutes the ordinary person's only real protection against exploitation or oppression by people with entrenched
power. In that sense, this purpose complements the purpose of supporting democracy, by making special efforts to serve groups of citizens who
otherwise would be ignored.

Some journalists see their mission as giving voice to people who share their own particular backgrounds, especially if those people have been excluded from the limelight. Usually these are younger journalists who, changing the demographic mix of the workforce, have entered journalism in recent years. For example, one African American print reporter told us:

I got into this business to try to help black people have better lives in this country, and I guess if I think of some large purpose that remains my large purpose. And I think by doing good journalism I can push that along somewhat. I mean maybe not as much as somebody who does things directly, a social worker or something, but I really do believe that information and truth and all those things can contribute.

A similar statement was made by Maria Elena Salinas, a prominent broadcast journalist in Miami. She told us that she is in the business to spread the news to the Latino community. She said that prior to her entry into the profession, there had been a void in news shows that were of interest to Latin Americans, and she believed she was helping to fill that void. Her mission included both covering the events that concerned Latin Americans and reporting the events in ways they would find especially interesting and useful:

Our main goal is to serve the Hispanics, or to inform the Hispanics in the U.S., even though we are also seen in Latin America. . . . We are trying to not just inform them but to help them in their day-to-day lives, somehow interest them. . . . We also cover a lot in Latin America, so that our main goal is to be a link to their countries of origin. And let them know what is happening in the country they now live in and in the community they live in.

Other journalists expressed commitments to serve a wide variety of unrepresented or underrepresented groups through extended reporting. The groups mentioned included women, ethnic and religious minorities, handicapped people, economically underprivileged people, and children, as well as nonhuman entities such as animals and the global environment. Some journalists believe that they can best fulfill such special purposes not only through their reporting but also by their very membership in the field.

The Mission of Supporting Democracy

Many journalists spoke of their desire to promote the values and processes of a democratic society—"[to help] people steer their destinies in a more democratic way," in the words of one reporter. This is a variation on the theme of empowering people, but when placed in the context of a democratic society, this focus has both social and individual significance. This purpose also underlines the urgency of preserving the press's autonomy and core standards: the news media can promote democracy only when they remain free, uncensored, and truthful.

Many of our participants expressed the belief that democracy is crucially dependent on open access to all the news for everyone. One reporter for a local newspaper said: "I've been a journalist as long as I can remember, and the reason was to go out, and to find out about things, and share that knowledge with people. Because, it's corny, but in a democracy, for people to remain free, they have to have knowledge, and somehow I'm a part of that chain."

Similarly, Tom Brokaw emphasized the societal importance of a "common base of information":

> I've felt strongly for a long time that we proceed best as a society if
> we have a common base of information. And what I've always
> thought was important about network television news is that peo-
> ple in the most remote corner of the state of Washington get the
> same [information] on a given day as people in a remote corner of
> Florida. This is a transcendent medium for this society, and I think
> that that's important. . . . The single greatest danger I know for a
> large and complicated free society is the absence of information.

The Mission of Promoting Social Change

A journalist can promote social change in at least two ways: through work in the domain (as with reporting or writing) and through work in the field (as with breaking a color or gender barrier, organizing for a union, joining management, or participating on an award committee). The domain work directly influences the memes that the news media transmit. When, during their coverage of the Watergate scandal, Bob Woodward and Carl Bernstein disclosed the chicanery of the Nixon administrations, they advanced a captivating and enduring way of thinking about government, and about the importance of relentless investigative reporting. Woodward and Bernstein's reporting changed our views of reportage and politics—in this particularly powerful case, the "we" including both the public and the profession—that is, the work had transformative significance within and beyond the domain itself.

The case of Bob Woodward effectively illustrates how a sense of calling evolves into a dedication to a mission and eventually a driving moral identity. Woodward told us about the spirit of inquiry that interested him even as a child and how this spirit grew into his lifelong passion for uncovering newsworthy secrets, what Woodward calls the "disposed files":

> [My father was] a small-town lawyer, a kind of revered figure who handled lots of problems for people. I discovered and looked up the divorce cases of my friends, and cases about the mayor, and about other figures in town—this small town. . . . And it was stunning that there was this sense in the town that everything is fine. . . . Simply put, everyone had a secret . . . not awful or untoward, but showed a gap between the public notion of who these people were and who they really were as revealed in the disposed files. So you see that as a young person, it sears itself into your brain as a truth that probably would apply to other institutions in town.
>
> I was a radio hand, and in that era you literally had to dial and tune. I started out by listening to short-wave radios, and there is that sense of mystery that you can turn to, turn it and listen and there is Hong Kong or Africa, or under the noise level is something interesting, and unexpected, at times exotic, and suggestive. Completely different languages added to the whole business as a young person, 8, 10, 11, whatever. You just see the possibility of a simple radio—more "disposed files," if you will. Secrets almost . . . I was always looking around.

After college, Woodward joined the navy as a communications officer. Again, his instincts for spotting suspicious discrepancies between the "cover story" and the actual truth kicked in: "I was in the Navy during the Vietnam War, in the last year I worked in the Pentagon, and it was so clear from my personal experience on the ship off the coast of Vietnam. . . . I saw that the gap between what was being said publicly and what was really happening was so wide, just like the 'disposed files.'"

With his drive for uncovering the truth clearly evident, Woodward looked for a job in journalism. One early stint was at the *Montgomery County Sentinel* in a Maryland suburb of Washington. There Woodward was able to dig in, to pursue his long-standing desire to "dig the dirt" and to perfect his craft:

> I started reporting and working on the DC government and what was in the files, and what the perception was about what was going on—that, you know, the food is healthy in the restaurants. Well, I found that rat shit was floating in the soup at the most famous restaurants in town, that they flunked their health inspections, that unsanitary conditions abounded. And here everyone was innocently going around to these restaurants. And we ran a series of front-page stories saying that—it's all about the gap. It's all about the "disposed files"—so that would lead you to the files.

Like any towering figure in any field, Woodward has borne his share of controversy and criticism, especially for some of his more recent writings. On the other hand, it is indisputable that he has done good work—indeed, great work—that has fulfilled the mission of the domain and has expanded the capacity of the domain to support a democratic society.

The Gap between Noble Purposes and Today's Practices

Unfortunately, this cannot be said about much journalistic work today. Carefully researched, profoundly written, power-challenging, democracy-supporting news stories now seem like the exception. Prominent journalists of our day have become media celebrities, as highly paid as captains of industry. Did they get there by chance or design? Did they get there by following or abandoning the lofty missions they profess? Was attaining fame and material success their real goal all along?

In a field where good work is frequently marginalized and trashy work is frequently rewarded, it is not easy to sustain a mission that reflects the domain's best traditions. This is why noble purposes do not always translate into noble practices: there are too many other constraints, ranging from the economic to the cultural, too many pressures from the various stakeholders in the enterprise. As we noted, it is possible that our participants were being disingenuous or perhaps self-deceptive when talking about the moral purposes that drive their work. But there may be better explanations for the contrast between journalists' avowed sense of purpose and the increasingly sorry state of journalism today. The first place to look is to the field—to the problematic external conditions that journalists must operate within today.

At the same time, we must look at journalists' conduct and practices as well. What if Woodward and Bernstein had been unsuccessful in digging up real sources but, in their belief that something was rotten in the White House, had proceeded to make up key elements of their stories? What if they were even right in the end—that there was something fishy, but they felt forced to use deception to report it? Perhaps they would have gotten away with this perversion of the domain's standards for a while, and they might even still have triggered the demise of a corrupt government.

Yet in this case, as in all moral matters, the ends cannot justify the means. The dishonesty at the heart of their story would sooner or later have been revealed. The free press relies on the public trust for its privileges (such as First Amendment rights) and for its influence (the power to sway opinion through its reporting). In any society, public trust withers when citizens lose faith in the intentions of key institutions. There can be no achieving democratic ends without means that abide by a consistent standard of truthfulness.

It is one thing to codify journalistic standards in a commission report or for an association charter. It is another thing entirely to conform to the standards in the newsroom or the public arena. Compounding matters, the standards themselves may be evolving—some might say disintegrating—as an alternate ethic of truth and responsibility emerges from a type of prevalent postmodern thinking that in some quarters has thrown the entire ideal of common standards into question.

Standards and Practices
of the Domain

Journalists today still profess allegiance to their domain's traditional standards—in particular, truthfulness and fairness. Eighty-four percent of our participants mentioned truth or fairness, or both, as key standards guiding their work daily. When complementary standards such as avoiding conflicts of interest are added to being truthful and fair, the figure rises to 92 percent. These are the percentages of journalists who, in the open-ended interviews, *spontaneously* told us how important the standards were to their work. If we had given our participants a forced-choice survey asking them to respond to predesignated standards of this sort, we have little doubt that the percentage would have been even closer to 100 percent.

Journalists themselves are acutely aware of their allegiance to the traditional standards. In the words of one: "The standards have been the same since I've been here, pretty much. [They are] always being refined and tinkered with, and different exceptions or new rules regarding this and that get established. But they have very high standards here and they adhere to them pretty well." Some, such as a print journalist we interviewed, believe that the standards are as strong as ever: "I actually think that the general public would be surprised at how much we think about the implications of what we're writing about, . . . [that the people here have] really great ethical standards . . . that journalists are ethical people." Other journalists worry that they are slipping: "One is that I really want somehow to convey to young journalists the sense of what I was lucky to be a part of at CBS news, before the industry changed, when journalistic values predominated." Virtually all agreed that journalists cannot stray far from the domain's traditional standards if they are to fulfill their missions.

As noted previously, the standards most commonly extolled by our study's participants were truth and fairness. "This is probably something that all journalists will tell you," said William Whitaker, "that you want to be fair and accurate and be truthful in passing on information." Other standards mentioned frequently were closely related: respect for sources, respect for the subjects of one's news stories, loyalty to one's audience, loyalty to one's fellow journalists, loyalty to the domain of journalism, and personal integrity (in the sense of avoiding conflicts of interest and other ethical breaches that could compromise one's objectivity).

As we will see, the exact meaning and implications of these standards are debated in the field today, but each of these notions evokes a shared sentiment among journalists and helps us understand the distinctive role of standards in contemporary news reporting.

Truthfulness

One participant spoke for most of the rest when he told us: "I'm passionate about telling the truth. I am honest to a fault . . . every last fact is critical." His views were echoed by another reporter:

> Well, number one, I feel responsibility to just tell the truth. Lots of times you have people telling you different things and you have to find the middle ground. And sometimes things are gray. You're interviewing people on two different sides, and they're each black and white. And sometimes the truth is in the middle. One thing that I've had to learn throughout the years of my experience is that you can't let your personal feeling get in the way of the truth. Because sometimes you might interview a person, you might personally admire that person and think they're a good person; but sometimes their storyline is not exactly the total truth. And I have learned that many, many times over. So I guess the first responsibility is to the truth.

Taken in its most literal form, as a *refusal to lie*, the standard of truth may be the closest thing to a universal value in contemporary journalism. The truth requires vigilance, hard work, and constant self-examination. Adam Michnik, the editor-in-chief of Poland's premier newspaper, *Gazeta Wyborcza*, has written:

> The only limitation to our freedom is the Truth. We are allowed to publish everything we write, but we are forbidden to lie. A journalist's lie is not only a sin against the principles of our profession, it is also a blasphemy against our God. . . . Nevertheless, this does not mean that we can feel superior, that we are the repositories of the ultimate Truth and that we are allowed, in the name of this Truth, to silence others. Simply, we are not allowed to lie. Even if it is convenient to our friends.[8]

The standard of truthfulness inspires such universal devotion among journalists that it overrides all but the most extreme dedication to particular groups and causes. Few if any journalists say they will invent or distort materials to help people with whom they are sympathetic. The truth is one area in which none seems tempted to use illicit means to pursue desired ends. Not one of our participants noted any conditions that could justify a journalist telling a lie. Instead, even those who identified most closely with a particular group accepted the standard of truthfulness as an absolute principle that demands their unquestioning allegiance, even when it might conflict with the interests of the favored group. Many of our participants believe that, in the long run, pursuit of truth and promotion of particular people's rights coexist in a journalist's mission. Salinas and the African American print reporter, as mentioned earlier, represent that convention.

Do some journalists believe that it is permissible to bend the truth in order to promote a worthwhile cause? We did not find examples of this kind of thinking among the eighty-five mature journalists we interviewed, but a handful of young journalists reported this about themselves or colleagues. Mainly, we found that journalists' commitments to particular causes or groups are expressed through their determination to widen the lens of the news, bring in other perspectives, balance their coverage, and avoid the biases and blind spots that occur when people from diverse backgrounds are excluded. This resolve is consistent with the traditional news mission of providing accurate and comprehensive reporting. As for the idea that some causes may be so urgent that they could justify a departure from journalistic truth, we found heated opposition and no support for such a notion. One reporter declared, in line with all the others we interviewed:

> Not only do I not want to crusade as a journalist, I don't want other people to crusade as journalists. [Regarding a coverage of AIDS that he disdained, he went on to say:] I thought that it was a crusade inspired by personal loyalties and I didn't trust what she wrote. I didn't trust her journalism. You have to ask a lot of questions and if your mind is made up, you won't ask them.

Some well-intentioned observers of the press, increasingly concerned about polarizing news stories that, they believe, are rending our social fabric, have advocated a "civic journalism" that could produce more "socially responsible" coverage. According to this philosophy, reporters should seek out positive, rather than negative, stories and write constructively about them. As discussed in Chapter 9, we found scant support for this approach among the journalists in our study.

Fairness

Journalists speak about fairness almost as much as about truth. In response to the question of what beliefs give meaning to the work, Barbara Gutierrez, the editor of a bilingual newspaper, said, "I try to be fair . . . fairness has to be . . . my rallying cry." Another passionately proclaimed: "I gotta tell you, I am absolutely, and I can say this right now, the fairest . . . I weigh things out on fairness, no matter how." Two-thirds of our participants spontaneously noted their commitment to fairness as a primary standard guiding their work. Reporters were a bit more likely to mention fairness than were people at the managerial level, but the difference was small.

What does fairness mean to a journalist? Even more than truth (where, as we saw, ideals such as accuracy and objectivity bestow diverging, though related, criteria), fairness signifies a number of distinct principles. We found that the major concerns cluster around two ideals: fairness to the subjects of stories (including sources that supply information or quotes for stories) and fairness to the audience.

In an essay for a *Media Studies Journal* collection called "What's Fair?" the *Philadelphia Inquirer* critic Carlin Romano analyzed the distinction between being fair to the audience through unflinching accuracy and being fair to subjects who may be harmed by unflinching accuracy.[9] He used the Clinton sex scandal as a case in point: "All the efforts in the world to make sure that reporting on Clinton's sex life is accurate would not address whether it is fair to Clinton—the human being—to report on his sex life, or fair to his wife."[10]

Every time journalists do a story on a sensitive matter, they must adjudicate between these conflicting claims to fairness. Each case is different, and each requires a judgment call that can be challenged.

Among the questions that arise on any investigative beat are ones like these: Where does the public's right to know stop and the subject's right not to be known begin? Should the cameras be turned on a criminal in the midst of a crime? on an adulterer in the midst on an illicit affair? or the victim of a horrible accident? The answers to such questions depend not only on whether the camera shots makes good TV but also on who the perpetrators are. There is a strong feeling among journalists that public figures should be treated differently from private citizens. One participant told us:

> I do feel a responsibility to the people I interview. Not so much politicians or people that are in the public eye that are used to it, but just ordinary people who you talk to, who really open up their lives and share their stories with you, and there are lots of times when I feel like telling people, 'Don't tell me this. Just hold onto this for yourself. You don't want to tell me this.' And I guess I feel responsibility to those people to get their message across in the way that I think they mean it. Instead of sometimes the way that they present it, if that makes any sense. I mean, when I deal with politicians, I truly do it just the way they present it. But sometimes I think with individuals, they're naive, and sometimes they don't know quite how to handle interviews, so I do feel more responsible to them to tell their story the way that I think they mean it to be told, rather than sometimes to sensationalize it. Because you can take little things out of context and make people look really bad if you want to.

This journalist's concern for protecting not only the truth but also innocent people who may reveal things open to misinterpretation perhaps implies some tradeoff between strict accuracy and respect for subjects' rights, but it does not imply a lessening of truth in the broader sense. The participant just quoted went on to say: "If you interview them for an hour, you can find ten seconds that might not exactly epitomize what they've been saying for the whole sixty minutes. But you could put it in there and sometimes you can have something sensational. But that's not necessarily the truth."

This last comment suggests that when truth is considered to be not just accuracy but accuracy-in-context, truth and fairness go hand in hand. The editor who waits to publish a scandal story until he gets comments from the story's subject is not only being fair to the subject but also giving the reader added information that may reveal a bit more of the truth. In this and other ways, fairness enhances truth.

Beyond the need for fairness in the investigation of the story, there is a need for fairness in the reporting of the story. Balancing opposing views, curbing one's personal bias, and refusing to be swayed by power and privilege are all standards that simultaneously serve truth and fairness. "I try to give a fair airing of the [opposing] values," said one reporter. Tom Brokaw told us:

> I don't have a personal agenda that I try to fill here every night. . . .
> I often tell people who worry that we're biased that that's the quickest route to failure that I know of. The audience is very perceptive, and when it thinks that you're trying to impose your views, it's not much interested in that. They're trying to get someone they can trust to give them a fair idea of what happened that day, or what's likely to happen.

To be sure, we encountered nuanced differences in emphasis among our participants. Some journalists believe that truth is best served by separating fact from opinion, whereas others believe that opinion adds essential context to facts. Some believe that partisanship and subjectivity contaminate truth, whereas others believe that pure objectivity is a myth standing in the way of truth. Some believe that the truth demands verified and absolutely confirmed accuracy; others believe that truth is best revealed by taking risks, allowing some mistakes, perhaps failing to verify some "irrelevant" details. Some believe that truth may require ignoring the interests of news sources, whereas others believe that fairness to subjects of news stories goes hand in hand with truthful reporting.

Yet, beneath these differences, there remains a broad consensus among journalists about the importance of affirming the basic standards such as truth and fairness. This consensus is more consequential than the differences; in fact, it may be the best hope for the ultimate salvation of the domain. Virtually all of our participants said that their own practice was continually influenced by the traditional standards of the domain. In a supportive climate, the main challenges in implementing these standards would be technical ones, such as figuring out how to verify a story, where to go for information, whom to believe, and what perspectives to note in the write-up. Indeed, techniques for discovering, confirming, and interpreting the truth—the "best practices" that the domain has evolved—are a major part of journalism's craft.

We were impressed to discover that the history of journalism has seen a steady movement toward the advocacy of practices that promote standards of truth and fairness. Over the years, all the field's professional bodies and leading practitioners have increasingly adopted both the standards and practices as their recommended mode of operation. Although many social critics charge that journalism does not follow (and may never have followed) these practices and standards, a look at how the field has evolved over time reveals a possible wellspring of strength and hope for the future of good work in journalism.

9

GOOD WORK IN
JOURNALISM TODAY

IN CHAPTER 7, we described pressures so formidable that many have lost hope for the future of good journalism. Then, in Chapter 8, we pointed to rivers of strength that still run deep within this troubled domain. Which of these two powerful, opposing forces is more likely to determine the shape of journalism's future?

To resist adverse pressure at decisive moments, people must draw upon the highest reaches of moral commitment and creativity. That is the story of human progress, and the history books are full of such inspirational accounts. In journalism today, lots of good work still gets done. While many journalists sell out or walk away from the field defeated, some are able to call forth sources of strength to prevail. What makes the difference? How do those who remain serious about the mission of their domain, who retain their sense of journalism as a calling, manage to accomplish work that is high quality, socially responsible, and yet commercially viable in today's media marketplace?

This combination is often difficult to achieve. Success in the business of journalism, unlike other fields, often means intentionally alienating those who pay for your services. A responsible journalist might have to produce critical stories about advertisers or risk boring or upsetting readers with unwelcome but significant new information. To fulfill this mission requires skill, creativity, and a mastery of journalism's most savvy strategies.

In this chapter, we describe the "winning" strategies of journalists who have been successful in the face of daunting pressures. Some of these strategies are deeply personal and moral. Others are brilliantly innovative. Still others consist of dogged applications of tried-and-true tricks of the trade. All these strategies are solutions that keep hope alive for the future of the domain—and have some relevance for many other domains as well.

The Strategic Power of Moral Consciousness

The purest version of journalists gaining control of their work is when they call forth inner moral codes that help them resist illegitimate pressures and remain focused on the truth-seeking mission. They intentionally use these codes as ways of thinking or cultivate mental habits that act as a cautionary "inner voice." Thereby, they can prevent the kinds of disastrous mistakes associated with acts of omission—that is, instances of going along with a corrupting trend.

An inner moral code can operate in a variety of ways. If it takes the form of an ethical code ("always report a story objectively"), it can preempt a whole range of problematic activities ("don't join partisan organizations that advocate on issues that you investigate"; "don't cover stories in which you have a personal stake, such as a financial interest, a family member, or some other source of possible bias"). One print journalist for a large metropolitan daily, referring to her moral value system, said:

> I try not to do anything that doesn't fit with my value system. I
> have a sense of propriety. I think the news business should be hu-
> mane, and not exploit people. I think that the news business has to
> keep itself in proportion, and not think that people have to have
> some obligation to talk to us when we're really, really we're just us-
> ing them as story fodder. I don't participate in journalistic "pile-
> ons." I don't do stories on things that are sort of just hot and
> faddish and trendy, just because they're hot and faddish and trendy
> . . . I have sort of a stiff spine.

The orientation may take the form of a cultivated mental habit. One writer for a national news magazine spoke of the importance of cultivating "curiosity, patience, an ability to put others ahead of self, myself—to engage with civic issues and personalities without feeling an obligation to become an activist or celebrity." An investigative reporter spoke of managing fear during his coverage of the civil rights turmoil in the South during the 1960s: "I kept reminding myself not to think catastrophically, not to let fear even enter my mind." Other journalists see detachment as essential to objective reporting. One seasoned reporter recalled:

> How unaffected I was myself emotionally by the fact that a person had died almost in front of my eyes. And instead, [I] had gone about this professional thing of what more can we learn, what do we know about all of that. That . . . has colored my entire professional life, the ability to detach myself.

Several journalists said that they take great pains to cultivate a mental distance from the stories they are covering. Daniel Schorr, a long-time CBS reporter and now a news analyst on National Public Radio, learned this mental habit from exemplars such as Edward R. Murrow and applied it to stories as emotionally wrenching as the Nazi death camps:

> When you write, you try—and we all try, making Ed Murrow a kind of model—you try to write with restraint, which is meant at the same time to reveal strong feelings under that restraint, that was sort of a typical trademark of Murrow's way of doing when he talked about Joe McCarthy or he talked about London, this is London in the midst of war. And it was always painful objectivity in the way it was done, but you would know it's masterful, because the guy clearly feels very strongly about it.
> I tried to imitate that . . . It was pretty strong stuff at Auschwitz, as I look back through my script, it was very strong stuff. There was a time, for example, when I was saying in my script, and this is where they came out of the gas chamber and then they pushed them into the ovens over here. And the ovens were running at a rate of sixty thousand a day, but they couldn't get all the people they were killing, so some of them were just burned from the ovens and thrown into empty trenches over here, which are now these places full of water. And if you run your hand along the bottom, you will come up with splinters of bone, and so on and so forth. I did that very journalistically. I didn't faint, I didn't feel overcome by it all, I didn't re-live the Holocaust. I just did my job.

In addition to cultivating an emotional distance from the events they cover, journalists must acquire a sense of perspective on their own work to remain objective. Several journalists told us that they frequently needed to remind themselves of the enormous power of the press and its potential to be used for good or for ill. Several mentioned cultivating a habit of inspecting their own activities to be sure that they were not abusing their power. An influential manager of a newspaper chain said that he guided his career by two principles—a love of fairness and a hatred of excess:

> I think that because of the ability to use the power of the press, I have always been conscious of the need to use it fairly. I don't mean to suggest that I have always achieved that or that journalism has always achieved that and has not made many mistakes. I think that it is a driving principle that I don't want to use that power in ways that hurt individuals or institutions. And yet don't want to shrink from the proper use of the power of the capacity to inform people about excess in police departments or systemic failures of institutions in the community. The schools, nonprofit organizations, others who may have taken advantage of their authority or power or influence. I think out of that approach to journalism, there have been two guiding principles. One of which is to seek out and report on excess and the other is to be ever conscious of becoming excessive at the same time.

Several women journalists stated that it was important to remind themselves consciously of their own worth:

> I've been in this business for . . . twenty-three years, but I still have to fight to keep my confidence, my self-belief. And I see that in women in various other capacities and areas, so I think that's something that we always have to kind of, "Am I really that good. Well, God, I have to be this good, I've been doing this for twenty-three years, I should have gotten something out of this." But you know, you still question yourself, and you question your ability, and I think—which is what I try to tell young ladies, girls, when I talk to them, "Believe in yourself."

Another female journalist emphasized the need for women to make special mental efforts to confront people whom they are investigating:

> All women have to get over the idea of confronting somebody. The idea of rejection: none of us like to be rejected, and this is a busi-

ness where you are rejected every day. And you have to understand why you're being rejected. Is it something that is something that you're doing? Is it something that you need to change, or is it something that makes you all the more valuable? Women have a very difficult time with rejection, very difficult time. And you build up certain walls to protect yourself from it.

A frequent refrain among journalists is the need to cultivate a love of hard work and a willingness to spend almost endless hours on a story. This is not unique to journalism, of course, but it is noteworthy because so many journalists identify it as an essential self-regulating strategy that they take great pains to maintain:

> The job's very demanding, and I wouldn't be able to do it well if I wasn't able to really submerge my desire to not work sometimes. There are sometimes you just want to put it down. And sit and watch a TV movie, or just relax and listen to some music or something like that but if there's something I have to do, I've got to do it. So that's really sort of where the nexus of discipline and capacity is.

Such remarks all testify to the capacity of seasoned journalists to carry on a conversation with themselves in which the key standards of the domain—distance, objectivity, fortitude—help to keep them on course when the going gets tough.

The Call of an Inner Moral Code: The Trials and the Triumph of Carol Marin

As noted in Chapter 8, Carol Marin is a highly respected investigative reporter for a CBS affiliate in Chicago and a contributor to *60 Minutes II,* the national weekly television news magazine. Marin's career itself became newsworthy during May 1997, after our interview with her. At the time, she was a coanchor and news reporter with NBC-owned Channel 5. In a highly publicized controversy, the station hired Jerry Springer, the nationally syndicated host of a salacious talk show, to do a series of commentaries for Marin's nightly news show. Marin objected to management that Springer's approach promoted a "cynical trivialization" of the news and violated essential journalistic standards, but her protests fell on deaf ears.

After some soul-searching, Marin resigned. At the conclusion of her farewell newscast, Marin's newsroom colleagues gave her a standing ovation.

Her coanchor, Ron Magers, resigned a few days later. The Chicago public expressed its support of Marin and its displeasure with Channel 5 by turning away from the station in droves. Most stingingly, this public spurning occurred during the critical "May Sweeps" ratings period. As a consequence, after only three days on the air, Springer resigned from Channel 5. By then, Marin already was preparing to move to the competition across town. In the Chicago area, there is widespread public perception that Marin's actions, which were extensively covered in the local news, affirmed in an enduring way the mission and high standards of traditional journalism.

Marin represents a particular kind of response to today's market-driven pressures toward sensationalism and trivialization of the news. She confronted the unwelcome market pressures through an explicit and unyielding protest. The protest led Marin to her peremptory solution of resignation, the ultimate act of moral resistance in a professional world. Her response was unquestionably brave and effective. It was ideally suited for the occasion. Such a courageous stand merits a prominent place among the best methods for meeting today's media challenges to good work.

In the aftermath of the Springer incident, the goodwill that Marin had gained among the Chicago public opened up a unique opportunity for her: a major local station offered her the anchor spot—and more importantly, editorial control—over its *10 P.M. News* show. Marin responded to this opportunity with energy and integrity. Under her direction, the show produced a string of probing, in-depth stories the equal of which have rarely been seen on local news shows. On several occasions, the show's investigative staff broke news that revealed new information on problems of pressing public interest, ranging from consumer issues to politics.

Unfortunately, Marin's seriousness of purpose and admirable public-mindedness did not translate into market success. Her show began with strong ratings, no doubt due to the attention generated by her fight over Springer. But after a few months, the ratings had dwindled to the point where Marin's *10 P.M. News* ranked a poor fifth among local offerings. The station canceled the show at the end of its eighth month.

What went wrong? A cynic might claim that the mass public is too simple-minded and depraved to provide a profitable local market for journalistic good work. But Marin and her critics have two other explanations, both of which ring more true to us. Journalist watchdogs groups, generally sympathetic with Marin's intent, gave her *10 P.M. News* low marks on its "production values," including its slow pacing and its paucity of local community color. In response, Marin complains that eight months was simply not a long enough time for her to develop a winning formula and a loyal following. These two explanations are not at all incompatible—indeed, the problems may well have combined to defeat the show.

We have made the point that breakthroughs in good work require a fortuitous conjunction of a domain ready for change, a talented individual capable of taking a creative initiative, and a field that is receptive (or at least not hostile) to the change. These conditions were not quite there for Marin's *10 P.M. News*. She could be faulted for not having the creative genius to come up instantly with a program format that both edified and entertained the Chicago public, but we believe that this is an unrealistic expectation for anyone. Creative success requires trial and error, time to make mistakes and correct them—in short, an incubation period during which the new ideas can be safely nurtured. Progress within domains requires fields that are willing and able to provide such incubation periods for promising new ideas. The failure of the *10 P.M. News* was a field failure, an incapacity to make enough of a commitment to the show to see it to fruition. Happily, the failure did not take Marin's career along with it: she is now an integral part of the esteemed *60 Minutes* news team.

Gaining Mastery of the Domain

Journalists are subjected nearly every day to pressures that challenge and test their professionalism. Thus, many develop "second-nature" practices that they can draw on reliably and that allow them to proceed with their primary mission of gathering and reporting the news objectively, fairly, and fully.

Consultation and Verification

A managing editor who trains many young reporters told us that every good journalist must develop "a method of systematically talking to everyone about something, and going back and going back, building for knowledge . . . figuring out what other people say happened, checking and cross-checking, absorbing others' motivations and personalities, and putting it together in stories."

Some methods for ensuring objectivity—for example, finding more than one source before reporting a discovery—have become standard practices in many newsrooms. Others must be invented by individual reporters. Tom Brokaw took the initiative to create his own method when he was a young investigative reporter working on controversial stories such as Watergate:

I had a buddy system. There was a really smart reporter exactly
my age from the *Wall Street Journal*, and we paired up. And we
became a kind of check on each other, as it were. And we would
talk a lot. And I recommend it to others now, as a system. When
(younger colleague) Brian Williams went down to cover the
White House, I said, "Find a print friend." Not somebody in television—you can find a lot of friends in television—but find
somebody (from print) who can help you and you can help him
or you could help her.

Similarly, Brokaw sought feedback from people who occupied different
roles:

The other system that I had is that I had on the Hill. When I first
arrived in town, because I was so unknown, I went up and made
the rounds in Congress and in the agencies and in the candidate offices, with Republicans as well as Democrats. On a regular basis, I
would call their offices, and if I had twenty minutes, I would run
up there and see them. And we would sit in the closed door and
talk about what was going on down there. And it was totally clear
to me that they had the same reservations that the nation did. So
that was kind of reassuring to me. They wouldn't say you guys have
really put yourselves over the line here. There was that whole question in their own minds. Republican partisans as well as more cen-
tered Democrats. So that was kind of the way you kept yourself on
course.

Much in line with these "buddy" feedback strategies, Bob Woodward
told us that, before going public with a story, he always obtains the perspective of the person or institution that he is investigating:

Because in the heat of the day, when things are getting late, and
you're trying to get on the air, and stuff is coming in, sometimes
you get, kind of myopia. And you need someone who's able to
stand back and say, I think you're going too far here or is that the
language you want to use. He came down last night and reviewed
very carefully our coverage of the Food Lion case, for example. It
was helpful to have, you know, somebody who represented the institution looking at it.

Persistent Probing

All reporters run into obstacles in reporting a story; often the bigger the story, the more pronounced the obstacles. One reporter explained: "I'm dogged. I think I will just stick with the story and continue to get an answer. A lot of the times when I get interviews it's difficult to get them and I will just go back and back and back at the person for the longest time and stroke them to get the interview." She then recounted how she had once obtained a story from a recalcitrant Latin American military officer:

> I was down in Nicaragua. The contra camps were closed and I
> speak Spanish fluently so I was sent down to see if I could get into
> the contra camp. They had been closed for months. . . . And no-
> body knew what was going on in there. . . . I found the colonel
> who could do that, who had charge of the news media, and asked
> him and he said no, he wasn't sure, nobody was going to be able to
> get in now, but I said, "When you do, I want to be the first one,"
> and so the next day—he gave me an appointment after three re-
> quests down there—the next day I was at his house that morning
> when he came out asking. When he came out for lunch from work
> I was . . . staking him out, asking, "Have you decided, have you
> taken my request, have you talked to someone about it?" When he
> came out to leave work to get into his car with his driver I was right
> there standing by the car, "Just wanted you to know I'm still very
> interested." I did that for three or four days. I was the first one to
> get in because I just wouldn't take no for an answer from him.

Another method for getting to the bottom of a cover-up is anticipatory fact checking—using what Woodward called "the disclosed files" (as described in Chapter 8). He described the "trick" to his great success:

> [It's been] getting ahead of them and thinking, "What's the story?"
> I systematically went through the DC government, when the DC
> government records were open, you can walk in and say "let me see
> your file" and just pull out the file cabinet. Systematically went
> through them, and there was incongruency between what they
> were supposed to be doing and what was actually going on regu-
> larly. . . . No one is going to have a press conference, nothing's go-
> ing to happen, but sitting there, mute in the files of the DC

government and the federal government. All you have to do [to un-root the lies and corruption] is to go to the records, check the occu-pancy of houses and apartments, and discover that there are 10,000 vacant apartments in DC. Look up a couple of them, visit them, and discover people living in lots of them.

Good work in journalism also means writing and producing the news in a manner true to the investigative reporting that has been done. The key is to see these activities as an integrated unit, as an editor noted: "It's not just the knowing, and it's not just the telling, it's a Siamese-twin rela-tionship between the two. The finding out *and* the telling."

Providing Context

With more and more competition for the audience's attention, journalists must vividly convey why a story commands notice. Crucial here is the ca-pacity to provide a meaningful context for an often restless and underin-formed readership. One print reporter told us:

Whenever I'm writing a story, I'm chasing the cats all over the place, trying to herd them in one direction while I write. I used to have tremendous trouble organizing my copy. And I learned a lot from some people around here, on how to do that. Believe it or not it took me many years to figure out the simple proposition that each paragraph has one topic in it. Cause I was trying to weave these complicated arabesques, in and out, and you can't do it that way. . . . I had, in order to make that really work, I had to learn how to put a structure on the facts.

An African American television journalist who was assigned to cover the O. J. Simpson trial for his local station talked about how he managed to communicate the full complexities of the case to his audience:

Trying to break down a complex issue, a complex story, into a very small, brief presentation and you have to find a way to get that is-sue or get that main point and present it in a way that everybody can say, "Oh, wow, I understand that." Sometimes just starting at A and going to Z is not the best way to do it. Sometimes you have to grab L, M, N, O, P out of the middle and put it up at the top be-cause that's the point that makes the most sense and that's what's easiest for people to understand and that puts it in perspective. So trying to find the best way to present the information is the most challenging but also the most fun part of the job.

Creating an Effective News Team

The atmosphere that pervades the gathering of the news is crucial to responsible reporting and writing. One editor for a large national newspaper talked about the challenge of creating an "open" newsroom where every motivated reporter has a shot at breaking the biggest story of the day:

> As an editor I had no earthly idea what was going on, outside my office and in other parts of the newsroom much of the time, let alone outside of the building in the world at large, which is why we have reporters and photographers, photojournalists, at work. So that they would forage and find out things that the editors had no earthly way of knowing about. And if the process was too top-down driven, where the editors either—because they valued their own experience, sometimes too greatly, or because in their own creative insecurity they had to demonstrate a level of knowledge that they did not honestly feel, journalists being inherently insecure individuals— they took too much control of the process and had meetings constantly to decide what to do and how to use the resources.

The Commitment of Two Domain Masters

People who make judicious use of strategies such as the ones just described come to occupy positions of power and prestige in the field; they then have the option of promoting the kind of work they believe in.

Maria Elena Salinas: Serving a Broader Audience

One such person is Maria Elena Salinas (introduced in Chapter 8), who is the coanchor and senior correspondent for the Miami-based nightly newscast *Noticiero Univision*. Her program is the most influential and frequently watched Spanish-language news show in the United States and is seen in thirteen Latin American countries. Salinas also hosts "En Contacto," a daily news commentary aired coast–to-coast on Radio Unica, a unique Spanish-language radio network. Also on Radio Unica,

Salinas manages a public service campaign to persuade Hispanic teenagers not to drop out of high school.

Salinas entered Spanish television news in the early 1980s, during its infancy. She had no television background, but that was not unusual for a Latina. She had studied marketing and merchandising at the University of California at Los Angeles where she also had taken a few courses in journalism. She explained: "For me, when I was a kid, the big thing was to graduate from high school. Because neither one of my sisters did. I started working when I was fourteen. I paid my own school by then because my parents were really poor."

What Salinas did possess was a command of both English and Spanish, as well as a bit of experience in front of a microphone while hosting community events and reading local radio news. She landed her first job at KMEX-TV, a Spanish language broadcast affiliate in Los Angeles. Salinas adeptly "learned on the job." Starting as a reporter on KMEX's local newscast and hosting a daily community affairs program called *Los Angeles Ahora*, she moved up the ranks to become the station's news anchor. In 1987 she moved to the national network Univision, where she soon became the coanchor of its flagship Spanish news show *Noticiero Univision*. "I was thrown into television," she related, "because I had done what they call in media 'rip and read news,' which, in radio, is when you take it off the wire, you pick a few stories and you say, 'This is what is happening in the world.' That was the only news that I had done."

During her rising career, Salinas's interest in news has never waned. "I truly believe that it is not possible to work in journalism if you don't have it in your blood," she told us. She has become adept at using captivating media techniques to deliver news stories in a compelling manner to a broad audience. Her skill has brought useful information to vast numbers of people who previously had no reliable source for up-to-date accounts of the society they are living in.

Tom Brokaw

Another example of a domain master is Tom Brokaw, who described to us the advantages of working for a company that occupies a leading position in the field:

> If you're number one, it gives you more resources to get your advertising base up, and therefore if it's more profitable, then you have more leverage in the company and you have more leverage in the

budget. And therefore, you can take more chances if you're number one. If you're number two or three, there's a real financial constraint that will come into play. And then there are all manner of ancillary reasons you want to be number one. It attracts the most talent. If we're number one, people want to come to work for us. When you're number three, they don't want to be on the number three network.

Reflecting on his proudest moment as a newsman, Brokaw revealed both the intense concentration and the domain-provided methods that have enabled him to rise to the top of his field. On the day that the Berlin Wall was torn down, he managed to have the only American TV crew on the scene, broadcasting this cataclysmic event live for the world. He described for us the strategies he used to report the event and, most importantly, to provide a meaningful historical and political context for his viewers:

> I remember vividly, I remember consciously just before we went on the air that wonderful phrase of the astronauts, *Don't fuck it up.* I mean, I remember hearing, Don't you know, this is a huge deal. There was enormous tension back here getting us on the air. The stuff was going on all around me. There was no more symbolic act of the end of communism than the fall of the Berlin Wall that we'd all lived with all of those years. And so I thought, I've got to tell (A) what's going on here, (B) how it happened, and (C) what it means in the larger terms. And there is a kind of almost out-of-body experience that you go through. At one point I started this riff that—I was conscious of my colleague standing off to the side of this platform with me, they were slack-jawed, and I went on for about three minutes in which I compared that moment with 1968 which I said, . . . in my lifetime, I always believed that 1968 would be the year that would be the boldest in my memory because of all the cataclysmic changes that occurred then.
>
> I ran it off—the assassination of Bobby Kennedy, the assassination of Martin Luther King, the invasion of Czechoslovakia by the Russians, the turmoil of the [Vietnam] War, the Tet Offensive in Vietnam, and the election between Richard Nixon and Hubert Humphrey that grew out of the turmoil of all that. And I did this kind of word-play description of all of that. And I said, "But think of what we've been through now." And I took them back through what had happened in the preceding twelve months. And I remember at the time, it was almost as unconscious as if I were speaking

in tongues. You know, it just welled up out of me. And went back
and looked at the transcript and the sentences parse, and it all
makes sense, and it was all correct.

And that was a pure product of all those years of preparing for
that moment. And that's how I felt the next morning when I got
up. I thought, you know, I was ready, it happened, and I didn't
screw it up. And all those years of hard work paid off in one moment last night.

Expanding the Domain Through Creative Innovation

From time to time, people launch major innovations that expand the capacity of the domain or transform the way it is practiced. This can be
done by creating a new institutional setting, inventing a new reporting
format, trying out a new method of discovery, or redefining the nature
and scope of the reporter's task. In our study the most frequently mentioned was CNN, the cable network created by Ted Turner to broadcast
news twenty-four-hours a day from all parts of the world. The success of
CNN transformed the field's expectations about what television news reporting could do. All of the journalists who mentioned Turner's CNN
saw it as a seminal achievement.

A more debatable transformation was the personalized form of reporting that Norman Mailer, Tom Wolfe, Truman Capote, and other literary
figures pioneered in the 1960s. The "new journalism" challenged the standard of objectivity by fusing the reporter's perspective with the coverage
of the event. Most of our informants rejected this model of news reporting, although many said that they had been influenced by it in their
younger years. Its main legacy seems to be that journalists now are aware
that they all have their own biases and that these biases inevitably will
shape what they cover and how they cover it. Rather than fight against
their biases, today's journalists compensate for them by using the kinds of
self-conscious distancing, checking, and balancing strategies that we have
described. In this way, the new journalism movement has led to a greater
sophistication in how journalists deal with subjectivity.

We found other examples of people who expand or transform their domains in our own study. Frances Moore Lappé, well known in the 1970s
for her book *Diet for a Small Planet*, founded a news bureau, the American News Service, dedicated to news about community building and the
preservation of a civil society. Unlike other news services, her organization was aimed at producing constructive stories that impart to readers a

better understanding of how our democracy works, what its possibilities are, and what ordinary people can do to participate actively in it.

To create a news bureau from scratch requires drawing on entrepreneurial skills—fund raising, marketing, and public relations—as well as an innovative journalistic vision and a willingness to depart from prior efforts. In our interview, Lappé said:

> I had a certain body of knowledge . . . and I pretty much walked away from all that and kind of reinvented myself. Or I am still in the process of reinventing myself. And so that is what I'm most proud of, that I don't rest upon my laurels. . . . I have taken on significant risks and stepped out there. . . . Not ever to be satisfied with where I am. . . . Not to get stuck is the basic thing.

Lappé's news service has teetered on the brink of financial insolvency from the day she started it. We cannot say whether it will be in or out of business by the time this book goes to publication. We do know that it is a noble effort, inspired by a dedication to the core mission and standards of the domain. Whether this particular effort succeeds in expanding the domain will depend on broader forces in the field. Will news chains with significant purchasing power see it in their interests to subscribe? Will consumers—the readers and viewers—indicate that this is the kind of news coverage that they want? Lappé's venture, however stellar its domain ambitions, may or may not conquer the market realities of the field at this time. The master entrepreneur Ted Turner has shown that it can be done for two decades, at least with an extraordinary concept such as CNN. This is the way of any progress: the unique blending of a creative individual, a domain that is ready to advance, and a field that is (or can be induced to be) receptive to something new.

Another "domain-expander" is Irving Kristol, who cofounded the prominent journal *Public Interest* to provide social and political analysis at a level of complexity that newspapers (and the educated layperson) can readily absorb. The journal has vastly influenced the framing of American social and political news in recent years. Kristol's particular genius was to recognize the need to make advanced scholarly ideas accessible to those who cover, write, and produce the news. "I founded them [*Public Interest* and a precursor] because I saw that there were gaps in the public discourse," Kristol told us.

Public Interest has played a powerful mediating role between social theory and journalists who—whether they are aware of it or not—rely on social theory to structure their reporting. The news profession itself was too fast-paced and too overburdened to stay current on social theory, so Kristol planned his journal to do that for them:

> The *New York Times*, I don't say this critically, feeds off magazines like the *Public Interest*. First of all, their reporters tend not to be sufficiently well trained. But they are journalists, there's no particular reason why they should be social scientists as well. In addition, they are very busy, and they don't read the scholarly literature. . . . So no, newspapers cannot do it. Nor news magazines for that matter. They just don't have the time to invest. We're lucky, we are parasitic on the academy. They are parasitic on us. We don't have the time to do longitudinal studies of this, that, or the other. On the other hand, people who are doing it, it turns out, would like to reach a larger audience. . . . I don't see any alternative to that system, really. And it does work. Sometimes it works better, sometimes it works less well. . . . It's very useful for them, to the degree that journalists read, which is not that great. They're very busy people.

Bob Woodward, whose work we have discussed at length, is another notable domain expander. Together with his colleague Carl Bernstein, Woodward forged journalism's old tradition of exploration and muckraking into a method of investigative reporting that rapidly became a mainstay of the domain. The method combined detective work with a sciencelike approach to establishing the reliability of facts and sources.

Of course, in breaking the story on Watergate, Woodward and Bernstein were far from the first to use this approach, and they could not have succeeded without the crucial support of management at the *Washington Post*. In this sense, their achievement was a collective one, drawing on both the domain's prior traditions and a supportive set of conditions in their own workplace. There has been controversy in this: "What hath Woodward wrought?" asked one social critic in the late 1990s, referring to the cynical stance that Woodward's journalistic progeny have adopted. Nonetheless, Woodward and Bernstein's approach was a seminal achievement—a domain-altering one—that spawned a generation of followers and imitators.

The Promise of Technology

Some journalists look to technology to help them do good work. Their challenge is to devise strategies for using the new technologies more wisely. Carol Marin put it this way:

I think the greatest challenge right now for us is that there is so much stuff you can yank down from a satellite, a medical feed for instance, but we know next to nothing about the origin of the piece of tape. It may for all we know be coming from some pharmaceutical company about the latest heart medicine and is really a sales pitch, not a science story. And so I think our discriminations have to be a lot tighter because of so much junk information. Look what happened to Pierre Salinger off the Internet [with reference to the cause of a plane crash]. Great journalist. Big find on the Internet. But no, it wasn't, it just looked like good information. I think we're dying in an avalanche of pseudo-information and it's becoming harder for all of us, not just in news, but in all categories from science to society, to figure out what is just a very carefully packaged sales pitch.

We can see how the journalist might emerge as more important than ever—assuming, on behalf of society, the crucial job of separating the "wheat" of news from the ever-accumulating trivial "chaff."

Some journalists see technology as a *solution* to the problems that their domain faces. They believe that technology can offer a way out of the stifling embrace of corporate control. They see the Internet, in particular, as a means of surviving the squeeze they find themselves in—that is, a way of realigning the market demands of stakeholders with the traditional noble purposes of their domain. They see the Internet as a way of withstanding today's incessant commercial pressures with their morale and standards still intact; and they see it as a way to reach a broader audience with more up-to-date, more accurate, more useful, and more serious information. Perhaps, indeed, the Internet can help journalism fulfill its potential as an open and democratic medium sustaining a free society.

Pluralization and Democratization

Jon Katz emphasized the freedom of discourse that the Internet's pluralistic nature makes possible. He sees a flourishing multiplicity of subcultures, each exploring their own version of the truth. They have never been subject to control before, because they have been too small and too obscure to notice. Now there are too many of them to supervise, so he sees them escaping the demands for conformity that have plagued much of the mass media:

The on-line world is just embryonic, it's a laboratory, with very interesting and distinct subcultures that have grown up out of sight

of academe or journalism or politics. And as a result, they are really
the freest subcultures, I think, in the country, because they've spent
years speaking absolutely fearlessly. They curse, they talk about sex,
they challenge God, they do all the things you can't do in mainstream media. So they have no experience of being inhibited, either
by the rules of academe or the conventions of journalism or the
anxieties of politicians. And I see them as incubators, really, for this
kind of free and unrestrained thought . . . [a] return to intellectual
freedom and democracy.

Another journalist pointed to the democratic benefits of cost savings
when news is presented on-line rather than through print or broadcast
channels:

I also see some hope with the new technology. . . . Maybe, we don't
know yet, you can survive more outside of the corporations, outside of big media. Because . . . I can do a story and actually put it
on the Web for the zillions to read at very low costs. I can put out
my Web magazine to get my message out. It is possible. It was not
possible before. People are doing that. You then have other outlets
for voices so the media world becomes less monolithic, which is
good, and you have more competition, more competing values,
more outlets. Independent people can think of life, maybe you can
survive without working for a big boss, without working for these
chains to really really do the things that you like. Prices are getting
cheaper and technology is getting better. It is possible.

The notion of the Internet as a force for pluralism and democracy is
not entirely futuristic. According to one participant, it has already helped
dissidents combat at least two totalitarian societies:

I've spent a lot of time writing and talking about the revolutionary
impact of the Internet because it's a many-to-many medium in
which every desktop connected to that network is in fact a printing
press and a broadcasting station and a place of assembly. So, during
Tiananmen Square [in China, in 1989] there were thousands of eye-
witness reports. You could get on Usenet. When the Serbian government closed down radio stations in '92 it was up on the Internet
almost immediately, so that's very democratic. We are seeing both

in the terms of monopolies and cartels in terms of government regulations and attempts to control that.

Dreamers see this potential realized across the board—that is, using the Internet to combat monolithic control of news wherever it exists, whether in a political dictatorship or in a corporate boardroom. In the words of one aspiring Internet journalist:

> So, will, ten years from now, we see a world that is dominated by a few powerful companies and a few powerful governments that can in fact control how individuals express themselves in this medium, or will we see a world in which that democratic trend continues—I think that's the most important question to ask. I think there are important implications of that. If that democratic trend continues, and anyone can be a broadcaster and an eyewitness, then questions of veracity and reliability of information become paramount.

A Challenge to Prevalent Mediocrity

Some see the Internet not only as creating an open, democratic news outlet of its own but also as transforming existing news outlets for the better. According to this view, a better product raises the level of competing products (or it eliminates them). One media owner commented that this is what happens when East Berliners become aware of how West Berliners are living: sooner or later, the old regime in the East must collapse or be torn down. One participant foresaw an Internet that one day would host timely and serious news programming. This would create an audience with higher expectations for its news consumption, which in turn would pressure all commercial news outlets to do a more serious job:

> I think there is some hope because of things like the Internet and the Web sites. I think it's all new now, and there's a lot of junk on it. But I think as time goes on, people are going to be more demanding because they have instant access. I think they're going to want more, because they can get it so conveniently. They're going to expect more. I think, I hope. And I think you'll see commercial news in a much different form. I don't think it will be anything like the six o'clock or the five o'clock news, or the ten o'clock news. I think there will be different channels devoted to the news, but

there will be no more of this personality-driven, high-powered
video stuff. It may be just somebody will read things into a camera.

For this participant, as for many others working in journalism, the
buoyant dream is reciprocal to the depressing reality that has come to
pass in recent years. Waxing ebullient about the possibilities, this participant spoke of drawing on his hopes to fend off the despair he would feel
if he were to accept the present set of circumstances:

> I think this so-called information age is going to get bigger and big-
> ger and bigger, as more and more people get on-line and are able to
> stay in their house and access a lot of things. All the new things we're
> doing with electronics, where you can punch up something on your
> TV set and get all the information in the world you want. I think it
> will be a big hit, I hope it will be a success. It will take away some of
> the sensational, commercial business. I hope. Otherwise, if it goes the
> other way it's just going to get pretty ridiculous. It's pretty bad.

Personalization of the News

Following a similar logic, Jack Driscoll, an Internet journalist, imagines
futuristic electronic means of conveying the news to people whenever and
wherever they want it. His inventiveness teeters on the line between
canny prescience and science fiction:

> We really need to think of different ways to convey news. One thing
> that's being looked at is how newspapers can be transmitted into
> your living room, your home, or whatever works for you. And so by
> the same token there may be forms of communication. For instance,
> Walter Bender [of the Media Lab at MIT] has this favorite little
> gumball trick, where gumballs are embedded with certain informa-
> tion. You put them into your computer somehow, and the informa-
> tion comes out onto your screen. For instance, if you're driving your
> automobile, you might be able to take something from your house
> physically—maybe gumball is not the right metaphor—carry it to
> your automobile when you drive to work or school or to the beach,
> activate this thing, and it produces audio. That audio might be e-
> mail that's been transcribed from written e-mail into voice; it might
> be news articles; it might be a program that's played on radio at 2:00
> in the morning, that was downloaded to your gumball or whatever,

because it knew that you had a passionate interest in parrots or something. It's sort of all packaged for you, and you just activate it as you're driving. Let's say you're doing scholarly work in physics. You might hear a lecture that some famous physicist has given and it was played on the radio at 2:00 in the morning.

The personalization of news through interactive electronic media was a theme that ran though the comments of our more optimistic participants. Ed Guthman, formerly a foreign correspondent with the *Los Angeles Times*, commented that if Bill Gates is right, "by that time (2010 to 2020) we will all be walking around with PCs that are wallet size and we can call up the front page of the *Wall Street Journal*. . . . It is going to be like this: you come home and say, 'What is the score of the UCLA game?' and it is all going to be voice activated." The consumer will control what news to receive and when to receive it, and the news will be more immediate. Guthman elaborated:

> Now this whole electronic thing is going to totally reshape the industry again. . . . I mean, at some point, the [*Boston*] *Globe* may decide, okay, we are a twenty-four-hour newspaper again like they used to be in the 1920s when they had fifteen editions a day. You could get a new edition of the *Globe* every two hours or something. And so they may start putting news out there, fresh news every day. I mean, you can go there now and click on the most recent news, but all you're reading is the wire stuff. It's the AP wires which run twenty-four hours a day. At some point, the paper may decide we're going to start becoming more like a wire, we're going to put news out there as soon as we get it.

The new technology's capacity to personalize the news may also enable audiences to create a menu of highly specialized programming and to move quickly, back and forth, across the menu of choices. One participant saw this as a superior way to acquire information, because audiences will be able to focus on the range of issues in which they have special interests. Eventually, through exposure to these specialized sources, audiences will themselves gain increased expertise, which in turn will spur media producers to aim for a higher standard of content in order to satisfy their then more sophisticated audiences. In the expectant view of this participant, shoddy and unethical media practices will then fall by the wayside, because audiences will no longer allow producers to get away with them:

What is becoming apparent is that the nightly newscast with Dan Rather and Peter Jennings and Tom Brokaw will become less and less relevant. They're still watched by several tens of millions of people, but they've become less relevant because people have gotten their news before they get there. . . . It's simply a changed world, and it's going to become more and more . . . for every aspect of news, you know, sports . . . and you already have sports channels. Psychology. Psychology channels. Economics. Economic channels. Diseases. You'll have disease channels. You'll have the heart channel. You'll have the kidney channel. I mean, it's just incredible.

So technology drives morality. The more you get, the more specialized the information, the more expertise you can bring to these things. As opposed to just the cheap ten-second sound byte on the ten o'clock news.

Community Building

The most utopian dream is the hope that the Internet will bring people together in like-minded communities, a notion that runs counter to the familiar (and not implausible) concern that the Internet will destroy social cohesion by making face-to-face encounters unnecessary. At least one of our participants believes that a medium can host and support virtual societies. Katz described a similarly positive vision:

I see the Web as a great, intense hive, in which ideas are absorbed and digested and then sent out all over the place and returned, changed and cross-pollinated and criticized and altered. It's a way people who are disconnected from one another form community— elderly people, disabled people, gay teenagers, academics doing research, you know, quilters, bee keepers, gardeners. One of my favorite on-line Web sites is a cockatoo chat [room,] petbird.com, where cockatoo lovers can finally get together and talk, for the first time, to other cockatoo lovers. Senior Net on America On-line is one of the first places where elderly people can come together in a community from all over the world, whether they can get out of their houses or not. I think you'd save countless lives of young gay people. Because they used to be isolated, they had a phenomenally high suicide rate. Now they can get on-line and talk to each other. Women are pouring on-line in mass numbers now, and women are community builders. And they're forming these communities, they're talking to each other, they're supporting each other.

Here we encounter the most ambitious hope of the journalist: the creation of a virtual culture, starting with the production, dissemination, and improvement of its memes. (We note especially the beehive metaphor and the verbs—*absorbed, digested, returned, changed, cross-pollinated, criticized,* and *altered.*) In a condition of free-flowing information, each group—indeed, each person—will arrive at the memes that are right for itself. The test of any meme will be the value, and the truth, that the meme brings to the group or person. This is the ultimate test for the news industry as well—a test that journalists working within the traditions of the domain would happily embrace.

We would be derelict if we closed this discussion without adopting a more external etic perspective, as described in Chapter 2. The Internet can be a force for democracy and pluralization, but it can also be used nefariously: the Web is as open to neo-Nazis and gay-bashers as to supporters of world peace. It can provide huge amounts of information written by millions of people, but in the absence of a sifting or editing mechanism it is difficult to know what users will make of this information—and utopian to think that they will be able to synthesize it intelligently. Other mass media have done little to eliminate mediocrity or enhance morality, and there are few signs so far that the Internet will be different. More personalized media are a likely dividend, but this trend can entail aspects of manipulation, personal attack, and loss of privacy. Communities might be built, but they could be divisive ones. And this "24/7" technology might encourage even more isolation—more "bowling alone." Technologies never have unequivocal consequences; how we use them is as important as how they use us.

One Blind Alley: Public, or "Civic," Journalism

There are lessons to be learned from the strategies that journalists spurn as well as those they adopt and from what people do not say as well as what they do say. The new technology, perhaps because it is relatively untested, has been warmly welcomed. But another widely advocated innovation, "public," or "civic," journalism (the terms have been used interchangeably), has received no such heady reception.

The notion of public journalism arose during the 1990s. It was supported by philanthropic foundations such as the Pew Charitable Trusts
and the Knight Foundation and promoted by an influential 1995 book,
Public Journalism and the Public Life.[1] The core idea was to combat the
cynicism and civic disengagement that many attributed to an irresponsible news media by aligning news coverage more closely to the priorities of
local communities. So, for example, in one early exercise of public journalism, the *Charlotte (North Carolina) Observer* made a conscious effort
to cover the 1992 city election by reporting citizens' views about issues
rather than their moment-by-moment preferences for candidates (the
usual "horse race" coverage). The paper's polls and news stories focused
on the substance of policy matters rather than on candidates' electoral
strategies. In another example, in the late 1990s the *Philadelphia Inquirer*
published citizens' own questions to candidates as well as the candidates'
replies, all on pages of the newspaper formerly reserved for editors, journalists, and other professional commentators.

Public journalism breaks with the domain's traditions in a number of
ways. First, it weakens the authority of experts (editors and journalists)
and strengthens that of ordinary citizens: public stakeholders begin to assume authority for selecting and framing the news. Second, it replaces the
norm of nonpartisanship with explicit advocacy for social action. Third, it
rejects the truth-for-truth's-sake ethic that has been the sine qua non of the
domain's traditional values. By its lights, stories that reinforce community
solidarity are to be encouraged; those that lead to alienation or polariza-
tion are to be discouraged. The skepticism of the hardened newshound is
tempered by a caring and engaged sense of community concern.

We found little if any sympathy for public journalism among our
respondents. Most ignored the idea, while the rest commented on it
disdainfully. Consider Carol Marin's harsh assessment:

> It's an utter corruption to believe that news is, by its nature, too
> negative and we need to make it more positive through partner-
> ships that seek solutions to the problems that exist rather than sim-
> ply identifying problems or issues. Once we become proactive on
> the solution side, we risk corrupting our own desire to tell the truth
> if our solutions fail.

The problem with public journalism is twofold. First, it establishes a
precedent for less benign attempts to control the press. In human affairs,
well-intentioned forms of social control often lead to abominations once

unscrupulous people get hold of the levers of power. There is no reason to think that control of the press would prove any exception. To undermine journalistic independence is to place the domain in grave jeopardy. Second, public journalism suggests that the absolute standard of truth should be compromised for a "larger social good." In the case of journalism, such a suggestion eats away at the standards of truthfulness that lie at the heart of the domain. No doubt this is why public journalism has been advocated primarily by people from outside the domain: insiders, and especially seasoned ones, recognize it for the threat it is.

Of course, if public journalism is construed as simply listening to a broader spectrum of the community about what should be covered, no one should object. Surveying public needs and wishes is nothing more than good business and good reportorial practice. It is a way of opening and competing for new markets, a classic entrepreneurial way to serve the public interest. This is precisely the way that the best news outlets—papers such as the *New York Times* and broadcast programs such as NPR's *All Things Considered*—have operated: with high standards, a keen ear to the diverse voices of the public, a rigorous guarding of journalistic independence, and marketplace success.

The idea of public journalism is still alive within academic and philanthropic circles, but dissenting voices have been heard even in these ivory-tower settings. In a recent dissertation, Sean Aday, a student at the University of Pennsylvania's Annenberg School for Communication, criticized the public journalism approach for losing sight of the unique and irreplaceable role of free journalism in a democratic society. He pointed out that public journalism's quest for community solidarity could tie the hands of journalists who want to ask sharp, unpopular questions about an immoral status quo. "How would a paper practicing public journalism have covered the Civil Rights Movement in Montgomery, Alabama, during the 1950s and 1960s?" Aday asks. "Was there a consensus opinion that 'Bull' Connor and Martin Luther King could share?"[2] Aday also pointed out that the press has a far more essential contribution to make than "civic boosterism." Above all, a democracy needs an institution that challenges the powerful, that gets beneath the official story to dig for truth, and that communicates this truth credibly and trustworthily. By abandoning the standards of nonpartisanship and objectivity, public journalism undermines this essential contribution.

In the view of our informants, public journalism falls short because, like all well-meaning attempts to control free institutions for worthy purposes (socialism, autocracy, censorship of any kind), it assumes that the ends can justify the means. Public journalism is willing to shade the truth—or, at the very least, to ignore, conceal, or slant large parts of the truth—for the sake of the "larger social good." This kind of well-intentioned path has been trod down many times in human history, all too often with disastrous results. Eventually the larger social good becomes defined by those with the greatest social power, for their own corrupt ends. By then, the protections once provided by a seasoned cadre of professionals with its own inner ethical compass are no longer available. In our view, it is a credit to our journalists' nose for moral hazard, and a sign that the core standards of journalism are still vital, that this well-intentioned experiment has so far met with skepticism.

The Ultimate Dream:
A Faith in the Traditions and Future of the Domain

When journalists look to the future, they see no miracles, but many believe that good work in their domain will prevail. They have faith that, with persistence and consciously wrought strategies, the domain of journalism will return to its traditional high standards, promoting truth and freedom for an open society, despite all current temptations and pressures toward corruption of its noble mission.

The seeds of salvation may lie in tough-minded recognition of the current situation. In sharp contrast to the blasé spirit of Hutchins's era, both journalists and observers of journalism are keenly aware of the threat to long-standing domain values and practices. Such recognition does not guarantee self-corrective measures, but it is surely necessary. The inventions of technology may potentially aid in the restoration of the classical purposes of the domain; but being fundamentally amoral and devoid of values, they will not do so by themselves. Strong, steady individual and group leadership and creativity will be essential.

In this spirit we close this chapter with hopeful quotes from two of our participants. Both look to a renewed alignment between the standards of the domain and the desires of the public. One print journalist said:

> I think tabloid is running thin. I think the public is getting tired of it. I mean, look at the talk shows that run into so much weird stuff and finally the public had enough. I have a great deal of faith in the public, that you can go so long so far, and then finally somebody says,

"Wait a minute." So I think that journalism will always be telling interesting stories in an interesting fashion, and doing some investigative work to keep everyone honest and on notice. And I think that we will stray, but we'll come back to this original path. . . . I think that is pretty much what journalism is. Always has been. Back in the days of newspapers, . . . there was the penny press, remember, and it sensationalized everything. Yet the *New York Times* continued to survive.

. . . I am not a dire predictor, nor am I a Pollyanna optimist. But I worry. With the conglomerates that now hold media power, where more and more is held by fewer and fewer, I fear we are becoming too cross-pollinated with commercial interests, and that news is becoming too homogenous and, worse than that, dumbed down. Still, I believe there are cycles in everything. In friendship, in professions, in labor, in management, in the economy, that bust things up just when you thought that they were as they would always be. Moreover, I still believe that there will always be some quest for honest information as uncorrupted by personal interest as it can be and still be done by human beings. And that there will be that need, that desire, and so the struggle to get it done.

The good-work methods examined thus far are solutions that journalists have worked out either on their own or with peers or mentors. We did not find a single instance of a strategy learned from a school of journalism, a training program, or a book or manual. It appears that the field has virtually no systematic way of imparting the methods that journalists actually use—or, if there are such ways, they are not particularly memorable or effective. The methods are journalists' private answers to the pursuit of their domain's mission. The people we interviewed had rarely or never articulated these strategies, for themselves or others, prior to our interviews with them. There is little communication about such methods across the field—either horizontally, among peers, or vertically, from manager to reporter or from trainer to trainee.

Could the good-work methods that journalists have devised for themselves be shared with others in the field? We believe that explicit and vivid articulation of these methods could be of great benefit to the future of the news profession, to those who work in the news field or are preparing to do so, and to the domain's central truth-seeking mission, itself essential for the preservation and flourishing of a democratic society.

Strategies *can* be learned. Young journalists in particular can benefit from the examples of people who have risen to the pinnacles of their field with success and integrity. To be sure, they will never emulate such examples in every particular: in the end, they will all find their own personal ways. Perhaps, with the right start, they will find a way to surpass the most shining examples of the past. If so, good work in journalism will have a future.

But that bright future—a domain defined by the good work of its most dedicated individuals—will not be secured unless forces of the field are also brought into alignment. We noted the struggles of dedicated practitioners such as Marin and Lappé in the face of hostile field pressures. New horrors arise almost daily in this besieged domain.

The debacle surrounding coverage of the presidential contest between George W. Bush and Al Gore in 2000 was largely a story of corrupting field forces. The major networks, for cost-cutting reasons, had abandoned their competitive practice of each doing its own polling research in favor of a jointly sponsored effort called the Voter News Service (VNS). As a result, every network news team received the same error-ridden information, with no independent means of fact checking. Reporters could do little more than pass along confusing, misleading, and often self-contradictory stories. This is hardly the ideal of good work. In this case—a close election, with voting still taking place in many parts of the country—the potential for mischief was enormous, and journalism's highly visible failure on this occasion will be a source of shame in the domain for years to come.

In this case, the adverse field force was an inadvertent collusion that extinguished competition, rather than the no-holds-barred competition that many of today's journalists complain about. But the source of the problem is the same: an excessively narrow, relentlessly bottom-line mentality that threatens to kill the goose in its quest for more golden eggs. Adverse forces of the field can be altered: public criticism and government pressure likely will force the networks to dissolve VNS and reestablish independent polling operations. As news consumers, and as a society, we need to express a habitual vigilance that will discourage those who control the field from making such misguided choices in the first place. Then journalists will once again be free to achieve good work.

PART FOUR

GOOD WORK
IN THE FUTURE

10

RESTORING GOOD WORK IN
JOURNALISM AND GENETICS

IN THE FIRST HALF of the twentieth century, two startlingly dystopian novels were published in England. In *Brave New World,* published in 1932, Aldous Huxley portrayed a highly stratified society of the future. Through test-tube fertilization followed by "Henry Ford–style" mass production and social conditioning, a castelike robotic society was created.[1] The Alpha Plus intellectuals ran the world, serviced in various ways by the Epsilon Minus Morons, who found contentment in their servitude. In *1984,* published in 1949, George Orwell imagined a world subjected to thorough thought control.[2] Against the background of continuing rivalry among three cold war–style megacontinents, individuals lost any semblance of independent thought or free will. They were programmed by an omniscient and anonymous Big Brother, who convinced them, via "double-think" and "newspeak," of such absurdities as "War is Peace," "Freedom is Slavery" and "Ignorance is Strength." A common theme of both novels was that traditional humanity, with its quirky emotions, aspirations, and spontaneity, could not survive under the totalitarian conditions that were likely to arise in the future.

Happily, we have so far avoided either of these dystopian fates. The more confident among us might even conclude that the two British novelists were naive; perhaps they were confusing the passing of British imperial society with the dissipation of human nature more broadly.

However, Huxley and Orwell had detected the most sensitive zones of modern life. Descended from a family steeped in the science of biology, Huxley was alert to the possibilities of controlling our bodies (and minds) through genetic manipulations. As one deeply and painfully immersed in the political cross fires of his time, Orwell was alert to the possibilities of controlling our minds (and bodies) through the manipulation of thought. To be sure, the Huxley of 1932 knew nothing about DNA, let alone genetic engineering or cloning; and the Orwell of 1949 could hardly anticipate the universal use of computers large and small, not to mention the Internet, the World Wide Web, or the rise of powerful multinational corporations for whom the literary world represents but an insignificant line in the annual report to shareholders. However, on the artist's intuitive level, they were alert to the memetic and genetic fault lines that have become ever more vivid with the passage of the decades.

We began our inquiry with a general interest in the "fate of good work" under conditions of rapid and often confusing changes. Like Huxley, we felt that the control of our bodies via our genes was one of the critical axes of our destiny; like Orwell, we felt that control of our minds via memes constituted the other equally vital axis. But our interest has always extended beyond the particularities of biomedical research and newspaper reportage circa 2000 to the generic set of issues facing anyone who is attempting to carry out good work in difficult times.

Revisiting Three Basic Questions

At the start of our inquiry, with an eye on the case of Ray Suarez (discussed in Chapter 1), we posed three questions that could arise at any time in the mind of a contemporary professional, and are especially likely to do so during periods of crisis:

Core Values: Why should my society entrust me with power and prestige?

Exemplary Beliefs and Practices: Which workers realize the calling best?

Sense of Moral Identity: How do I feel about myself when I look in the mirror?

To an extent that we had not anticipated, both geneticists and journalists voiced strong agreement about the values and standards of their respective callings. As scientists, geneticists are bent on discovering the nature of the fine structure of the biological world. They respect work that is scrupulous, honest, open, and original; they honor those among their peers who have carried out the most original, pathbreaking work. They are most critical of those who are secretive, cut corners, and fail to make a bona fide contribution to knowledge. Those in clinical or therapeutic positions naturally emphasize the healing implications of their work; but they, too, embrace the scientific ethos.

Journalists also forge a contract with society. In return for certain privileges and constitutional protections, they are expected to be truthful, objective, and fair to all whom they cover. Many also feel an obligation to protect democratic values and to make sure that diverse and often powerless groups are fairly represented in the news. They respect work that is adequately researched, appropriately contextualized, and expressed crisply and vigorously; they disdain work that is derivative, shoddy, biased, and reported clumsily or insipidly. The respect of one's peers, as epitomized by the Pulitzer Prize, is as important to journalists as the Nobel or Lasker Prizes are to biomedical researchers.

The divergence between the two groups comes through in the third hypothetical measure—the so-called mirror test. Most of the geneticists with whom we spoke felt positive about their work. They enjoyed what they were doing, thought it was important, and believed that it was, or soon would be, contributing to the public's health and well-being. Misgivings were minor, though some of the informants—and particularly the younger ones—did voice concerns about the actions or values of less scrupulous colleagues.

We encountered a far more unsettled picture among the journalists. While most expressed pride or at least satisfaction about their own work, they were decidedly downbeat about the profession as a whole. The forces they discerned at the workplace were at odds with values they personally cherished. Even if they personally could still look at themselves in the mirror, few indicated their belief that the profession as a whole could pass such a reflective self-assessment.

Yet, just as the golden age of genetics may shield troubling storm clouds, the severe straits of journalism may harbor promising signs. A certain amount of conflict or tension can be productive in a domain. The most respected journalists have banded together in various ways to stipulate what is central to their calling, document trends, and create models that can guide both rookies on the beat and crusty professionals who may have lost their passion or sense of direction. The very threats to the integrity of the journalistic calling may stimulate leading professionals to dig in their heels, take a stand, and launch a revolution (or counterrevolution) in standards. Instead of heading steadily downhill, perhaps the field will succeed in turning a corner and pushing the domain in a new and more positive direction. Most practitioners believe it is preferable to work in a well-aligned profession such as genetics than in a poorly aligned one such as journalism. Yet we do not in any sense equate alignment with either goodness or happiness. Indeed, it may be a sign of dynamism when a profession exhibits poor alignment between, say, the goals of practitioners and the demands of the marketplace. We suspect that certain professionals—and they may be among the most impressive—are suspicious of seamless alignment and on the lookout for areas of misalignment toward which they may exert their passions.

Five Levers for Good Work

Because journalism has been under pressure during recent decades, we have searched that domain, particularly, for levers, or moves, that can encourage good work. In some cases, the good is clear; in other cases, the potential is less evident or the moves might be counterproductive in light of the domain's core values. In the absence of equivalent pressures, the domain of genetics currently holds fewer examples—for good or for ill—but we have nonetheless considered the steps toward good work that geneticists might take if the circumstances warranted such action. Thus, we now review the ways in which resourceful journalists or geneticists can influence their chosen domain or field.

Creating New Institutions

The most dramatic way practitioners can influence a realm is to create a new institution, one designed to embody the values they cherish. Prominent among the institutions that we have already described is the American News Service, launched by Frances Moore Lappé and her colleague Paul Martin DuBois. Other examples of relatively new institutions that attempt to cover the full range of news straightforwardly and nonsensationally are National Public Radio, a high-quality source that is among the fastest-growing news outlets in the world today. C-Span, which presents "gavel-to-gavel" coverage of important political events; and Ted Turner's CNN, which provides round-the-clock television coverage of news in the United States and most other nations. Some magazines have been focusing on serious stories and avoiding glitz, such as *Hope,* which presentsuplifting personal sagas, and *Double Take,* which specializes in photographic essays.

A different form of innovation focuses explicitly on the quality of journalism. A prime example, as mentioned in previous chapters, is *Brill's Content,* a monthly publication that presents itself as a watchdog of the American press. To ensure a guarding of the guardians, *Brill's Content* itself has an ombudsman who serves a two-year, nonrenewable stint. The first was the respected journalist Bill Kovach (introduced in Chapter 7), then the curator of the Nieman Fellowship at Harvard University, itself a "trustee" institution in journalism.

The Internet opens the possibility of updating the news, not merely hourly but on a minute-by-minute basis. Among the widely praised sites doing high-quality, cutting-edge work are *Slate, Salon,* and *Cybereditions.* Although most Internet sites are currently modeling themselves on print or broadcast exemplars, they are offering far more opportunities for comment by and interactions among users. It remains to be seen whether such sites can simultaneously maintain high quality and attract sufficient revenue through advertising or subscription rates, thereby flourishing.

A different innovation, which we examined in Chapter 7, has been introduced by the Internet "journalist" Matt Drudge. In our view, the *Drudge Report* has exceeded the boundary of what should qualify as journalism, since its inclusion of gossip represents the kind of expansion that strikes at the domain's soul and threatens to destroy it. To be sure, not all such innovations survive; they are as prey to decline as any other novel undertaking. The impact of such institutions should be judged in terms of two criteria: the work—good and not-so-good— they accomplish and the long-term impact they have on those who do the work and those who are served.

Over the past few years, many new institutions have arisen in the area of genetics. For our purposes, the most provocative are the for-profit biotech companies with a strong focus on cutting-edge research: among them, the best known are Celera, under the direction of Craig Venter, and Human Genome Science, under the direction of William Haseltine (see Chapters 4 and 6). There is no question that such companies have led the way in investigating—if not creating—new areas of science, new forms of information delivery, and new pharmaceuticals; and that their successes have stimulated not only other private companies but also research funded publicly or by foundations.

Yet, without pointing fingers at specific companies or leaders, we mention doubts that have been raised about these trends. First, such companies cannot make profits unless they patent information that might more properly remain in the public sector (in 2000, fifteen thousand biotechnology patents were pending in the United States alone). Second, they are pressured to engage in those activities (for example, curing diseases prevalent in developed countries) that are likely to lead to profits. There is also the temptation to work on problems that fall well outside the province of "pure" science; for example, Celera recently acquired a code-breaking company that eavesdrops on other nations.[3]

Fortunately, other newly created institutions have arisen to address precisely these concerns. The Council for Responsible Genetics, based in Cambridge, Massachusetts, is a watchdog group that focuses on events in this fast-breaking area of study (see Chapter 6). It commissions studies of controversial issues and reports its findings in accessible publications. Among the topics it has investigated are genetically modified foods, the patenting of genes, the risks of gene therapy, "designer genes," and the controversial status of cloning. Of particular interest, in light of the dual focus of this book, is the recently established *Gene-Media Forum,* which promotes public dialogue about genomic research and its implications for society. The *Forum* promises "a diversity of views," plus the "fullest coverage of the social and political issues, as well as the science of the genetic revolution."

Expanding the Functions of Existing Institutions

In the present highly competitive climate, nearly every journalistic and genetic organization is on the lookout for new activities that may serve clients, address unmet needs, and, it goes without saying, increase profitability. Spurred by criticism of journalistic coverage, many newspapers, magazines, and broadcast outlets have added the function of "ombudsman" or "ombudswoman" to their staffs. When James D. Watson was appointed the first head of the publicly funded Human Genome Project, he requested that 3 percent to 5 percent of the annual budget be put aside to address social and ethical issues arising from research on genetics. Perhaps stimulated by this example, Celera's Venter has also commissioned studies of the ethical aspects of biological research.

It is easy to envision expanded functions of existing institutions, but the ultimate merit of these experiments is not always evident. For every observer who praises the communitarian impulse that underlies civic journalism, there are others who endorse the blurring of genres favored by Patricia Smith or the populist sentiment endorsed by Matt Drudge. In our view, the norms of a calling evolve gradually over a long period, and for good reasons. Well-intentioned efforts to change those norms often minimize the seasoned rationale for their existence and the risks entailed in trifling with them. As school reformers have discovered in the last decade, it may well be easier to create a new institution that attempts to preserve traditional norms in its own way than to bring about changes in an existing institution by fiddling with those norms.

Reconfiguring the Membership of Existing Institutions

Few trends in American society have been more dramatic than the efforts to diversify the workplace, and particularly to bring traditionally under-represented groups into leadership positions. Many believe that diversification is in itself a positive goal, and even those who disagree nevertheless recognize that it can improve the quality and the appeal of products.

Still, diversity is often difficult to achieve. Among geneticists there are relatively few women, and even fewer minorities. Scholarship and fellowship programs have made some demographic inroads, but the obstacles to diversification remain formidable. With the blurring of lines between pure research and business, both public and for-profit institutions employ people from a greater variety of backgrounds: pure scientists, applied scientists, and marketing and entrepreneurial types now rub elbows. Yet, white males remain the dominant group.

When it comes to making decisions about controversial issues in genetics, diversity takes on a different complexion. Ideally, most people would want such decisions to be made by a representative group of the broader population; indeed, most interviewees denied having special expertise for dealing with questions like whether to clone human beings or whether to pursue the possibility of "designer babies." Yet, practically speaking,

many of these issues are technical ones, and few laypeople have the expertise or inclination to become deeply involved—until these issues show up
in court or on daytime television talk-shows. And because many scientists
spend little time educating the public, responsibility for these consequential decisions may fall between the cracks.

Probably because the training is much briefer and the commercial benefits more tangible, the ranks of journalists have been more successfully
diversified in recent years. Much credit goes to pioneers like Maria Elena
Salinas and Ray Suarez, who by example and networking have broadened
the ranks of the organizations with which they are affiliated. Still, greater
success has been achieved in front of the camera or in illustrated newspaper columns (where the dividends for African American, Asian American,
or Hispanic American faces are more evident) than in the business end of
the enterprise.

Reaffirming the Values of Existing Institutions

Perhaps the strongest lever for good work resides in those organizations
that already embody it. The National Institutes of Health is admired
around the world for its generous and politically unbiased support of top-
quality science; and other, less headlined institutions, such as the
Carnegie Institute of Washington, are also widely praised. When it comes
to the press, there is considerable regret about once-admired broadcast
outlets such as CBS News or long-admired publications such as the
Louisville Courier-Journal and the *Times of London* having declined in
quality or gone out of business altogether. There is still esteem, however,
for a few publications—for example, the *New York Times*, the *Economist*,
and the *Wall Street Journal* (and their counterparts in Continental
Europe)—that have retained their high quality and continued to be innovative over the years. Most of the journalists to whom we spoke would
move to these publications if offered a job. Alas, though, it is far easier to
destroy a great publication than to create one. The single embarrassing
episode involving the *Los Angeles Times* and Staples, which we discussed
in Chapter 7, was so damaging to its credibility that some observers question whether the *Times* can regain its lofty stature.

Excellence is generally transmitted from one individual to another
through lineages of mentors and their apprentices. One of our informants, Stephen Engelberg of the *New York Times*, described the tremen-

dous influence exerted by Bill Kovach (introduced in Chapter 7) on a whole generation of reporters at the *Times*. Kovach had a special knack for spotting young talent. From the first, he trusted reporters and gave them responsibility, increasing the challenges as rapidly as the fledgling journalists could take them on. He acknowledged the quality of their work often and generously. At the same time, he made his high standards—and the standards of the *Times*—absolutely clear to all.

In Engelberg's phrase, Kovach embodied the "intellectual dress code." According to the code, "I care about each and every sentence in this paper and I care how we get them, and I have very clear views of how they are to be gotten." Kovach supplemented this code with an ethos about personal relations. It was vital for the journalists to work together supportively rather than ruthlessly. Kovach protected the members of his team: "Make the calls, and I'll back you," he told them. But Kovach let it be known that those reporters who could not cooperate with their peers on the team would ultimately get in trouble.

Taking Personal Stands

When prominent, well-informed practitioners make moves that affirm the values of a domain, and when they resist encroachment on their own and their colleagues' legitimate prerogatives, others take heart—especially budding professionals. Young journalists pay attention to Bill Kovach and to night-time anchors Peter Jennings and Tom Brokaw; young geneticists monitor the words and deeds of James Watson and Craig Venter. On the other hand, if leading figures succumb to pressures—for example, from corporate stakeholders bent on short term-profits—others are likely to become confused or disillusioned.

When things are proceeding well in the domain—as they are, for the most part, in genetics—then the best thing practitioners can do is to carry out their jobs in an exemplary manner and help younger workers do the same. When conditions are less than optimal, however, those in leading positions are placed in a quandary. They can ignore the situation and hope that conditions will improve, or they can take more proactive steps to help "right" the situation.

In recent years, many journalists have spoken out about the declining situation in their domain. They have given speeches, written articles and books, and participated on the Committee of Concerned Journalists.

They have worked with private foundations that have a journalistic portfolio, including the Ford Foundation, the Pew Charitable Trusts, and the Knight Foundation. Embodying the standards of their craft, they have refused to publish scurrilous stories and—ignoring the pressures of priority—have withheld other stories until sufficient confirmation could be obtained. They have populated symposia sponsored by the Nieman Foundation at Harvard, the Poynter Institute in St. Petersburg, and other comparable journalistic think tanks. These efforts all encourage journalists to maintain the core values of their profession and to remind the public of the importance of these values in a democratic society.

Scientists can take comparable steps to ensure the health of their domain. For example, they can accept relatively low paying and unglamorous positions in government service, in an effort to support the continuing high quality of government-funded science. The Nobel laureates Harold Varmus and James Watson at the National Institutes of Health, as well as their colleague Bruce Alberts at the National Academy of Sciences, have led the way with that public commitment. Other scientists can teach in local high schools, as Leroy Hood and his associates have done (see Chapters 4–6). They can address ethical issues in their lectures and writings, as MIT geneticists Eric Lander and Jonathan King (Chapter 6) have done. They can refuse to patent genes discovered in their laboratory, as Stanford University's Paul Berg has done. Also, they can decline money for certain kinds of advisory tasks or equity in companies where they carry out research, as several of our respondents have done.

The ultimate statement by a disillusioned professional is to resign.[4] While a tradition of resigning on principle exists in the British Isles, such practices—never common—are increasingly rare in the United States. Even when Secretary of State Cyrus Vance resigned in 1980 following a failed mission to rescue Americans held hostage in Iran, he did not explain the reasons for this unusual action. More commonly, people leave projects or professions quietly, satisfying their own conscience but avoiding public confrontation or the appearance of ungracious behavior. Among our subjects, neither the journalist Ray Suarez nor the biologist Jonathan King expressed their displeasure publicly. We note, however, that a protest or resignation—whether public or silent—may prove ineffectual. Indeed, in a number of instances that we have described, younger workers who attempted protests were ignored or silenced.

Toward Authentic Alignment:
Maintaining an Essential Tension

Every practitioner aspires to work in a well-aligned domain—that is, one in which personal aspirations are consistent with the enduring values of the domain, the current roles and institutions in the field, and the interests of various other stakeholders. As we have seen, journalism currently stands as a poorly aligned realm, while genetics seems to be almost blessedly well aligned.

Yet the alignment in genetics may be short-lived and too highly vaunted. After all, the balance of power that still rests significantly on the scientists' side could shift over to managers and portfolio handlers. Scientists themselves could be corrupted, by the temptations of power, to compromise their scientific integrity and perhaps even the health of their experimental subjects. Shareholders could become impatient with companies that show more promise than profit, and the public could be repelled by experiments that go awry or by uses of technology that are repressive, inhumane, or deadly.

The domain of genetics does not stand alone, though, in facing less glowing times. Earlier declines in other domains are all too obvious. If one of our respondents is right, and "the media are an early warning sign for every domain," then a short-circuited golden age may be the rule from cyberlaw to dot.coms to scientific research in genetics. Still, there is no reason to believe that such cycles are inevitable, that there must be an endless alternation between golden and dark ages. Indeed, it should be possible to have authentic, relatively enduring alignments. The solution is to retain an essential tension within a domain.

The very concern journalists entertain about the fate of their profession is a potential source of power. Threats to the integrity of journalism can stimulate seasoned professionals to articulate the essence of their calling, to draw a line to indicate what is acceptable and what is not, and to act decisively against individuals and institutions that trespass on it. Journalists *have* unique skills and understandings; *if* they can vividly demonstrate the costs of the deterioration of their profession, they may well succeed in strengthening and reconstituting it. If journalists band together around their deepest beliefs, they will discover that they have a great deal of power, and they may successfully reorient the domain.

In contrast, the affairs of geneticists are going so well that they risk becoming smug, self-satisfied, or greedy. More important, they are likely to miss or minimize the various danger signs. The best insurance of continuing vitality in a domain like biological science is vigilance with respect to potentially disruptive conditions. In our view—though not, we admit, in the view of all other observers—the finest moment for geneticists was the Asilomar Conference, where scientists voluntarily suspended their activities for a while, until they felt assured that experiments in genetic recombination would not be harmful. This hiatus proved to be a brilliant investment—it bought a quarter century of confidence in the area. (As a cautionary contrast case, we recall the Congress of Vienna of 1815, which bought peace for so long a time that Europeans forgot the horrors of war.)

As long as we humans live on this planet, we can expect strains, conflicts, crises. The more we anticipate these trials, the more honestly we deal with them, the greater the likelihood that we will survive them. Therein lies authentic alignment. We should be suspicious of superficial alignments that mask looming storm clouds, and we should take preventive action to thwart those potentially massive misalignments that will be difficult to repair.

The Public Task

It is probably utopian to expect geneticists and journalists, who are just as human as everyone else, to resist single-mindedly the temptations society provides. In the last analysis, it is the responsibility of the community as a whole to encourage and reward those aspects of the enterprise that are most likely to result in beneficial outcomes for everyone. It is imperative for basic science to continue at reasonable levels of funding, so that scientists who are attracted by fundamental questions concerning life and disease are not marginalized by peers whose orientation is more immediate and market driven.

Of course, basic research is not necessarily beneficent; it uncovers horrible as well as helpful things. The important difference, however, is that for the "pure" researcher truth, in and of itself, is relatively more important than for a scientist who is competing for market shares. The former is responsible only to the rules of the domain and the needs of society; the latter must also satisfy shareholders' financial stake. This split allegiance of profit-conscious scientists makes questioning the implications of their own work—a difficult task under the best of conditions—all the more challenging. It is all too easy for engaged practitioners to see *only* the beneficent facets of their work. It is up to the rest of us to make a less self-serving judgment about good work and to construct a society that encourages its cultivation.

The same line of reasoning applies to journalists. It is certainly tempting to sit back and simply wait until the journalists sort things out, expel the violators, and restore effective and thoughtful coverage. But while we wait for the stables to be cleaned, the coverage of the news will continue to deteriorate. What is worse, talented young journalists will be deterred from entering the domain in favor of flashy, opportunistic people uninterested in the careful, fair-minded coverage of important matters. For these reasons, publications and broadcast outlets that do preserve the important values of journalism must be protected. We can all offer support by, for instance, subscribing to them, giving them to relatives and friends, or contributing generously to fund-raising drives. In addition, individuals and institutions that deliver shoddy journalism should be held accountable. We can do so by writing letters of protest, canceling subscriptions, and supporting legislation or regulations related to the objectionable practices. Adherence to the First Amendment does not entail reflexive support for work that undermines the values of journalism.

What we collectively expect from the media and from science will likely come true. Even if they wanted to guarantee everyone protection from unfortunate consequences, journalists and scientists are too closely implicated in their work to do that. So it is up to us as members of society—stakeholders in the largest sense—to decide what the future will be like. Certainly, traditional wisdom warns us against making imprudent choices. The danger is that with all goodwill, we are cheerfully encouraging trends that might turn the information inside our bodies and minds into a chaotic jumble. And then *1984* and *Brave New World* will no longer seem quaint period pieces.

11

GOOD WORK IN
THE WIDER WORLD

THE TRENDS WE HAVE DESCRIBED regarding the news media and genetics are by no means unique to these two domains. The forces that threaten good work are placing stress on nearly everyone, from electricians to pharmacists, from teachers to judges. Rapid technological innovations, new forms of ownership, and changing social expectations on the part of both producers and consumers make it difficult for any of us holding a job to live up to the values of the domain, the values of society, and our own system of values. The same time pressures impinging on journalists and geneticists are forcing doctors to shorten their appointments with patients and lawyers to bill clients for five-minute increments. Changing patterns of ownership affect not only newspapers and genetic laboratories but also medical, legal, and even educational institutions. In these latter, formerly staid domains, liability is more of an issue than ever before, advertising has become accepted, and the financial bottom line holds sway.

Three Threats to Alignment

Three developments are placing pressure across the gamut of professions. In addition to already familiar instances from journalism and genetics, we now draw examples from four professional realms mentioned at the start of this book, especially in Chapter 2: medicine, law, teaching, and artistic crafts.

Promethean Technology

In Greek mythology, Prometheus sacrificed himself for the good of the human race, stealing fire from the hearthstone of the gods and teaching people its uses. Human beings learned how to forge metals with fire, but in punishment for his presumption, the gods chained Prometheus to a rock where vultures tore endlessly at his liver. Promethean achievements are apt metaphors for humankind's uneasy relationship with the technology it has invented.

Myths aside, it is not difficult to discern the reasons for this unease. At each stage of human evolution, our ancestors developed a set of beliefs, a lifestyle congruent with the technology of the era. Hunters built cultures based on independence and autonomy suitable to hunting; warriors organized their lives around heroic virtues; traders praised quick, risk-taking minds; and farmers extolled the value of patience and hard work. Whenever such alignments are fractionated by a technological advance, the old values and lifestyle are disrupted. The former virtues no longer make sense, and people are torn between allegiance to the new technology or to the old virtues. When the new values of a mercantile class were spreading through ancient Greece, for instance, members of the old aristocratic families whose wealth and lifestyle were based on farming—which included Plato—could not help but feel that a golden age was passing.

Cycles of destruction and renewal have always alternated in history. As the economist Joseph Schumpeter and others have observed, episodes of "creative destruction" are often needed to break out from stagnation.[1] But there is no question that in the past few centuries, the pace of change has increased exponentially. As little as a century ago, most jobs had been practiced for millennia, and people knew what to expect from them. Now numerous occupations employing many millions from Singapore to Silicon Valley are of such recent vintage that no one really understands their parameters—which are changing yearly anyway. Electronics, computers, robotics, nuclear physics, and molecular genetics have so changed the landscape of human activity that stable bearings are elusive.[2] So even as we cherish the savings in time and effort that technological advances have brought, we would be prudent to consider their possible side–effects.

This is especially true when changes are occurring so rapidly that there is no chance to evaluate their potential drawbacks and their clash with deeply held values such as having a suitably paced lifestyle, nurturing a sense of community, or encouraging children's respect for their elders.

In earlier chapters we extensively discussed the disruptive effects of "warp speed" technologies on journalists' established practices, and we suggested that the current alignment in the domain of genetics may be tenuous, partly because no crude facts have yet materialized to disrupt the dreams of perfect health promised by the doctoring of genes. At this point, we need to look even more closely at the questions that Promethean technologies pose not only for geneticists but also for the rest of us.

Once genetic engineering starts in earnest—as it no doubt will—we may well expect a host of troublesome issues to come to the fore. Even the genetic alteration of fruits and vegetables, which at first seemed like a simple and innocuous process, has lately come under increasingly harsh criticism by a variety of constituencies, especially in Europe. Nor should we (particularly in America) assume that such resistance is necessarily ill founded. Sound scientific reasons may support the need for us to refrain from certain kinds of experiments that might harm other species or the ambient environment. Also, we might need to consider such subjective issues as a belief in the sanctity of life as it has evolved over the millennia.

The enormous competition among leading geneticists and genetech companies brings with it dangers as well. As new technologies pour forth at dizzying rates, speed becomes a dominant concern: all seek to be the first in identifying the function of specific genes, first in patenting, first in publishing, first in optimizing profits. As a result, the work-related issues of accuracy, context, and consequences become relatively less important. The scientists (and the rest of us) risk confusing good work with fast work. And a domain once characterized by common principles and common pursuits could become wracked by litigation, ill will, and domination by a few monopolistic powers.

The cascade of new technologies affects other domains as well. Consider, for example, the effect of the Internet on higher education. Whereas nearly all education once occurred face-to-face, the new technologies now promise education at a distance. "Distance learning" is in principle available to all at much less cost, and credits or even degrees can be awarded rapidly to unprecedented numbers of consumers. The appeal of such delivery is undeniable, and it may be that the results are on par with those connected to the age-old routine of lectures and tests on campuses. Yet, in this new equation, neither students nor teachers have any way of ensuring contact with the intended people. That is, the teachers may be reviewing work submitted by someone other than the enrolled students; in turn, the enrolled students may be having their questions answered by a graduate student, a fellow student, or even an ingeniously programmed computer. And students' opportunities to work side by side with gifted teachers and to observe how they formulate problems or conduct new research are obviously minimized. Indeed, thanks to technology, pressures are already mounting to demonstrate any "value added" by "live" education.

The classic professions of law and medicine also take on new contours as a result of information now available on the Web. Patients can research their own diseases, clients can research their own cases, and anyone can join chat groups composed of like-minded people. Without doubt, these new sources of information will keep professionals on their toes, and that is to the good. But the value of information gleaned on the Web is uneven at best, and advice purveyed by anonymous sources can be worthless or even dangerous. There is also the risk that clients will feel so well informed that they will come to regard the professionals merely as aides hired to carry out their bidding (as in, "Just write me out a prescription for Perganol"), rather than as experts capable of seasoned judgment. Still, professionals may be understandably reluctant to attack these alternative demotic sources of information directly—especially if the same professionals are supposed to defend the First Amendment.

Many artists and craftspersons are attracted to new technologies. They often succeed in disarming the mechanistic potential of these media and find stimulation for their own imaginations. Yet the struggle between established and new practices often produces havoc, at least temporarily. For example, the success of photography discouraged many aspiring painters from developing their skills. What happens to draftsmen or architects who have worked for decades to master a craft, only to discover that a computer program creates blueprints that are indistinguishable from theirs? Or to artists whose works are excellent but who lack the ability, the will, or the connections to promote themselves on the new technologies? What happens to museums if there is no longer an original object, and the ten millionth version is identical to the first? Or when all new work can be instantly downloaded and shared and there is, as a result, no royalty (and, hence, no livelihood) for the creative artist?

Ownership and Sharing of Information

Creators have always striven to acquire and protect privileged access to the knowledge they originated, uncovered, or synthesized. Even in the Stone Age cultures of New Guinea, men tried to preserve ritual lore that women were not supposed to hear about, and vice versa. In more complex civilizations, each craft or profession learned to guard jealously the secrets of its guild. The knowledge of how to graft a lemon tree or fire an earthenware bowl was a valuable possession the bearers sought to hoard among only their families and to transmit solely to a few committed apprentices. As trade expanded, knowledge of far-off events such as migrations, wars, floods, and harvests became increasingly valuable, and shrewd merchants could use such information to anticipate fluctuations in the price of merchandise. Now we have a phrase to designate this resource—*intellectual property*—and a branch of law to protect it, but the phenomenon to which it refers is as old as knowledge itself.

In a small city-state such as Athens it was possible, at least in principle, for the entire citizenry to act as a collective medium of information by debating issues in public, as well as exchanging, interpreting, and discussing the news of the day. To be sure, this ideal was never fully realized. Nevertheless, we owe to the Greeks the profound and cherished idea that the commonwealth would prosper if each person had access to the truth and could act on it.

The Greek ideal, or its analog in nineteenth-century American town meetings, is clearly unfeasible in a nation-state, where numbers and distances make it impossible for people to keep abreast of what they should know by meeting fellow citizens face-to-face. Hence those people—that is, we—must increasingly rely on communications mediated by print and broadcast. As we have noted already, news that has been packaged in the media is more readily selected and controlled by a small number of powerful people. The steadily increasing concentration of newspapers and broadcast stations in fewer and fewer hands is one of the obvious threats to good work in the news media.

Beholden to a large number of anonymous stockholders, today's owners—unlike their often family rooted predecessors—must measure the success of their investments solely by quarterly profit statements. In turn, managers often feel bound by a solely financial gauge of their success, partly because of the focus of the corporation and partly because of the stockholders' lack of personal attachment to the conglomerates packaging the news. After all, the everyday citizens who own a few hundred shares of AOL/Time Warner/EMI (once Time Warner and, before that, Time, Inc.) are unlikely to feel a surge of pride through association while reading a thoughtful editorial in one of its magazines. So the diffusion of ownership to society at large may have resulted in a subtle corruption of the media: instead of becoming more responsive to societal needs, the media have been narrowed to their main function of providing profits.

The Web—that changeling brainchild of the Pentagon—is supposed to revolutionize the ownership of information so that all the news will be in the public domain, accessible to everyone. According to some scenarios, the magnificent confluence of information will create a memetic fusion that would put a hydrogen bomb to shame: all the brain cells on the planet resonating together to the same pattern of information. Or the thousands of media outlets will balance one another out and the truth will emerge in a magical, Darwinian fashion. But neither of these exalted outcomes is likely. Because we can absorb only so much information, the more "information" that is placed on the Web, the less useful it becomes—unless it has been edited, organized, and interpreted by "infomediaries" that we learn to trust.

Changes in the ownership of media pale when compared to what has happened in genetics. Until little more than a decade ago, we would have met blank stares if we had mentioned *genes* and *ownership* in the same sentence. Scientists had a proprietary interest in their work only in the symbolic sense of intellectual ownership—who discovered what, who published it when and where. Scholarly competition and the pursuit of fame (by no means weak motives), plus the joys of discovery and understanding, were the main rewards that kept geneticists toiling in their labs.

The situation is totally different now. At faculty gatherings formerly elbow-patched professors who now head biotech firms can be overheard telling of their desire to retire as soon as they can sell $200 million worth of stock options. The Parliament in Iceland recently ceded to one company the right to create a database from all of Icelanders' medical records, and it is considering selling for an astronomical sum all the information contained in its inhabitants' genes to a pharmaceutical firm.[3] Jeremy Rifkin, the critic of unbridled genetic research mentioned in Chapter 6, believes that patents on our genes, cells, and organs could one day be held by a few gigantic multinational corporations. In less than a generation, genetics has become a mover and shaker in business. Until now, the scientists themselves have had a major say in what information was procured and how it was to be shared. But what guarantee—indeed, what likelihood—is there that future captains of the biogenetic industry will behave responsibly—and any more responsibly than, say, the executives of tobacco companies, or savings-and-loan institutions, or global media corporations?

Questions of ownership loom large in other professional realms as well. The independent physician or the small private medical group has been largely replaced by huge medical complexes, often profit-making in goal, if not always in reality. Even those that retain nonprofit status are under enormous pressures to seek greater returns and to cut costs. Physicians whom we've interviewed almost universally report a loss of autonomy, as they are reimbursed according to the number of patients they can squeeze into a brief period. They complain that they cannot rely on their professional judgment in the face of powerful strictures to avoid expensive procedures. Lucrative rewards go to medical personnel who agree to work with pharmaceutical companies or other industries; these for-profit institutions provide remuneration for the use of their products, work conducted in their laboratories—whatever will benefit the corporate bottom line. This is not to say that most physicians have sold out; rather, it is to emphasize that, in the absence of counterforces, only those with strong ethical codes can withstand corporate pressures. At least as disturbing, large numbers are leaving the medical profession altogether. The entrance of for-profit enterprises into education—from preschools and day-care facilities through colleges and universities—has produced increasing pressures to reduce costs, cut corners, and advertise their products with hyperbole. Not-for-profit institutions have found it infeasible to ignore these commercial enterprises. The result is a spreading commodification of the vast majority of traditional educational institutions. The eruption of privately funded schools for kindergarten through twelfth grade has heralded the "marketization" of young people's minds.

Colleges and universities now compete with one another in offering attractive financial packages for the best students, providing lavish services in dormitories and across their campuses, and (unrealistically) promising an education that will result in excellent jobs and lifelong prosperity. Courses by star teachers are taped and sold to individuals or to franchised educational operations. The situation with artists is equally intriguing. Artists now have a greater chance than ever before of bringing their works directly to the public's attention, without the need for intermediaries or infomediaries (such as galleries or agents). Many artists now maintain their own Web sites and 'display' their works—thus jeopardizing their own livelihood, since others can readily and cheaply print virtually perfect reproductions. When this happens, the value of the original works is destroyed. As a reaction to the possibly unbridled dissemination of valuable works of art, powerful encryption procedures will in all likelihood be devised and mandated. However, these controls on distribution are likely to benefit the media-controlling multinational corporations—AOL/Time Warner/EMI or Disney, for instance—rather than the individual creators.

Dumbing Down

To attract a large audience, any medium must beam its programs to the most widely shared taste (as rated by "sweeps"), which usually means the lowest common denominator in the marketplace. So when information becomes a mass commodity, the media are inevitably pushed to provide news that appeals to the broadest possible audience. Publishers, editors, and producers are then evaluated almost entirely on the basis of the fraction of the total audience they are able to attract and retain. At first blush, this arrangement may seem democratic—let the market decide what is most worthwhile. On closer examination, however, this seemingly fair attitude may conceal serious drawbacks.

Not all information is equally easy to grasp. Some of it can be understood by almost any adult—for instance, results of sports events, news of an earthquake in Turkey, or accounts of a British royal wedding or funeral. Other news relating more complex events will interest fewer people, because the meaning is less readily understood by the majority—say, a decision by the Federal Reserve to change interest rates or a scientific controversy about global warming. Only a few readers or listeners may have the motivation to find out about complex and apparently remote events, even though these may in fact have momentous consequences for everyone concerned—for instance, Central American economic developments that may result in political unrest and mass migration, or the pros and cons of germ-line therapy or of encryption codes on the Web.

Certainly, the people who track complex news may also be interested in the more accessible popular stories about sports results, earthquakes, or royal affairs of state. But people accustomed to a diet of simplistic news generally are not interested in decoding and absorbing information that requires more complex processing, or they cannot do so. In light of this asymmetry in the populace, the rational choice for media owners and producers is to aim for the lowest common denominator. If size of audience determines the bottom line, there is no contest.

One solution to this scenario may be a fragmentation of the market, with "higher-end" outlets such as National Public Radio appealing to a more educated, globally oriented elite, and Fox Broadcasting catering to those in search of the most dramatic, late-breaking stories. This scenario will not unfold by itself, however; it will take innovative investors (or underwriters) and risk-taking journalists to make it happen. And there is a cost to the body politic when members of a community no longer share the same information, as they may have during the seemingly idyllic mid-century period or in the agora of classical times.

The dumbing down of genetics is less obvious, but the forces are detectable there as well. The money invested in genetic engineering is attracted to the most promising sources of profits: curing the diseases of the wealthy, discovering cosmetic breakthroughs, and finding the keys to prolonged life. As the best recruits in the field are pushed to focus on immediate payoffs, market pressures are more likely to undermine the domain's long-term growth potential. Already, some of the "pure scientists" working in university laboratories and research institutes feel alienated from the hustle-and-bustle of the biotech and pharmaceutical firms, to which so many of their young peers have been attracted. But the flow of groundbreaking ideas is apt to slow down or even dry up if the more idealistic, disinterested exploration that tends to characterize the best basic research becomes a backwater shunned by the most talented and original young minds.

The undiluted pressure for profits threatens to trivialize other domains as well. Certainly, dumbing down can be readily observed in the arts. Whether it is the trend toward publishing only potential best-selling authors, mounting only blockbuster shows at museums, or avoiding complex documentaries and esoteric "foreign-style movies," there are unmistakable shifts toward marketing only those items that stand to make enormous profits. And the trends continue unabated—even after the glitzy, overrated, and simplistic "safe bets" have lost substantial amounts of money. To be sure, there are countertrends as well: small publishing companies that cater to niche markets, self-publishing opportunities, movies and videos that can be made for a tiny fraction of what Hollywood customarily bankrolls. And the individuals or teams involved in creating such forms do, in fact, often gain much satisfaction (and, at least occasionally, significant profits). Yet, it seems likely both that many of the most talented individuals are siphoned off to the mass market and that many others are discouraged from participation altogether. When one of us mentioned to Jonathan Miller, the noted British artistic director, that we intended to study good work in theater in America, he quipped, "Good luck! There is no serious legitimate theater in North America."

Dumbing down may be less immediately manifest in the classic professions of law and medicine. And yet, one can discern unsettling signs as well. Public interest law, a viable option for young lawyers thirty years ago, is faltering in this country. Now recent graduates of law schools are attracted by the huge salaries and comfortable perks of big Wall Street firms or media companies, and their knowledge and skills have become more narrowly specialized in a few technical areas. This law is not "dumber," perhaps, but it satisfies the needs and greeds of the wealthy, rather than the less glamorous but patently more pressing needs of the poor and the defenseless. Community medicine and medical care for the third world or for diseases that strike primarily the poor and the weak also attract fewer young physicians than these altruistic career paths did some decades ago. Lest we lose our most talented practitioners to the most high paying pursuits, it is important to buffer aspiring workers from the lures of easy rewards and to introduce pursuits that they might come to value more in the long run.

What Good Workers Can Do

Faced with powerful societal trends, what can the individual aspiring worker do? What do *you* do if you wake up in the morning and dread going to work, because the daily routine no longer satisfies your standards? In terms of an overall framework, the answers are easily stated. But execution requires all the skills and luck any of us can muster.

Expanding the Domain

The first option involves recomputing or reconfiguring the current contours of the domain: clarifying the values on which it is based, bringing new knowledge to bear on the tasks, or instituting better procedures to serve the profession's purposes. Consider a reporter who feels he cannot do a good job because he is not given enough time to investigate stories properly or to secure corroborative or conflicting testimony. The reporter may elect to focus on topics he knows well, develop a network of trusted sources to facilitate his task, or use cell phones, e-mail, or the Web for immediate help. Or consider a scientist who feels pressured to cut corners in an investigation so that she can publish before her rivals. In response, the scientist can initiate research in an area that is less competitive, create a journal in which scientists could publish preliminary notes indicating precisely where more research needs to be done, or establish a new norm by voluntarily sending her preliminary data to rivals as well as colleagues and asking them to return the professional courtesy.

Such domain-expanding options are open to workers in every profession. Artists who fear that their works will be distributed for free can band together to create a Web site where people are charged a small sum for each viewing, or they can exhibit only with gallery owners, museums, or copyright licensees who will pay them a reasonable royalty or per diem. (Unions for artists may come back into fashion!) Physicians disturbed by the poor quality of information on unregulated Web sites can create a more reliable site and charge a modest fee for its use. Elite law school graduates who recognize the need for defending indigent clients can create special pro bono wings of their firms. And educators who believe that face-to-face contacts with students are precious may refuse to participate in distance-learning schemes or may set up portable offices (for instance, at Borders or Starbucks) where they can interact directly with young people who need tutoring but cannot afford to pay for it.

Reconfiguring the Field

Another option is for professionals to work directly with individuals and institutions already in place to confirm the domain's crucial norms and values. A news reporter disturbed by the decline of investigative reporting may lobby to reinstitute the "spotlight" feature of earlier days or ask management to hire an ombudsman. A university-based scientist who deplores the loss of students to biotech firms may develop a set of guidelines that restrict worktime off campus or reward students who remain engaged in full-time research and teaching.

The option of working innovatively with individuals and institutions is available to all professionals. Physicians can lobby executives of their managed-care organization to put aside time for patients who need extra attention or who cannot afford current rates. Newly hired lawyers can stipulate as a condition of their employment that they be allowed to spend a proportion of their time on pro bono work. Museum directors can reallocate entrance fees or museum-shop profits and support artists working in media with easily threatened original works. And educators can voluntarily restrict advertisements to descriptions produced by non-biased third parties (for example, the College Board), rather than permit claims that cannot be verified or that are blatantly hyperbolic. High school administrators can decline deals with soft-drink companies to carry certain products in exchange for funds.

There is no sharp line between expanding the domain and reconfiguring the field; these categories shade into one another. Today's new domain knowledge can lead to the field alteration of tomorrow, or vice versa. The proliferation and pursuit of options, not the labeling efforts, are what matter.

Taking a Personal Stand

Sometimes it is not feasible to create a new institution or to reconfigure an existing one. To preserve personal integrity, some workers must confront their situations by themselves and either fight against or withdraw from jobs that are no longer aligned with their values.

Occasionally a personal stand can send ripples through the entire society because of the stature of the person involved. A good example is Linus Pauling, who received a Nobel Prize for having developed the quantum mechanical bases of chemistry. Pauling became convinced during the cold war that it was impossible to do good work in science without taking responsibility for its intended or probable use. Hence, he took a leadership role in expanding the realm of science by circulating petitions, leading peaceful marches, and exhorting other scientists not to let themselves be co-opted by projects that supported the development of new weapons. Finally, when he felt he was not making enough headway, Pauling took part in demonstrations that led to his being harassed by police, the FBI, and Congress. The State Department withdrew his passport, thereby handicapping his research on the structure of DNA. A similar path was taken by Benjamin Spock, the pediatrician whose child-rearing guide for years sold more copies than any other book except the Bible. During the same cold war era, Spock felt that it was irresponsible for a physician to worry

solely about children's colds or diarrhea when an ever-growing nuclear ar-
senal threatened to extinguish all life on earth. He tried to work through
the American Medical Association, ran as a third-party presidential candidate, and finally took to the streets. Spock also ran into trouble with legal
authorities as a result of his deeply held convictions. And there are more
controversial examples. In 1971, the security analyst Daniel Ellsberg risked
being jailed when he distributed the secret "Pentagon Papers," containing
details about U.S. involvement in Vietnam, to a few leading news outlets.
And by electing to publish these classified documents, the *New York
Times* and the *Washington Post* risked financial and legal penalties.

A readiness to put ourselves on the line obviously will not always result in positive outcomes for us. No one is irreplaceable, and there seems
to be an endless supply of willing practitioners who feel no compulsion
to honor the tacit contract that binds them to their domains. On the
other hand, resigning need not lead to giving up professional goals. Indeed, the challenge for "domain departers" is to find—or create—institutions or causes that allow them to achieve what is essential to maintain
integrity. Two noteworthy examples are John Gardner, who inspired the
creation of several influential grassroots civic organizations, and the consumer activist and third-party presidential candidate Ralph Nader, who
has challenged conventional governmental and corporate practices repeatedly over the last several decades. Several options are available to scientists who are unhappy about trends within their specialties. For
example, they can publish individual critiques. In the area of genetics
this is the option followed by insiders like Mae-Wan Ho (see Chapter 6)
or by relative outsiders like Rifkin. They can band together to create an
organization like the Council for Responsible Genetics, which has issued
the following guideline: "No individual, institution, or corporation
should be able to claim ownership over species or varieties of living organisms. Nor should they be able to hold patents on organs, cells, genes,
or proteins, whether naturally occurring, genetically altered or otherwise
modified."

Students associated with the Pugwash group—a politically oriented
scientific association concerned with issues of atomic energy—have
developed an oath:

I promise to work for a better world, where science and technology
are used in socially-responsible ways. I will not use my education
for any purpose intended to harm human beings or the environ-

ment. Throughout my career, I will consider the ethical implications of my work before I take action. While the demands placed
upon me may be great, I sign this declaration because I recognize
that individual responsibility is the first step on the path to peace.[4]

Finally, raising the ante on these exhortatory moves, it is possible to implement legislation that prohibits certain practices. It would be possible,
for instance, to ban for-profit medical or research institutions from pursuing certain kinds of research, such as human cloning, genetic engineering, or the tracing of a target population's genetic profiles. Similarly,
regulations might stipulate that only trained physicians could head medical organizations. Such options do not seem likely in the United States
today, but practices like desegregation of schools or government funding
of medical care for the aging seemed unlikely a century ago.

The Need for Coherent New Visions

The difficult choices we must make in the future may be impossible to
make unless our society develops a common set of priorities, or shared set
of values, that will justify the sacrifices that wise choices often entail in
the short run. To develop a joint vision is the task of national leaders. But
if our leaders lack the courage such a task requires, the burden to articulate tomorrow's vision falls on our shoulders. If everyone claims to be too
tired to pick it up, we shall face the future without map or compass.

There is a strong possibility that in twenty-five years a small minority
of the world's people—those in the United States, some European countries, and East Asia—will be trying to maintain an enormously energy-
intensive lifestyle in competition with the overwhelming majority of the
world's population. As those with fewer resources clamor to be admitted
to the palace of material affluence, the fortunate elites may be indulging
addictions barely related to authentic needs and luxuriating in a constant
stream of vicarious entertainment while gradually losing contact with
what happens in the rest of the world. The hard-won power of science
may be harnessed to ensure the survival of the fortunate few at the expense of the rest of humankind. *Brave New World* and *1984* might have
been premature, but these meme and gene dystopias could all too easily
be realized.

The path of least resistance—entropy or inertia—is constantly at work in history, as well as in the physical universe. Overcoming entropy in human affairs is not easy; it takes not only faith in a vision of a better way to live but also a commitment to translating that vision into reality. Yet the old signposts may prove inadequate to indicate the best direction for development. If we wish to envision an alternative to inertia, we must consider which values could serve as a map to the future.

Every culture that has endured and that has advanced the human condition through art or knowledge has had a coherent view of the universe. The cosmologies that the Chinese, the Indians, the Aztecs, or the Judeo Christian West invented may appear inadequate or even bizarre in hindsight. But they did provide direction to people's actions and a justification for their lives. Most of these value systems were harsh and unfair, justifying the power of men over women, the old over the young, the rich over the poor. Now it is fashionable to condemn these ancient civilizations for their faults. But condemnation tends to be ahistorical and decontextualized, because it not only ignores the conditions under which our ancestors had to struggle to survive and the limits to their knowledge but also wrongly assumes that their shortcomings were due to the lack of good intentions. In any case, there is no record of a human group prospering without a coherent set of values based on a cosmology—flawed and preposterous as those guiding frameworks might seem in the "age of the smart machine."

To venture a bold simplification, we could say that American culture has been made up of an uneasy combination of two main ingredients: the religious values that led the Puritans to New England and are replicated in many forms (for example, Mormonism or Islam) and the secular legacy of the Enlightenment that inspired the framers of the Constitution. The conflict between these two streams of values is illustrated, for instance, by the debate concerning the teaching of evolution in the public schools. The Christian cosmology dates the beginning of the world at about 4000 B.C.; the secular cosmology, about a million times earlier. These discrepant dates stand for two apparently irreconcilable sets of ideas that polarize the value system of our culture. It is revealing to note that according to recent opinion surveys, the U.S. population is about evenly divided among those who do believe in evolution and those who do not. In any case, neither of these value systems proves very useful in helping our culture decide how best to deal with the future of information.

The religious system does provide applicable rules, but its cosmology seems irrelevent to the problems at hand. The Catholic Church has been in the business of managing memes for close to two millennia: the Index of Forbidden Books was one attempt to control the information shaping the minds of the faithful, and the trial of Galileo marked another. Religious censorship was never very successful in the past; it will be even less so in the era of the World Wide Web. As exemplified by the controversies surrounding birth control and abortion, religions have also been keenly concerned with the fate of the human body—if for no other reason than because it is the seat of the soul and thus contains a fragment of divinity. With enough ingenuity, observers can derive from the tenets of the various religions their respective stances on which genetic manipulations are permissible and which are not. Of course, only those observers who are also believers in a particular religion—or in one interpretation of that faith—will feel bound by the conclusions drawn.

Nor does the secular value system provide tenable principles. The fundamental faith of the Enlightenment has been that human reason unhampered by dogma and convention would ultimately prevail over the mysteries of nature. When grafted onto a market economy and a democratic polity, these assumptions have bred that ultra-individualism which is the essential ethos of the United States. There is no need to praise its evident advantages; the question is whether it can suggest credible and useful guidelines for building the future.

Concerning the media, we have seen that one of the major values guiding journalists is the provision of information people need to improve their lives. This is a straightforward application of Enlightenment principles to the domain. Applying the tenets of democracy, it assumes that all needs are equal. Consequently, the task of journalists is to dig up and present all the news that potentially could be of use to anyone. We have seen how this stance is threatened by the changes in technology, ownership, lifestyle, and patterns of consumer demand. But even if journalists were to implement these fundamental values, would the values prove equal to meet the challenges of the future?

One tacit assumption is that each bit of information has the same right to exist as every other. This value is deeply entrenched in U.S. culture, from the First Amendment to the free speech campus demonstrations of a generation ago. The American Civil Liberties Union reminds us of the right of pornographers and fanatics to express their views, on the grounds that privileging some expressions over others is the first step on the slippery slope that ends in the destruction of individual rights. While the constitutional protection applies to opinions, in a subtle way it has been expanded also to cover the realm of facts. Postmodern scholars, for example, have been busy trying to erase the epistemological divide between facts and opinions, indeed between history and literature, between science, common sense, and common nonsense.

While much of this leveling of the value of information is done in the name of the Constitution, one can only imagine the disbelief of the framers of that venerable document if they could see how their inspired ideas have been applied. Two hundred years ago there was no need to qualify what freedom of speech included: a common value system and the social controls imposed by close-knit communities ensured that excessively outrageous ideas would be rejected. Freedom of speech—as any other form of freedom—is of little use without a solid base of shared values. "To be really free," Cicero has been quoted as saying, "you have to become a slave to some laws." Even the freedom of play is based on rules. If you are bound for a specific destination, side trips can be a pleasant diversion. But if you lack even a rough destination, everything becomes a side trip, and you may easily become lost or disoriented. Nor are our current value systems any better suited to helping us resolve conundrums in other domains. Do we owe equivalent medical care to all individuals regardless of their means, or is there a rough justice entailed in providing privileged services for those with financial or political power? Should legal justice favor the highest bidder, or should we attempt to even the playing field and provide protection for those who are weak and indigent? Is the marketplace the ultimate arbiter of aesthetic value, or should the government (or other agencies) provide support for those who dare to proceed in a nonpopulist direction? Should those with the most assets be allowed to purchase the best education, should adequate funds go to those who are able but needy, and should all education be given away "for free" on the Web? Neither religious values nor those of the Enlightenment nor a brilliant combination of the two provides ready answers to these puzzles.

A Midlife Medical Crisis

The following hypothetical composite, using two characters who are discussing many of today's actual trends and events, is based on a conversa-

tion one of us recently had with a physician colleague. We use the rhetorical device of an imagined dialogue to reveal the dilemmas and the options many practitioners—and, in fact, we as a society—now face. Let us,
then, introduce Rick Sutton, a thirty-nine-year-old cardiologist who
works for a large HMO in Boston, and Cynthia French, an acquaintance
and a retired physician who was visiting her grandchildren.

On Wednesday afternoons, Rick regularly golfs with his medical partners. When he comes to the nineteenth hole, he often orders a scotch and
relaxes with his friends. On the day we eavesdropped, he ordered a double-
scotch, sank into an oversized chair, and began to talk with Cynthia.

CF: Rick, you look depressed.

RS: Well, Cindy, perhaps I am. Twenty years ago, I was so excited I
couldn't wait to get up in the morning. I loved learning about medicine,
studying the body, understanding the science (not that I understood all of
it!), and helping patients. Arrowsmith, Marcus Welby—all that stuff.
Now that seems like a distant memory. Everything has gone downhill. I
don't even recognize my profession anymore. Sometimes I dread going to
work. The guys who run our place, they tell me whom I can see, how
much time I can spend, which meds to use, whom to refer and when to
refer—and, increasingly, when *not* to refer. My secretary and I spend
more time filling out forms than we do seeing patients.

Two of my closest buddies have left medicine entirely—one retired
early (you remember Phil); the other is making twice as much money
working for a new drug start-up. He never gets beeped on the golf course,
and he gets stock options too. I don't know how long I can take this life
anymore. And I'll tell you this—when my son Mark (that's the ten-year-
old) said the other day that he wanted to become a doctor, I had to bite
my tongue to keep from shouting, "No way!"

CF: That's a mouthful, Rick. I feel badly for you. Sorry to say, I've
heard that story a lot recently. I spent a wonderful life in medicine, and
I'd hate to feel that opportunity would be lost to you and others who'll
come after you.

RS: It's a different time, Cindy. You were lucky to have been born when
you were!

CF: Perhaps. But let's think about this a bit more. You mentioned a number of reasons for going into medicine. Do those still hold?

RS: Well, let's see. I still feel wonderful when I can detect a disease in its earliest stages, when I can make a difference for a patient or his family. I'm still helpful to patients—when I can see them for long enough. Certainly the science continues to advance. Somehow, though, the style of life isn't what I expected. I feel like I'm struggling to keep up. And there are so many other options that seem more attractive—more money, less aggravation.

CF: Do your colleagues feel the same way?

RS: That's interesting. As I mentioned, some have already left medicine, and others are complaining as bitterly as I am. But I can't say it's a blanket condition.

CF: Forgetting for a moment about your Mark, what would you say to young people who had lost relatives to, say, heart disease, and really wanted to go into medicine?

RS: Good question. I'd have to fight my initial cynicism and become more thoughtful. I guess I'd tell them to think very carefully about what professional path to follow—basic research, treatment-oriented research, full-time hospital work, maybe even working for a tech or biotech company. I'd ask whether they'd be prepared to work long hours with inadequate nursing support, not give their own children everything that they wanted, put up with bureaucratic red tape—

CF: (interrupting) But you know, Rick, that list could include other options, too—like Doctors Without Borders. Have you heard about Paul Farmer, one of your colleagues who set up Partners in Medicine and spends a good part of each year working with victims of tuberculosis and AIDS in Haiti? Randolph Whitfield, the ophthalmologist who provides eyecare in fifteen sub-Saharan countries? The band of physicians who are working politically to ban for-profit medicine in your state?

I just read in the paper about a doctor in California who took a stand against his HMO and now travels on his bicycle with his battered black leather medical bag from one patient to another. He calls himself a "conscientious objector!"[5]

RS: Now that you mention it, my college classmate Charlie Harris recently went to business school, not to open a business but to learn how to set up his own ten-person partnership, where he won't have to operate by some huge HMO's rules. And I ran into someone I'd interned with, who has moved to a Native American reservation and is working exclusively with that population. Said he'd never felt more fulfilled. Oh yes, and when I worked two years ago with inner-city high school students who wanted to learn something about medicine, I got more fun out of that than anything else I've done professionally in the last five years.

CF: Bravo! That's the Rick I know. You hinted before that you don't have as much money as you'd like. Are there some things you and Alice need that you really can't afford?

RS: I have to admit that a net family income of over two hundred thousand dollars a year shouldn't feel inadequate . . .

CF: Now, if you could phrase that a bit more positively, Rick, think of where it might lead!

The Foundations of a New Vision

Though it originated in a conversation that one of us recently had with a physician colleague, this brief dialogue is evidently a rhetorical device. Starting with the example of Ray Suarez in Chapter 1, we have approached the same underlying question in numerous ways: How can individuals who want to engage in good work do so during tumultuous times? The imagined example of Rick Sutton makes concrete the conversations that thoughtful professionals all over the world are having with themselves and with one another. The conversation also introduces four key elements that could lay the foundation for good work in our time. (If mnemonics are of any help, we can speak of the "three *DEs*—development, decency, and democracy—and the one *ED*, education.)

Development of the Individual

Across diverse cultural traditions, it is recognized that the optimal development of a person requires first satisfying the most basic needs (food, shelter, sex), then addressing higher-order needs (companionship, competence), and finally attempting to cultivate more sophisticated capacities (generosity, forgiveness, self-discipline). The most developed individuals exhibit a sense of autonomy and maturity, while at the same time maintaining a connection to the wider community, to vital traditions of earlier times, and to people and institutions yet to come. Development involves a measure of freedom from the limitations of biological heritage; it allows a person to develop unique potentialities while at the same time contributing to the well-being of the community.

It is useful to distinguish two lines of development: *competence* and *character*. If people are to become experts, they must develop skills, techniques, and understandings that are central to their chosen professions or crafts. For instance, Tom Brokaw and James Watson, as well as the Rick Suttons throughout our society, can go to work each day because they have mastered the key skills involved in journalism, biology, and medicine, respectively. In addition to this competence, we look as well for marks of character. Individuals with strong character have an inner set of values, a moral compass, on which they rely when facing issues that are ambiguous, difficult, or threatening. A person of character will not always make the proper decision, but at least he or she will have the discipline to judge whether a course of action was, in retrospect, well motivated and judicious.

But character and competence are not enough. They are important personal strengths, but development involves more than perfecting individualistic virtues. Optimal development of a person involves fulfilling two potentials that we all have: *differentiation* and *integration*. A differentiated person is competent, has character, and has achieved a fully autonomous individuality. This is the highest goal of Western cultures. An integrated person is someone whose goals, values, thoughts, and actions are in harmony; someone who belongs to a network of relationships; someone who accepts a place within a system of mutual responsibilities and shared meanings. In many Eastern cultures, it is integration that is held to be the highest goal of human development. A future worth striving for, in our opinion, is one where a person can develop both differentiation and integration to their fullest extent.

In the imaginary dialogue with Rick Sutton, Cynthia French is in effect teasing out these components. She reminds Rick that he has skills that allow him to perform medical work expertly; she asks him to look to his inner sense of purpose and value, as it prompted him initially to select the domain of medicine. And she challenges him to reflect on the potential for helping those in need that the physician's craft makes possible. Expressed more generically, good work is whatever advances development by supporting the fulfillment of individual potentialities while simultaneously contributing to the harmonious growth of other individuals and groups. When the two components are out of kilter—when individual interests run rampant, or when conformity to social needs and pressures thwart individual expression—the quality of life suffers.

This notion of development applies to many entities at different levels of complexity, ranging from molecules to nation-states. For instance, domains themselves can develop. Journalism, genetics, and medicine are continually giving rise to ever-finer differentiations. The challenge is to maintain integration. Consider, first of all, integration within the domain. For example, can discoveries about genes be linked productively with considerations about ecology? Can current newspapers work effectively with Internet sources and outlets? And then, consider integration between the domain and the broader society. Given an ever-greater number of news outlets, is it possible to have citizens who share the same information on which to make informed decisions? If data about gene function are available commercially from many different sources, can we ensure that information is used for the benefit of citizens, rather than to categorize, stigmatize, or even induce eugenic policies? No matter how skilled professionals become, and how much fame and gain accrue as a result, they are not doing good work unless they take such questions seriously.

It is difficult to look in the mirror and like what we see unless we can combine—in our lives, in our work—the full development of individual potentials with commitment to a greater whole. Neither great wealth nor other gifts of fortune are needed to lead a life worth living. Instead, a simple set of goals may be more worth pursuing: a *decent* profession, a *decent* living, a *decent* life. No one who practices journalism or genetics, law or medicine, art or teaching should have to take vows of poverty; but the privilege of engagement in exciting work should cause practitioners to reflect on whether they need to become wealthy celebrities. As no less an authority than the conservative publisher Irving Kristol reminded us, it is not far-fetched that television stations and newspapers (and their employees) should be satisfied with modest profits, nor is it entirely fanciful to think that geneticists might keep their distance from corporations and follow strict guidelines for personal involvement in profit-making enterprises. In most countries and at most times, these ideas would not be fanciful. Alas, they are becoming increasingly so in the United States at the dawn of the third millennium—a country where, in the words of the original corporate titan John D. Rockefeller, everyone seems to want "just a little bit more."

Democratic Processes

None of the social conditions in this book have been either foreordained or carved in granite. It is in our power to create the kind of society that we want, in the way that we want to. The genius of the original Greek system, confirmed two thousand years later in the fabled town meetings of New England, is that individuals of goodwill, working together, have the capacity to tackle and solve seemingly intractable problems. Authoritarian solutions are easier to impose, but only those solutions that the stakeholders work out patiently and revisit periodically are likely to survive.

As it is not easy to have such continuing discussions among millions (or even billions) of people, we now resort regularly to representative democracy. When voters are engaged and representatives are honorable, the system can work well; but too few examples of well-working systems can be cited today. In practice, we concede operation of domains to the professionals themselves, intervening only when their practices clash too powerfully with the "general will." We contemplate censorship when the media show no restraint; we ban human cloning when we no longer trust the scientists' judgment; we impose regulations on physicians or medical institutions when the core values of the Hippocratic oath seem to have become obscure or lost.

But other democratic entities are possible. In between a tightly knit guild, on the one hand, and a simple "up-down" vote on the Internet, on the other, we could constitute a regulative body composed of people drawn from neighboring domains—people who are knowledgeable but disinterested. Or each domain could choose to be supervised by a senate of retired professionals. There are many former doctors, scientists, journalists, and other workers who are attracted to being—in the phrase dear to Jonas Salk—a "good ancestor." Could not members of each domain elect their most distinguished elder colleagues, and give them some real power over the direction of the field? Such an arrangement might slow down the pace of innovation—but would that be a terribly bad thing?

In addition to noting that democracy is, at a minimum, the least wretched form of government, Winston Churchill said that the American people always do the right thing—*after* they have considered every other alternative. Whether in America or elsewhere, we *can* have a society in which good work is an everyday reality; the only question is whether we have the will to make that happen before it is too late.

Education as Key

Our society knows a good deal about developing competence; indeed, few would question that most of our practitioners, and particularly the ones we have studied here, do well on that score. But strong character is difficult to achieve, particularly at a time when religious, communal, and family traditions and values are weak and uncertain, and the principal messages conveyed by the mass media are irrelevant at best. Accordingly, many people look to schools—private and public, elementary and secondary, undergraduate and graduate—as forgers of character. However, it is unrealistic to expect schools to accomplish this alone, particularly when they are being asked to do so many other things, often with inadequate resources.

But even when a reasonable moral character has been formed, a further issue arises. A person must be able to deal not only with situations that have arisen before but also with new ones, including ones that could not have been anticipated by mentors or classical texts. In the particular cases examined here, a continuing integration is called for between professional skills and a person's sense of character. It takes a lifetime to achieve such an integration. The people we personally admire are the ones who can, figuratively, continue to look in the mirror *over time,* instead of becoming gradually degrading Dorian Gray portraits: for example, the scientist and environmental activist Rachel Carson, who wrote *Silent Spring;* the college president, scholar, and one-time U.S. attorney general Edward Levi, who helped restore the Justice Department's credibility after Watergate; the internationally renowned cellist and promoter of international understanding Pablo Casals; the legendary tennis player and dedicated civil rights activist Arthur Ashe. And we can all think of such people's less well known but similarly skilled, dedicated, and courageous counterparts among today's workers.

Our study has suggested a number of educational processes that can increase the likelihood of good work. Of great importance is the moral milieu of graduate or professional school and of people's first jobs. If these formative experiences occur in places where good work is at a premium, then many younger workers will "get the message," while those who do not can be sifted out. Relatedly, the privilege of being part of a professional lineage is invaluable. Beliefs and practices associated with exemplary good workers—for example, Edward R. Murrow and James Reston in journalism—are often passed on not only to students or protégés but even farther down the lineage to "grandstudents" and even "great-grandstudents." Familiarity with admirable mentors or paragons can make a significant difference to young workers tempted to trim their values to fit current fashions. As the much-admired elementary and secondary school principal Deborah Meier has said with reference to her young charges, "We have to be their Joe DiMaggios." The example of Mike Tyson cannot be refuted simply by a critique; however, the counterexample of Muhammed Ali may be persuasive to an ambitious young athlete.

Professionals' education must be complemented by that of the broader public. The issues raised in this book are familiar to those who follow the national political and cultural scene, but they are not nearly as familiar as they should be to the general public. We hope that this book can help bring the issues to the attention of more people. A good start would be if the phrase *good work* were re-energized and entered into everyone's personal lexicon. If journalists, geneticists, or other professionals—idealistic beginners or crusty old-timers—were to read and debate these pages, we would be delighted. If programs designed to foster good work were to be created, we would eagerly offer our help.

Final Words on Good Workers

Like the authors, most readers of this book are neither journalists nor geneticists. It might be tempting to think of this book as addressing problems of "others' domains" that should be solved by "those people." Needless to say, such a write-off would be shortsighted. Nearly all of us are subjected to many of the same pressures and opportunities that exist in journalism and science. We can recognize ourselves in the quandaries faced by a journalist like Ray Suarez or a genetics researcher like Arno Motulsky. And we have probably overheard, or taken part in, a conversation like the one between our two fictional physicians. After all, each of us is dealing with a world in which change is rapid, market forces and opportunities are extremely powerful, and concepts of time and space are being rapidly altered. We should be able to recognize ourselves in these portraits of "the other."

What would we say to aspiring young workers—or to put it to the acid test, what would we say to young people for whom we have some responsibility? If invited to write such a letter to younger relatives or to our own children, we might share the following thoughts:

> You—like the rest of us—will find it very difficult to stay on course unless you feel loyal to an enduring tradition. Sometimes your loyalty or trust may be based on religious faith and at other times on the assumption that traditions devoid of wisdom would not survive the passage of time. If you are lucky, you learned such sustaining beliefs in your family, and you may not even be aware that you have absorbed them. To complement these beliefs, you will need to gain a parallel anchoring in the traditions of your domain, as embodied by teachers, mentors, or paragons whom you admire and from whom you have learned. Without strong foundations in traditions that give meaning to the future, it is hard to keep up professional values under the pressure of countervailing forces. And so, as often as needed, unclutter your mind: Revisit those codes, documents, and exemplars that are integral to your domain—whether they are as ancient as the words of Moses, Hammurabi, or Hippocrates, or as recent as the mission statement of your favorite organization.
>
> Next, seek the support of others who share the same purpose. Very few people have the fortitude to act consistently against the grain of the organization to which they belong—or to resist the field that has wandered from its core values. We are social animals, after all, and we need to feel that our behavior makes sense to others. So find allies, inside or outside the job, or—in the style of a social entrepreneur—consider starting an organization of like-minded peers. If you belong to a lineage—a vertical line inspired by a mentor you admire or a horizontal collection of colleagues you feel close to—that membership will often suffice to help you withstand even powerful temptations to "sell out."
>
> But having strong principles and support may not be enough. You will also need a third vital ingredient—the resolve to stick by

your principles. Knowing what should be done and having the means to do it are useless without personal commitment. In the last analysis, no one else is responsible for upholding the values of your work. Either you live up to the implicit covenant that justified professional status, or you do not (and in that case, you would continue a life of furtive deception). What Harry Truman said in the Oval Office applies to all of us in our less august surroundings—"The buck stops here." Sounds difficult? Not really. For the joy we derive from doing our best work, according to high standards, is rewarding enough, even if we must sometimes struggle in lonely confusion.

You and I have listened to the music of someone who intuitively understands this—the folksinger Ani DiFranco. By her midteens, she had decided that folk music had fallen into ritualistic modes of expression, losing its vitality and purpose. As she started writing and playing music that was meaningful to her, she was ignored by the music establishment. Her solution was to start her own label, Righteous Babe Records. She went on to write and play what felt right, recording, pressing, and distributing CDs on her own—and she has been very successful. Such examples are everywhere, in every realm—a dozen books could be filled with their stories. But you may not have to struggle in that way if you find what is important to you, see whether it can be pursued through existing channels, and if not, work with others to create conditions that allow that form of self-expression. All of us who believe in good work can find inspiration in what the anthropologist Margaret Mead said: "Never doubt that a small group of committed people can change the world. Indeed it is the only thing that ever has." And let's remember the way that Garrison Keillor signs-off on the radio feature "Writer's Almanac"—"Be well, do good work, and keep in touch."

AFTERWORD

Good Work in 2002

BOOKS ABOUT contemporary trends often have short half-lives. Their analyses risk being as timely as yesterday's newspaper. The hardcover edition of *Good Work* appeared in bookstores in early September 2001, barely a week before the attacks on New York's World Trade Center and the Pentagon. Naturally the authors—as well as many readers—have wondered about the extent to which the findings reported here remain relevant in what many view as a new age of terrorism. In this Afterword to the paperback edition, we relate our own impressions about "good work" in light of recent events, using the occasion as well to give a report on our continuing studies.

It has become a cliché to say that "everything has changed since September 11." When it comes to Americans' understanding of global political and religious forces, our feelings of vulnerability, our decisions about travel and holidays, this remark may well make sense. However, if other momentous events—the Great Depression, the Holocaust, the destruction of Hiroshima, even the Vietnam War and its political aftermath—did not drastically alter the way we live, we may question whether 9/11 will. Most adults still spend about half their waking hours at work. To what extent have our work lives changed in the months since the terrorist attacks, and what changes are we likely to experience in the future?

Realignment in Journalism and Genetics

In the domains we studied, genetics and journalism, the relative importance of issues was profoundly affected by the attacks. During the summer of 2001, the most important policy decision facing newly elected President George Bush was whether to allow research on embryonic stem cells. It would be an exaggeration to say that this issue has disappeared from the radar screen, but it is fair to observe that genetic research has become less central in policy discussions. Huge increases in expenditures for defense and security have decreased the federal money available for biological research. Moreover, the focus of such research is shifting to concerns about bioterrorism. Private funding of genetics research remains as dependent as ever on the overall health of the economy and on products or techniques that have the potential to earn significant profits. How long will this hiatus last? Probably not long. Scientific and financial interests committed to genetech research are preparing a new bid for legitimacy, even as conservative interest groups are exerting pressure to outlaw research on human cloning. The distant clouds we saw when *Good Work* was being written are becoming more visible daily.

In this context, popular perceptions of genetic research have changed. The public is now more fully aware of the essential ambiguity of all scientific discoveries: genetics breakthroughs can be used to cure or alleviate diseases, but they can also be used to create or spread new kinds of toxic agents. Companies like Advanced Cell Technologies have put forth the dramatic claim that cloning has the potential for curing or alleviating the most debilitative diseases, but members of the health establishment, including Harold Varmus, former head of the National Institutes of Health, have expressed suspicions that these claims are based more in the need to secure venture capital than in the quest for scientific breakthroughs. Craig Venter, former head of the genetics research corporation Celera, was pressured to leave his position even in the wake of his triumphant contributions to the decoding of the human genome, reportedly because his interest in the informational components of genetic discoveries ran counter to Wall Street's focus on profitable new drugs. Venter is now devoting his time to the Institute of Genetic Research, a not-for-profit organization.

Understandably, print, broadcast, and photo journalism have all received a much-needed shot in the arm since September 11. For the first time in many years, ordinary Americans cared deeply about events in remote parts of the world. Concerned about the possibility of war, the dangers of anthrax, the Taliban, Islam, and Osama bin Laden, Americans demanded news coverage that was detailed and accurate. And at least for a time, the American media rose to the occasion. Although tabloid coverage did not evaporate, there was a surprising and reassuring resurgence of quality journalism around the country. Papers like *The New York Times* and *The Boston Globe* (owned by the *Times*) dedicated unprecedented amounts of coverage to "A Nation Challenged." Indeed, given the indifferent performance of our national investigative agencies prior to September 11, many of us came to feel that our best reporters know and understand more than our leading spies. And with the kidnapping and murder of *Wall Street Journal* reporter Daniel Pearl in early 2002, we were all reminded that knowledge sometimes comes at great cost.

Economically, the journalism industry came up short in 2001. But then, quality news coverage is expensive. The corporations that own most major news outlets reported far reduced profits and even losses during the last months of 2001. By one estimate, an extra $100 million were spent in the final months of the year, and $500 million in advertising revenues were lost. Whether management will continue to accept such a financial change of fortune is uncertain.

September 11 clearly had an impact on the alignments of these two professions, but it is too early to tell whether the new alignments will last. The profession of genetics is somewhat less well aligned: there is less money available, the money is more likely to be targeted, and citizens have a more ambivalent attitude toward scientific discoveries, recognizing perils as well as promise. In contrast, the profession of journalism has become somewhat better aligned. Citizens have been reminded of the importance—and fragility—of accurate investigative reporting, and many journalists have been reenergized to pursue the core practices of the profession in line with its traditional values.

Alteration in the Status of Other Professions

How has the rest of the working world changed since September 11? To begin with, professions that address clear public needs have experienced growth. In addition to journalism, we can single out human services, the military, and, indeed, much of government service as professions that have attracted more interest since the terrorist attacks. After many years of being degraded in the public consciousness, public servants—fire fighters, police officers, EMTs—are once again seen as performing important and needed functions. In contrast, professions that are seen as more frivolous or less essential—for example, those involved exclusively in making money—have taken a hit in public esteem.

Young people making career choices have also been affected by the terrorist attacks and the national reaction to them. On college campuses, far more students are considering careers in public service, intelligence and counterintelligence, and teaching. The nonprofit organization Teach for America reported a threefold increase in the number of applicants in the final months of 2001. In contrast, the appeal of venture capital, investment banking, advertising, and other Wall Street–Madison Avenue pursuits has lessened. Law schools report a surge of interest in public service and public interest law, and ROTC has returned to many college campuses. In the summer of 2001—when news of Congressman Gary Condit's sex life dominated the airwaves—who could have predicted such an abrupt shift in public consciousness?

Challenges to the Power of the Market

A major thesis of *Good Work* is that market forces have assumed overwhelming importance in contemporary professional life, and that increased emphasis on profitability has caused tension for employees. Since 9/11, the pervasiveness of the "bottom line" has hardly been undermined, but two unanticipated counterforces have significantly complicated the situation.

The terrorist organization responsible for the attacks of September 11 could not have functioned without a large amount of capital—Osama bin Laden is (or was) certainly a man of means. Yet the airplane attacks themselves were a low-budget operation, costing only a few hundred thousand dollars by most estimates. And the suicide bombers, whose willingness to sacrifice their own lives shocked and outraged the world, were educated members of the middle class, not poverty-stricken illiterates. In the midst of an age that has been described as "postideological" and even "posthistorical," a religious ideal of unanticipated power has gained tremendous importance in global politics.

The fall of the Enron Corporation further undermined the primacy of market forces in the public mind. Enron was the seventh largest corporation in the nation, heralded for its innovation and widely emulated in the world of finance. It turned out that Enron's success had been fraudulent, a deception that involved not only the executives of the company but the collusion of the Arthur Anderson Company, one of the five principal accounting firms in the world. The collapse of Enron had effects that went beyond the loss of jobs and retirement funds for thousands of employees, spreading disillusionment about corporate accounting throughout the world.

During the preparation of *Good Work,* one of us quipped that if the market were the only operative force in American life, then, ultimately, accounting would be the only profession that remained. When money dominates every sphere of life, society depends on accurate reporting of financial conditions—on "transparent" financial operations, to use the current phrase. The Enron collapse gave unexpected substance to this quip. If accountants—professionals charged with an accurate and disinterested reporting of monetary transactions—are no longer trustworthy, then the primary basis on which the society operates is undermined.

It is worth noting that financier-turned-philanthropist George Soros has long expressed views consistent with our analysis in *Good Work.* A triumphant product of the market system himself, Soros has stressed that market mechanisms alone cannot bring about a viable society. Soros has devoted much of his philanthropic enterprise to the promotion of systems that counterbalance the unmitigated power of the market.

Taking Stock

It is far too early to say that the nature or provenance of good work has changed in recent months. The newspapers are filled with reports of ethical dilemmas similar to those we've described, numerous cautionary tales of people who do not rise to the challenge of carrying out good work, and inspiring examples of those who do carry out work that is both excellent in quality and socially responsible. Large corporations continue to put the bottom line first, and to put pressure on reporters, physicians, and scientists who refuse to cross certain ethical boundaries. Corporate consolidation continues in the biotechnological and media sectors, as does wholesale patenting of genes. But at the same time, new government and medical school guidelines prevent or publicize conflicts of interest in biomedical research. We hope that such measures will reduce the likelihood of unnecessary deaths, such as that of Jesse Gelsinger, who died as a result of a high dose of gene therapy. And the public uproar that has greeted reports of plagiarism by well-known authors and journalists shows that there is still a demand for straightforward reporting.

The events since September 11 do underscore the fluidity of alignments that we posited in *Good Work*. We had suggested that all alignments and misalignments are temporary, and recent events have underscored that assertion. What we had not anticipated was a shock that would affect not just individuals or professions but a whole society: a Damascene experience that few Americans could escape. Such trauma tests a society—and, to borrow a term from earlier generations, it tests whether it can be a Good Society.

So far, the Good Work Project is largely an American phenomenon, but translations of this book will make our ideas available abroad. In January 2002, we conducted three workshops on good work in Copenhagen, and we have reported on this work in several other European and Asian countries as well. We hope that readers and researchers around the world will join us in exploring the set of ideas put forth in this book.

Finally, we record with sadness the death in February 2002 of John Gardner, the twentieth-century American leader to whom we dedicated our book. Carrying out Good Work would not be possible without role models who inspire us to think boldly and to reach beyond our comfort zones. We are proud to have had the privilege of knowing John Gardner. His inspiration will continue to guide us, as it has so many thousands of our fellow citizens.

Appendix A

Information About the Good Work Project

Since 1995, three teams of investigators, under the direction of Howard Gardner of Harvard University, Mihaly Csikszentmihalyi of Claremont Graduate University, and William Damon of Stanford University, have been researching the ways in which leading professionals in a variety of domains carry out good work. *Good work* is used in a dual sense: first, work that is deemed to be of high quality and, second, work that is socially responsible. Through intensive one-on-one interviews, the researchers have investigated several domains, including journalism, genetics, business, jazz music, theater, philanthropy, and higher education. Pilot studies have been conducted of medicine and the rapidly emerging domain of "cyberlaw," with plans to explore these areas more fully in the future.

In addition to this central line of study, several other related lines of investigation have been launched:

1. The Origins of Good Work project is an examination of teenagers who excel in extracurricular activities.
2. The Dedicated Young Professionals Study focuses on those who have just begun (or will soon begin) promising professional careers.
3. The Good Work in Interdisciplinary Contexts is conducting studies of exemplary research institutions that feature interdisciplinary work, as well as secondary schools and colleges with admired interdisciplinary programs
4. The Role of Contemplative Practices investigates the ways in which contemplation or meditation influence how professionals carry out work.
5. The Encouraging Good Work in Journalism project, carried out in conjunction with the Committee of Concerned Journalists, is currently developing a "traveling curriculum" for use in newsrooms around the country.

6. Good Work as Transmitted through Lineages examines how the principle of doing good work is passed down through continuous generations of teachers to students or from mentors to less experienced professionals.

7. Good Work in Other Societies, a project spearheaded by colleagues at Denmark's Royal Danish School of Education, investigates good work in Scandinavia and Latvia. In the future, additional international components will be added.

The Good Work Project is issuing a variety of books, reports, and related documentation. A series of reports on several of the lines of research previously mentioned is available on-line or for purchase in hard copy. For further information on the Good Work Project, please visit the project Web site at goodworkproject.org or contact

Howard Gardner
201 Larsen Hall
Harvard Graduate School of Education
Cambridge, MA 02318
E-mail: hgasst@pz.harvard.edu

Appendix B

Methods for
Studying Good Work

Before interviewing respondents, we obtained background information from publicly available sources, from informants, and, when possible, from the respondents themselves. By the time of the interview, the interviewers were already well informed about the subject, and they could adapt the protocol as needed to secure the most important information. Subjects were also asked to participate in a Q sort, in which they rank-ordered thirty values held by them and by other professionals. Here in alphabetical order are the values:

Broad interests
Challenge
Courage, risk taking
Creating balance in one's life
Creativity, pioneering
Curiosity
Efficient work habits
Enjoyment of the activity itself
Faith
Fame, success
Hard work and commitment
Honesty and integrity
Independence
Openness
Personal growth and learning
Power, influence
Professional accomplishment

Professional conduct
Quality (of work)
Recognition from one's field
Rewarding and supportive relationships
Searching for knowledge
Self-examination, self-criticism
Social concern
Solitude, contemplation
Spirituality
Teaching, mentoring
Understanding, serving others
Vision
Wealth, material well-being

Each interview lasted anywhere from one and a half to three hours. It was tape recorded and transcribed verbatim. Respondents were asked whether they could be quoted directly by name or preferred to remain anonymous, and whether they were willing to be identified by name as a participant in the study. They could also indicate when comments are "off the record." Following the transcription, respondents were sent a copy of the protocol and permitted to make changes that more accurately communicated what they wished to say.

Independent of the domain under investigation, respondents were probed in eight general areas:

1. Goals and purposes
2. Beliefs and values
3. The work process (areas of pride, personal qualities)
4. Positive and negative pressures in the area of work
5. Formative influences (childhood, training)
6. Perspectives on work (training of next generation, areas of like or dislike)
7. Community and family
8. Ethical standards

Within each of these areas, more specific questions were posed. These questions could be adapted in light of the particular domain, the role assumed by the subject in that domain, and the particulars of his or her life and career. Sample protocols are reproduced as Appendices C and D.

Put succinctly, the task of data analysis in this study was to distill the transcripts—which sometimes ran up to fifty single-spaced typed pages—to categories, numbers, and ultimately empirical findings. Once the transcript was prepared, it was converted into a *reading guide*, or in essence a reordered transcript. Independent of where it emerged in the interview, material was placed under the category to which it properly belongs. In case of doubt, material was placed under two or more categories.

The next and crucial step was to convert the reading guide into a *coded reading guide*. This step involved a radical condensation and categorization of the interview material into eleven distinct headings. For the study reported in this book, the following headings were used:

1. Independent variables: type of work, role; gender, age; racial/ethnic background
2. Larger purpose (ultimate goal or mission of the professional)
3. Goals, obstacles, strategies: For our study, this was the most important category. For each subject we identified several goals, principal obstacles that threaten attainment of goals, and the strategies devised to address those obstacles.
4. Opportunities, obstacles converted into opportunities
5. Supports (at work or at home)
6. Transforming moments (pivotal in the respondent's career)
7. Positive or negative changes in the domain, field, and workplace
8. Initial involvement in the domain
9. Formative influences (persons, groups, activities)
10. Mentors and antimentors
11. Contemplative activities

Each of these headings was, in turn, broken down into independently coded topics. For example, with respect to journalism, "changes" were subdivided in terms of whether they involved technology, values, format, rewards, or other. Twelve coders were trained across the three research labs. Several reliability tests were conducted in each laboratory and across laboratories. Following this training, pairs of coders, called "subteams," were responsible for the data selected for a given code; in the case of strategies and obstacles, three-person teams were used. Given the challenge of coding qualitative data, it was not easy to obtain high agreement among the coders. Over various trials, we achieved stable reliability scores with a range for Cohen's Kappa of .47 to .62. We believe that this level of reliability is adequate for the claims made in this volume.

Once the coding was completed, it was possible to ask many kinds of questions regarding the data. Because all of the data are available online, it is possible, using software called Nud*ist, to generate new questions and to obtain ready, if provisional, answers. We hope that these data collected, at a time of dramatic change in professional lives around the world, will remain as a valuable resource in its own right and for comparative purposes.

Here, with selected examples, are some of the types of findings that can emanate from a study of this sort:

- *Counts of variables of interest:* Investigators can ask how many respondents had mentors or "antimentors," or at which age subjects first became involved in a domain.
- *Proportions:* The number of strategies listed by respondents is of interest, but it may be more revealing to know the proportion of strategies that simply maintain domain practices and the proportion that might expand the potential of the domain.
- *Relations between independent and dependent variables:* Investigators can determine whether those who are creator-leaders feel a greater sense of agency than those who are midlevel practitioners in a domain.
- *Comparisons across domains:* Many of the most revealing findings emerge when investigators can compare response profiles across domains. For example, we compared respondents' impressions of changes that they are observing in their domain. This comparison allowed the conclusion that geneticists are far more optimistic than journalists about the future course of their profession.
- *Comparisons across project studies:* As noted in Appendix A, the Project on Good Work is composed of several lines of research. Illuminating comparisons are emerging between the reports of veteran professionals and those of people who are just entering the professions. See, for example, Papers on Good Work, Paper #5, "Good Work among Dedicated Young Professionals," by Becca Solomon, Greg Feldman, and Marcy LaLacheur.
- *Comparisons across cultures:* So far our study has been restricted largely to the United States. We have the good fortune, however, of collaborating with Hans Henrik Knoop, an investigator in Denmark. Knoop his and colleagues are using the just-described good work research methods to study professions in Scandinavia and Latvia. See, for example, Papers on Good Work #7 "Good Work in a Complex World: A Cross-cultural Comparison," by Hans Henrik Knoop and Howard Gardner.

A more detailed description of the data-analytic methods used in the journalism study is available on Papers on Good Work #3: "The Empirical Basis of Good Work: Methodological Considerations," by Howard Gardner, Mihaly Csikszentmihalyi, William Damon, and Mimi Michaelson.

Appendix C

Journalism Interview
Protocol

I. Opening: Goals and Purposes

1. What kinds of things are you trying to accomplish in your work right now?
2. Is there a goal in your work that gives meaning to what you do that is essential to making your work worthwhile?

    a. What is it?

    b. Why is this goal important?

    c. Are there other comparable ones?

    d. How do you know when they have been met?

3. In your work, to what or to whom do you feel responsible or loyal?

II. Beliefs and Values

4. Are there specific qualities that have contributed to your achievements? (qualities = attributes: e.g., determination, persistence)

    a. Qualities that hinder achievements?

5. Which of your personal beliefs contribute to your achievements? (beliefs = worldview: e.g., belief in truth, justice, fairness)

    a. Personal beliefs that hinder your achievements?

6. Do you feel that your beliefs conflict with the dominant values in your area of work?

7. Would it be different if you were working on your own or in another organization?

III. The Work Process (Personal Level)

8. What of your work are you most proud?

   a. To what do you attribute your success in this endeavor?
   b. May we have a copy of this work?
   c. How important is creativity for your work?
   d. What qualities are instrumental to your creative process?
   e. What role does reflection play in your creative process?
   f. What qualities inhibit your creative process?
   g. Is it necessary to take risks?

IV. Positive and Negative Pressures in Your Area of Work

9. Reasons that make it difficult for you to achieve your goals?

   a. Constraints of workplace?
   b. Relate a specific situation?
   c. Unique to your area of work?
   d. Practical economic concerns/money?
   e. What roles do prestige and fame play?

For Gatekeeper: How do you approach the challenge of managing creative and ambitious people?

   a. Are there incidents when you have to put priority on the institutional needs?
   b. Does this produce conflicts with individual needs of people working with you?

(Work Process: Institutional/Organizational Level)

10. What kind of work is rewarded/discouraged?

   a. Is innovation/creativity rewarded?
   b. What are innovations that have changed your work process?
   c. How do you work differently from when you started?
   d. Does your job allow for time alone, to reflect?

For Gatekeeper: What kind of work do you reward or discourage?

V. Formative Background

(Childhood/Adolescence)

11. Reflecting on your formative years as a child or adolescent, what influences do you view as most salient in the way you approach your professional work?

   a. Influence of family background?
   b. How you spent your time as a child? What would a person have seen if they shadowed you for a day when you were a child?
   c. As a child, were you intensely involved in one or more activities? Which ones?

d. Influential religious and spiritual factors?

12. Do you remember the first time you thought of yourself as a (respondent's profession)?

(Mentors/Training)

13. What attracted you initially to your area of work?

14. Describe your training.

15. Have you had any mentors who have significantly influenced how you approach your work and/or how you have made crucial decisions in your career?

   a. An influential book, experience, or project?

   b. Any "antimentors"?

   c. Weaknesses of your mentors?

VI. Perspectives on Your Area of Work

16. What do you like about your area of work? dislike?

   a. What does your area of work do well? not so well?

   b. Example of a piece of work you respect? don't respect?

   c. If you were in a higher position of authority, how would you do things differently?

   d. What direction do you see for the future of your area of work?

   For Midlevel Practitioner: What direction do you see for the future of your own career?

   e. Does your work serve the public?

(Training the Next Generation)

17. How well does your area of work train young people to have the qualities that you think are important? How would you train them differently?

   a. How would you advise a young person who is thinking about a career in your area of work?

   b. Promising or warning signs of a young person in your area of work?

   c. What would you change about young people in your area of work?

(Respondent's Work with Young People)

   d. Is it important for you to work with young people?

   e. What's important for you to transmit through words or deeds?

   f. What are you learning from the people you mentor?

VII. Community and Family Relationships

18. What do you consider to be your principal community/communities?

   a. Do you retain ties with communities in which you grew up?

   b. Are you an active member of communities outside of work?

c. To what extent is your family related to your work?

d. How do you balance family/private life and work?

e. Do religious or spiritual concerns play an important role in your life?

VIII. Ethical Standards

19. Some people say that the standards in your area of work are more ethical than they used to be, and some say they are less ethical. What has been your experience?

20. Can you tell me about an incident in your area of work where you weren't sure about the right course of action?

    a. How did it become clear to you what to do?

    b. How do you deal with beliefs/practices you disagree with?

    c. Has it become harder to do work that you consider to be responsible and ethical?

21. Are there things that you would not do in your profession, even though it is not illegal?

IX. Closing

22. We are coming to the end of our interview. Is there anything you would like to add?

    a. Check notes for things left out.

    b. May I follow up with you in the future?

Appendix D

Genetics Interview
Protocol

I. Introduction

1. What attracted you initially to your area of work? your subfield?

   a. Is that still what appeals to you about it?

   b. If you hadn't become a (respondent's profession), what might you be doing instead?

2. In lay terms, what kinds of things are you trying to accomplish in your work right now?

3. What do you like about your work? dislike?

II. Conditions of the Domain/Field: Past, Present, Future

4. Which of the many changes in (respondent's area) have affected your experience of your work the most, either for better or worse?

   a. (if appropriate) If you were in a higher position of authority, how would you do things differently?

   b. Thinking about work that you respect, what are the common denominators? common denominators of work that you don't respect?

5. What direction do you see for the future of your area of work?

   a. This sounds like such an exciting field; under what circumstances would it cease to be, for you?

   For Gatekeeper: What is your involvement with where the field is going?

III. Beliefs and Values

6. Would you say that there are any personal beliefs or core values that guide your work? (beliefs = worldview: e.g., belief in truth, justice, fairness)

   a. What experiences or influences were most important, in forming these beliefs/values?

7. Are these values the same as or different than the values of colleagues and others in your field?

   a. (if in conflict) What effect does this have, if any, on pursuit of your goals?

   b. Would it (degree of consistency) be different if you were working on your own, or in another organization? (i.e., is this specific to respondent's institution?)

   c. What about if you were working in a different (business/noncommercial) setting?

IV. Goals and Responsibilities

8. In your (life's) work, is there an overarching purpose or goal that gives meaning to what you do that is essential to making your work worthwhile? What is it? (If unclear, probe for self vs. other orientation; universalism vs. particularism.)

   a. (if unclear) How does this connect to your day-to-day work?

   b. Are there certain tactics or techniques that have helped you achieve your goals in your day-to-day work? (Probe for strategies.)

   c. In what ways do reflection/contemplative practices help you in your decision making?

   d. What experiences or influences were most important in forming this goal?

   e. How do you know whether you are on track/making progress toward this goal?

9. Have you ever been torn between conflicting responsibilities (divided loyalties), in your work? (e.g., personal vs. institutional, funder vs. the public, funder vs. scientific integrity)
   (If needed, probe for universalistic/particularistic purpose.)

   a. Please describe.

   b. How do you resolve the conflict?

   c. (if needed) In your work, who or what do you feel most responsible to?

V. Opportunities and Supports

10. What are some of the things that have helped you to reach your goals? (Probe for most important opportunities or supports.)

11. Are there specific qualities that have contributed to your achievements? (qualities = attributes: e.g., determination, persistence)

a. What about qualities that have held you back or made it harder to pursue your goals?

VI. Obstacles, Pressures, and Rewards

12. Reasons that make it difficult for you to achieve your goals? What are the biggest pressures that you face, where you work?

    a. External difficulties coming from funders, government?
    b. Any difficulties from colleagues, your institution?
    c. (Probe, if respondent mentions difficulty balancing work and private life.)

13. How do you go about dealing with these difficulties and pressures? (Probe for type of strategy [domain mission, etc.; proactive, reactive, etc.].)

    a. How did you come to deal with them in this way? (Probe for learned/devised.)

14. What is your work environment like; is it generally supportive or constraining? (Probe for collegiality, competition, autonomy, dispersion of resources.)

    For Gatekeeper: How do you approach the challenge of managing creative and ambitious people?

    a. Are there incidents when you have to put priority on the institutional needs?
    b. Does this produce conflicts with individual needs of people working with you?

15. In your institution, what kind of work is rewarded? What kind of work is discouraged?

    a. Is innovation/creativity rewarded?

    For Gatekeeper: What kind of work do you reward or discourage?

VII. Formative Background

16. Reflecting on your youth, what were the salient influences on your broader professional goals and the way you approach your work? (*Note:* Influences on values and goals may have been described earlier.)

    a. How has your family background influenced the way you approach your work?
    b. How did you spend your time as a child? What would a person have seen if they shadowed you for a day when you were a child?
    c. As a child, were you intensely involved in one or more activities? Which ones?

    If the question was not adequately answered at the start of the interview:
    What attracted you initially to your area of work? your subfield?

17. Who has had the greatest influence on your approach to work and/or how you have made crucial decisions in your career?

a. Would you consider any of them mentors? How did they affect you? What did you learn from them?

b. Any "antimentors"? How did they affect you?

c. An influential book, someone you didn't know personally?

d. An experience, opportunity, or project that was transformative?

For Midlevel Practitioner: What direction do you see for the future of your own career?

VIII. Training the Next Generation

18. (if needed, preface with probe "a.") What's important for you to transmit to young people through words or deeds?

a. (if needed) To what extent do you work with young people?

b. How important is it for you to work with young people?

c. What are you learning from the people you mentor?

19. How well does your area of work train young people to have the qualities that you think are important? How would you train them differently?

a. How would you advise a young person who is thinking about a career in your area of work?

b. Promising or warning signs of a young person in your area?

c. On balance, what is your impression of the young people entering your area today? (or) In what ways if any are they different than in the past? What would you change about young people in your area?

IX-A. Ethical Issues in the Area of Work

20. Do you have ethical concerns about your area of work—things that you worry about?

a. Are your concerns shared by others? (e.g., the public, the scientific community)

b. How would you like to see them handled?

21. Are there lines of research you would discourage? What about possible lines of research in the future that you can imagine discouraging?

a. What is the scientist's responsibility for preventing them?

b. (If respondent says that scientists must go where the science leads, probe, as with the following.) Is there anything you yourself would not do? Anything you would counsel your students not to do?

IX-B. Ethical Dilemmas (See chapter 5, section on "Dilemmas.")

X. Closing

If time permits:

How do you spend most of your time, at work?

What was your training like—formal and on-the-job training, or both?

What of your work are you most proud? (Request a copy.)

For Gatekeeper (if necessary): What about in your current position?

    a. Why? (Probe for relation to overarching goals.)

    b. To what do you attribute your success in this endeavor?

    —Did you do anything special to prepare for it or make it possible? (Probe for strategies.)

    —Were there any particular resources you drew on? (Probe for supports.)

22. We are coming to the end of our interview. Is there anything you would like to add?

    a. Check notes for things left out.

    b. May I follow up with you in the future?

NOTES

Chapter 1

1. See M. Csikszentmihalyi, *Flow: The Psychology of Optimal Experience* (New York: HarperCollins, 1990), and M. Csikszentmihalyi, *Finding Flow* (New York: Basic Books, 1997).

2. E. Erikson, *Identity and the Life Cycle,* Psychological Monographs, vol. 1 (New York: International Universities Press, 1959).

3. Reported by P. F. Drucker, *Management Challenges for the Twenty-first Century* (New York: HarperCollins, 1999), p. 175.

4. A. O. Hirschman, *Exit, Voice, and Loyalty* (Cambridge, Mass.: Harvard University Press, 1970).

5. Quoted in A. Etzioni, *The Third Way to a Good Society* (London: Demos, 2000), p. 47.

Chapter 2

1. E.g., D. Yankelovich, "New Rules in American Life: Searching for Self-fulfillment in a World Turned Upside-down. *Psychology Today 15*, no. 4 (1981): 35–91.

2. P. Kutumbiah, *Ancient Indian Medicine* (Bombay: Orient Longmans, 1962).

3. F. Garrison, *An Introduction to the History of Medicine*, 1929).

4. T. Kuhn, *The Structure of Scientific Revolutions* (Chicago: University of Chicago Press, 1970).

5. G. Gaizler, *A Bioetika alapkerdesei* (Basic issues in bioethics) (Budapest: Magyar Bioetikai Allapitvany, 1997), p. 362.

6. E. Durkheim, *The Division of Labor in Society* (1893; reprint, New York: Free Press, 1964); E. Durkheim, and *Suicide: A Study in Sociology.* (1897; reprint, New York: Free Press, 1951).

7. K. Marx and F. Engels, *The German Ideology: Including Theses on Feuerbach and Introduction to* "The Critique of Political Economy" (1845; reprint, Amherst, N.Y.: Prometheus Books, 1998), p. 547.

8. T. H. Luhrmann, *Of Two Minds* (New York: Knopf, 2000).

Chapter 3

1. Plato, *Dialogues, in Great Books of the Western World,* vol. 7, ed. R. M. Hutchins. (Chicago: University of Chicago Press, 1952), p. 362.

2. Ibid., pp. 340–341.

3. E. Huntington, *Mainsprings of Civilization* (New York: Wiley, 1945).

4. F. Galton, *Hereditary Genius: An Inquiry into Its Laws and Consequences* (London: MacMillan, 1869).

5. C. J. Williams, "Nazi-Bred Children Uncover Roots," *Boston Globe,* 30 January 2000, p. A17.

6. G. A. Miller, "The Magic Number 7, Plus or Minus 2: Some Limits on Our Capacity to Process Information," *Psychological Review* 63 (1956): 81–97; G. A. Miller, "Informavors," in *The Study of Information,* ed. F. Machlup and U. Mansfield (New York: Wiley, 1983).

7. H. A. Simon, *The Sciences of the Artificial* (Boston: MIT Press, 1969).

8. J. Tooby and L. Cosmides, "The Past Explains the Present: Emotional Adaptations and the Structure of Ancestral Environments," *Ethology and Sociobiology* 11 (1990): 375–424, p. 408.

9. H. Gardner, *Intelligence Reframed* (New York: Basic Books, 1999); R. J. Herrnstein and C. Murray, *The Bell Curve: Intelligence and Class Structure in American Life* (New York: Free Press, 1994).

10. R. Dawkins, *The Selfish Gene* (Oxford, U.K.: Oxford University Press, 1976).

11. M. McLuhan, *Understanding Media* (New York: McGraw Hill, 1964).

12. P. Inghilleri, *From Subjective Experience to Cultural Change* (New York: Cambridge University Press, 1999); F. Massimini and P. Inghilleri, *La Selezione Psicologica Umana: Teoria e metodi d'analisi* (Milan, Italy: Libreria Cooperativa IULM, 1993).

Chapter 4

1. E. Schroedinger, *What Is Life?* (1944; reprint, Cambridge, U.K.: Cambridge University Press, 1967), p. 46.

2. Ibid., p. 77. See also R. Pollock, *Signs of Life* (Boston: Houghton Mifflin, 1994), p. 56; G. Stent, *Nazis, Women, and Molecular Biology* (Kensington, Calif.: Briones Books, 1999), p. 236.

3. V. Bush, *Science: The Endless Frontier* (Washington, D.C.: U.S. Government Printing Office, 1945), p. 1.

4. Q. Avery, C. McLeod, and M. McCarty, "Induction of Transformation by a Deoxyribonucleic Acid Fraction Isolated from Pneumococcus Type III," *Journal of Experimental Medicine* 29 (February 1944): 137–158.

5. "Probing Heredity's Secrets," *New York Times,* September 12, 1963.

6. M. Brakha, "The Twenty-first Century: A User's Guide," *Newsweek,* 1 January 2000, p. 26.

7. P. Hilts, *Scientific Temperaments: Three Lives in Contemporary Science,* New York: Simon and Schuster (1982).

Chapter 5

1. J. D. Watson, *The Double Helix* (New York: Atheneum, 1968).

Chapter 6

1. J. Rifkin, *The Biotech Century: Harnessing the Gene and Remarking the World* (New York: Tarcher, 1998).

2. Quoted in L. M. Krieger, "Genetic Research Pioneers Take on New Threat," *San Jose Mercury News*, 2000.

3. R. Merton, "The Matthew Effect in Science," *Science 159* (1968): 56–63.

4. H. Garrison and S. Gerbi, "Examining Employment Data Is Useful in Assessing Biomedical Ph.D. Training," *The Scientist*, 12, 7 (1998), p. 9.

5. Quoted in *The Economist*, August 14, 1999, p. 11.

6. D. Cohen, *Science*, 1999, p. 1000.

7. N. Anki, "Patent Applications Booming in Biotech," *Boston Globe*, 30 August 2000, p. D1.

8. Rifkin, *The Biotech Century*, p. 2.

9. K. Alibeck, *Biohazard* (New York: Delta, 2000); D. Suzuki and P. Knudtson, *Genethics* (Cambridge, Mass.: Harvard University Press, 1990); M. Ho, *Genetic Engineering: Dream or Nightmare?* (Bath, U.K.: Gateway Books, 1998).

10. George Klein, personal communication, April 21, 1999.

11. G. Kolata, *Clone: The Road to Dolly and the Path Ahead* (New York: Morrow, 1998).

12. Alibeck, *Biohazard*.

13. D. Curiel and P. Reynolds, "Gene Therapy Death Highlights the Remaining Challenges, *Helix* 2 (2000): 21–25.

14. L. Silver, *Remaking Eden* (New York: Avon Books, 1997) pp. 10–11.

15. A. Dembner, "Research Integrity Declines," *Boston Globe,* 25 August 25, 2000, p. C1.

16. Ibid.

17. R. Pollack, *The Missing Moment* (Boston: Houghton Mifflin, 1999), p. 189.

Chapter 7

1. K. Lasn, "Free to Be You and Meme: A Toolkit for Corporate Culture Jammers," *Utne Reader* 94 (1999): 31–33, 32.

2. Ibid.

3. P. Starobin, "A Generation of Vipers: Journalists and the New Cynicism," *Columbia Journalism Review* (March–April 1995).

4. D. Hewitt, "Filling Time with Second-Rate News Magazines," 21st Annual Frank E. Gannett Lecture, Media Studies Center, New York (Arlington, Va.: Freedom Forum World Center, 1998), pp. 1–11, 9.

5. P. Arnett, "Goodbye, World," *Monumental Shift*, part 6 of The State of the American Newspaper, 1999.

6. H. Evans, "What a Century!" *Columbia Journalism Review*, part 7 (January–February 1999).

7. *New York Times*, 26 December 1999, arts section, p. 52.

8. D. Shaw, "Special Report: Crossing the Line," *Los Angeles Times*, December 20, 1999, p. 1.

9. M. Frankel, "The Wall Vindicated," *New York Times Magazine*, January 9, 2000, p. 23-25.

10. G. Overholser, Editor, Inc., part 7 of *The State of the American Newspaper Series*, sec. 5.

11. B. Kovach and T. Rosenstiel, *Warp Speed* (New York: Century Foundation Press; 1999), p. 11.

12. Ibid.

13. D. McClintick, "Town Crier for the New Age," *Brill's Content*, November 1998.

14. Konner quoted in A. Sullivan, "The Scoop," *The New Republic*, October 30, 2000.

15. McClintick, op-cit.

16. McClintick, ibid, p. 127.

17. *Boston Globe*, 25 February 1998.

18. C. Lydon, transcript of *The Connection*, 23 June 1999 (Boston: WBUR, NPR, 1999).

19. Ibid.

Chapter 8

1. B. Franklin, *Apology for Printers; including: "On the Providence of God" [and] "In the Government of the World"* (undated; reprint, New York: Privately printed, 1967).

2. Commission on Freedom of the Press (Robert M. Hutchins, chair), *A Free and Responsible Press* (Chicago: University of Chicago Press, 1947).

3. Hutchins, 1947, p. 22.

4. Ibid., p. 26.

5. J. Fallows, *Breaking the News* (New York: Pantheon, 1996).

6. Hutchins, 1947, p. 35.

7. W. Damon, "Moral Development," *Scientific American*, August 1999.

8. A. Michnik, "After Communism, Journalism: Ten Commandments for a Decent Journalist," *Media Studies Journal* 12, no. 2 (1998): 104–113, 107–108.

9. C. Romano, "All Is Not Fair in Journalism: Fairness in People vs. Fairness to the Truth," *Media Studies Journal* 12, no. 2 (1998): 90–94, 93–94.

10. Ibid., p. 94.

Chapter 9

1. D. Merritt, *Public Journalism and the Public Life* (Hillsdale, N.J.: Lawrence Erlbaum, 1995).

2. S. Aday, "Public Journalism and the Power of the Press: Exploring the Frame-setting Effects of the News." Ph.D. diss., Annenberg School of Communication, University of Pennsylvania, Philadelphia, 1999, p. 201.

Chapter 10

1. A. Huxley, *Brave New World* (1932; reprint, New York: Harper and Bros., 1946).

2. G. Orwell, *1984* (New York: Knopf, 1949).

3. A. Pollack, "Supercomputers Track Human Genome," *New York Times,* 28 August 2000, p. C1.

4. A. O. Hirschman, *Exit, Voice, and Loyalty: Responses to Declines in Firms, Organizations, and States* (Cambridge, Mass: Harvard University Press, 1970).

Chapter 11

1. J. Schumpeter, *Capitalism, Socialism, and Democracy* (New York: Harper Bros., 1942); C. Christensen, *The Innovator's Dilemma* (Cambridge, Mass.: Harvard University Press, 1997).

2. B. Joy, "Why the Future Doesn't Need Us," *Wired* (March–April 2000).

3. M. Enserink, "Start-up Claims Piece of Island's Gene Pie," *Science* 287 (February 2000): 951.

4. Quoted in *Science* 286, November 19, 1999, p. 1475.

5. J. Glionna, "Rural Doctor Drops HMO, Regains Career," *Boston Globe,* 26 December 2000, p. A17.

INDEX

HOWARD GARDNER is the Hobbs Professor of Cognition and Education and the chairman of the steering committee of Project Zero at the Harvard Graduate School of Education. Also, he is an adjunct professor of neurology at the Boston University School of Medicine. He is the author of eighteen books, including *Frames of Mind, Creating Minds, Leading Minds, Multiple Intelligences,* and *Intelligence Reframed.* He has been honored with the MacArthur "Genius" Award, the University of Louisville Grawemeyer Award, and eighteen honorary doctorates. He lives in Cambridge, Massachusetts.

MIHALY CSIKSZENTMIHALYI (pronounced "CHICK-sent-me-high") is currently a professor at the Drucker School of Management at Claremont Graduate University in Claremont, California, and is a former professor and chairman of the Department of Psychology at the University of Chicago. His previous books include the best-selling *Flow, Being Adolescent, The Evolving Self, Creativity, Finding Flow,* and *Becoming Adult.* He is a member of the National Academy of Education, the American Academy of Arts and Sciences, and the National Academy of Leisure Sciences. He lives in Claremont, California.

WILLIAM DAMON is a Professor of Education and Director of the Center on Adolescence at Stanford University. He is also a Senior Fellow at the Hoover Institution on War, Peace, and Revolution. Damon's books include the prize-winning *Greater Expectations, The Moral Child, Some Do Care,* and *The Youth Charter.* He is editor of *New Directions for Child and Adolescent Development* and *The Handbook of Child Psychology.* Damon is a member of the National Academy of Education and the Board of Advisors of the John Templeton Foundation.